# CINEMA-(TO)-GRAPHY

## FILM AND WRITING IN CONTEMPORARY COMPOSITION COURSES

EDITED BY

# ELLEN BISHOP

BOYNTON/COOK PUBLISHERS
HEINEMANN
PORTSMOUTH, NH

**Boynton/Cook Publishers, Inc.**
A subsidiary of Reed Elsevier Inc.
361 Hanover Street
Portsmouth, NH 03801–3912
http://www.boyntoncook.com

*Offices and agents throughout the world*



The editor and publisher wish to thank those who have generously given permission to reprint borrowed material:

"Reading the Right Thing" by Joseph Harris was originally published in *Reader* 27 (Spring 1992). Reprinted by permission of the Editor.

**Library of Congress Cataloging-in-Publication Data**
   Cinema-(to)-graphy : film and writing in contemporary composition courses /
edited by Ellen Bishop.
       p.   cm.
     Includes bibliographical references.
     ISBN 0-86709-458-3 (acid-free paper)
       1. English language—Rhetoric—Study and teaching.   2. Film criticism—
Authorship—Study and teaching.   3. Report writing—Study and teaching.
   4. Motion pictures in education.   I. Bishop, Ellen.   II. Title: Cinematography.
   PE1404.C49   1999
   808′.042′07—dc21                                                98-54808
                                                                    CIP

Editor: Lisa Luedeke
Production: Vicki Kasabian
Cover design: Jenny Jensen Greenleaf
Manufacturing: Louise Richardson

Printed in the United States of America on acid-free paper
03  02  01  00  99  DA  1  2  3  4  5

*I'd like to thank all the contributors to this anthology for their good, hard work as teachers and for their patience and good humor with my editing.*

# Contents

# Introduction

This anthology began with the recognition that although virtually everyone teaching in undergraduate English language-based departments seems to be integrating film (and other visual media) into their composition courses, almost no one is writing about it. What's going on out there in all those classrooms? Surely by now, after the acceptance of film studies into the mainstream of graduate and undergraduate programs during the 1980s and the widespread recognition of film as the premier global cultural medium, the one everyone attends to, there would be a lively conversation about who was doing what and how they were doing it with which texts. But, to my surprise, and to the surprise of many of the authors represented here, little has been written about it. So, this collection of essays is first of all designed to begin to fill that gap.

I had also imagined this anthology as primarily a practical guide for teachers, instructors, and TAs who staff either composition or film studies courses and who are interested in integrating the two in their classrooms. This collection fulfills that intention. It offers a substantial perspective on how English teachers across our current educational scene, from community college to ESL classes to undergraduate courses in both large research-oriented and small teaching-oriented universities and colleges, are integrating film and other visual media with student writing.

I'm saying "integrating" film purposely here as opposed to "using" film, because the two are significantly different. Simply "using" film in the composition classroom, or "using" writing in the film classroom, is what all the authors represented here are resisting, in one way or another, even if on occasion they use the word *use* to describe the connection of film and writing in their courses. As the title of the anthology, *Cinema-(to)-Graphy,* indicates, the relationship between film and writing is much more complex and interesting than the simple "use" of one in the other's territory would suggest.

Recognition of this complexity has come to the film and composition classroom with the highly politicized cultural studies emphasis on interdisciplinarity, the significance of all cultural texts—(not just canonized literature) the theorizing of textual influences on readers (and vice versa), and the production and reproduction rather than the simple transmission of knowledge. Cinema and writing have taken on new, complicated theoretical meanings that the authors in this anthology all address in both their theoretical planning and their classroom practices.

To address this complex activity of integrating film and writing, the authors represented here, to varying degrees and depending upon the sophistication and specific needs of their students, are all designing courses that weave these together: (1) the old, new critical, and standard film theory emphases on the rhetorical and formal structures of the text and its medium; (2) the heightened and heavily theorized politics of the text and its writers and readers that cultural studies, riding the wake of the poststructuralist wave, has brought to English departments; and (3) the becoming standard logic of deconstructive analyses. The results are sophisticated classes that produce undergraduate critical thinkers who are well prepared to participate responsibly in the complex and often tense multicultural global village we all live in. As many of the authors will illustrate, these students develop demonstrable understandings of the ways that film and verbal texts produce meanings, reveal their own motivations, and are subject to the interpretive strategies of communities of readers and *their* particular historical and cultural positions as well.

The essays have been loosely divided into four sections based on where the authors locate themselves on the field between film and writing. Their official film or composition affiliations and the student populations each writer works with have also figured into this organization, although all the authors, I think, would be quick to qualify any compartmentalizing of their fields or the work they do in their classrooms. These essays, if anything, resist any easy categorization; all of them begin to unfold both theoretical and practical questions that arise from the conversation between film and writing, cultural studies, and undergraduate students. They produce useful knowledge about how the dance of critical thought about culture, human beingness, film, and writing can be enabled in diverse classrooms. Finally, these essays give readers specific views of the authors' courses and what happens in them: the nuts and bolts of teaching composition with film and vice versa.

The first section, "Critical Frames," consists of three essays that each examine some of the larger questions concerning the foundations of conventional thought about composition and film. Pat Caillé's essay, "Interpreting the Personal: The Ordering of Their/Our Own Reality," uses a set of contemporary documentary films to bring together questions about the efficacy of the "liberatory" personal narrative in the composition classroom with questions about the interpretations of documentary films to "investigate the ways in which the meshing of autobiography and interpretation not only produces knowledge but also establishes power and authority" (8). She makes these theoretical issues available to her students by asking them to consider their own writing, their relationships to the films they view, and the production of knowledge in both film and essay form. She also frames some of the larger problems or "pitfalls" of the simple "use" of film in the classroom rather than its integration, a theme that will be repeated often in the other essays.

In the second essay, "Writing Images: Some Notes on Film in the Composition Classroom," Daniel Wild takes up one of the issues Caillé also raises: the dilemma of undergraduate students who are asked to "write themselves into the university" (as David Bartholomae [1985] has named this activity), before they have acquired the skills to do so (22). Indeed, the composition classroom is where students should ideally begin to develop a "self-reflexive understanding of [writings'] discursive functions, an understanding of the student writers' role within this discourse and an emerging sense of the scope of intellectual practices in writing" (23). Like Caillé, Wild also wants students to learn to question the categories of established intellectual thought as they are learning them rather than simply learn to reproduce them. When film as a serious cultural medium is integrated into the composition classroom, Wild continues, questions of "reading" as well as writing come to the fore, since film is not a medium that is "read" easily in all of its imagistic complexity. Using a student's response to the recent film *12 Monkeys* (Terry Gilliam 1996), Wild raises some provocative questions about the hegemonic strategies of "reading" films and the complexities of grammar and time in the construction of narrative. Referring to the work of French philosopher Gilles Deleuze, Wild gives his readers a glimpse of the complexity of the categories of reading and writing with words and images that challenges simple assumptions about these activities.

In *"Rear Window:* Looking at Film Theory Through Pedagogy," Edward Maloney and Paul Miller offer a concise overview of the short history of film in the composition classroom, noting the shifting interests in both fields between formal structural or rhetorical properties of texts and their political and cultural contexts. Given this history, they propose a threefold approach to integrating film and composition:

> to give students tools to analyze film; to facilitate students' recognition of the value of film as a cultural text that has something to say about the society in which we live; and to help students see film as a model for, or at the very least a parallel of, the writing process. (34)

They go on to describe how they used the 1954 Hitchcock thriller *Rear Window* to emphasize both the text and the context at work in the meaning-making processes of filmic and narrative composing. This film is well suited to both discussions of text and context since it plays thematically and visually with the perspectives of the characters and the viewer, requiring the viewer to understand multiple contexts within the story. The nature of the mystery in the film also invites close readings, as many of Hitchcock's films do, thus encouraging an examination of the formal structural and rhetorical properties of the text and its medium. The authors then turn to *Pretty Woman* (Garry Marshall 1990) in conjunction with the Cinderella fairy tale to foreground the larger cultural patterns or contexts of meaning reproduced in films that encompass both whole films as historically located texts and their readers as also located within particular cultures. By combining their insights from *Rear Window,* students were able to produce papers that displayed an awareness of all three dimensions of the texts, including their senses of their own location with respect to the Cinderella story.

The second section of this anthology, "Methods of Reading Race in the Film and Composition Classroom," is composed of four essays that take up the larger issues of combining the formal rhetorical, political, and cultural contexts of film and writing through specific focuses, one way or another, on the issue of race. At once timely and close to home, race is also a particularly difficult issue for undergraduates to address. Each of the essays offers a way of critically framing this topic for students within the particular classroom the authors find themselves in.

In "Representing Student Culture: Field Research and John Singleton's *Higher Learning,*" Donna Dunbar-Odom offers a methodology that begins to address some of the questions posed by Maloney and Miller about how to make the cultural contexts of texts and student writers visible to the students. Her approach is to offer the "field research" framework of ethnography along with an emphasis on close reading, the core of the old new-critical reading strategies, and some basic film terms to give her students a way of developing their own critical languages about race and about the culture of education. Singleton's films, like Hitchcock's although from a different genre perspective, are very reflexive and so offer students ample opportunities for developing their close-reading skills. By asking her students to examine their own experiences of higher learning along with the film's representation of it, both framed within an ethnographic perspective, Dunbar-Odom enables her students to produce lively, interesting, and increasingly sophisticated essays. She argues that

> the possibilities of the film itself [*Higher Learning*] are less important than the possibilities enabled by juxtaposing film literacy and field research to move composition students toward a more sophisticated understanding of research, analysis, culture, and writing. (55)

Like the other authors represented here, Dunbar-Odom thinks not in terms of privileging one cultural medium or way of reading and writing, but rather in terms of locating students within the field of play between texts, mediums, ways of seeing, reading, writing, and cultural perspectives.

The next essay in this section, my own, begins with the sometimes tense politics of multiracial and multiethnic classrooms, noting the difficulties that students all too often have when the issue of race is brought up. I offer several of my assignments for the class and discuss them. I chose to approach the topic indirectly by setting up a complex conversation between two films, *Cry Freedom* (Richard Attenborough 1989) and *A Dry, White Season* (Euzan Palcy 1987), and the original novel version of the latter. All three texts focus on the end of apartheid in South Africa during the late 1970s. By first offering my students opportunities to develop and use critical reading frameworks that foreground the rhetorical and filmic aspects of the texts along with a sense of the political context of South Africa, I enabled them to develop their own critical languages for talking about race before I asked them to read such controversial and close-to-home films as Spike Lee's *Do the Right Thing* and John Singleton's *Higher Learning*. By comparing three versions of the "same" story, they were also able to surface the issue of "truth" within a postmodern context as it is entwined with perspective and politics, and to ask questions about the languages of race and the languages of film without immediately falling into the dangerous polarizations of simplistic thinking that often arise when students are tense or seriously insecure about what they are saying and the ways they are tenuously trying to say it.

The next essay in this section, Joe Harris' "Reading the Right Thing," also invites students to write about Spike Lee's *Do the Right Thing* through a focus on critical *reading* that resonates with Wild's earlier discussion of the interconnectedness of reading and writing. Harris wants his students

> to get a sense of what it is like to go back to re-view a scene in a movie, to look at it once again not simply to relive the experience it offered you the first time around (as we all do when we watch TV reruns or get a copy of a favorite movie from the video store) but to try to see or understand it in a new way. And I want them to get a practical feel for how hard it is to switch media, to use writing to "quote" or describe what happens in a film. And, finally, I want them to see for themselves how viewers of the same scene can often describe and understand it in strikingly different ways, and, when that happens, to get a sense of what might be involved in arguing for one view or the other of it. (72)

He chooses a complex, highly reflexive film that is also very controversial as a text, which will enable his students to develop close-reading skills of its sophisticated rhetorical dimensions, to resee their own initial readings of the film after class discussions focused on students' writing about the film; and to work with, to respond responsibly to, the increasingly sophisticated arguments presented from different points of view from different discursive positions. He focuses his class on the different readings of the film that different students produce, asking them to examine and rethink and rewrite their responses based on how their own perspectives shift in light of what the others have to say. By also raising questions about the nature of responsible argument as opposed to assertion, he deflects the tendency toward polarities and tension by opening up this issue for investigation. He also deflects the students' quick relativistic assertions about assertions that "everyone has a right to their own opinion"; one of the most entrenched sacred cows of undergraduate composers.

The next essay, "Reading Multiculturally and Rhetorically: *Higher Learning* in the Composition Classroom," by Johanna Schmertz and Annette Trefzer, also takes into account the tensions many students feel around issues of race. Their classrooms are predominantly white and rural with a significant Native American minority population. Also, they note, "as the geographic and economic isolation of our students promotes monolithic 'white' identities [even among the Native American students], it also renders print culture somewhat irrelevant" (86). One third of these students are required to take developmental reading and writing courses to qualify for college-level work.

Schmertz and Trefzer propose a threefold approach to teaching film and writing to these students, one that is similar to Maloney and Miller's but adapted to their particular educational context. Like the authors of all the essays in this anthology, they juggle the cultural and political contexts of the films and the students while also raising the issues of the rhetoricity of film and the categories of thought the students bring with them. Because "teaching a multicultural agenda in a fairly homogeneous classroom can unwittingly strengthen rather than weaken students' feeling of alienation and their ideas that their own identities are not being acknowledged" (88), Schmertz and Trefzer begin with a pedagogical approach to teaching empathy. Drawing on the theory of Jacques Lacan and the work of Constance Penley, Trefzer asks her students to "identify" with a student character in the film and then, in a journal entry, to explain how they see and understand the character's problems. The film offers enough different characters—black and white, rich and poor, male and female, and homosexual and straight—to mix the issues of identity, racial and otherwise, across the borders of bodies, and to break down the easy monoliths of "whiteness" and "blackness." After the students have read the characters in Singleton's *Higher Learning* through this lens, they move on to close readings of the rhetorical dimensions of the film, and finally to complex analyses of the film's cultural context by writing about reviews of the film and examining the ways that it constructs its audience.

The next section of the anthology, "Other Classrooms, Other Students, Other Methods," continues with four more essays that integrate film and writing for specific student populations: Dulce Cruz's essay, "Mapping the Use of Feature Films in Composition Courses"; Loretta Kasper and Robert Singer's aptly named "Inherit the Text: An Interdisciplinary Perspective on Argumentation"; Kate Chanock's "Using Film to Teach Coherence in Writing"; and Victoria Salmon's "Educating *with* Rita." The pedagogical approaches are more directive than those in the previous essays, but this is due to the requirements of the students being served. The sense of a complex and productive tension between the rhetorical dimensions of films, the political and cultural impact of them, and the students' implications within that interaction as culturally located writers and readers continues to form the basis of the work the students are asked to do.

What makes these essays and the classes they represent different are their specific student populations. All five authors teach nontraditional students. Many are ESL students who are also just learning American culture. Many come from third-world or Asian or Middle Eastern or African countries with cultural traditions and rules that are vastly different from those in the United States. The authors therefore tread a complicated line between indoctrination and informed instruction where the space of cultural difference can open up. These teachers are also charged by the institutions they work for both to make the hegemonic ethical and political systems of American culture explicit for their students, and to teach the "basics" of American or "Anglo" argument and writing.

Dulce Cruz, whose students come from all over the world, and who is herself the "only Latina" in her department, uses a variety of foreign films in conjunction with American films to illuminate aspects of both the formal, rhetorical properties of writing and film across cultures, and the ways films construct images and narratives within complex cultural frames of reference. She notes:

> It is, perhaps, even more complex to teach college composition as a culturally constructed process that consequently entails encoding and decoding as a context-specific experience. But that difficulty is diminished, I have found, if the polemics of that stance are integrated into the discourse of the class, and if I consistently emphasize to all my students that their cultural uniquenesses are welcome, that their ways of making meaning are as valid as our nebulous "United States mainstream" ways, and that they're certainly as worthy of being incorporated. (100–101)

Kasper and Singer also explicitly teach "argument." However, they tackle this too often objective and universal aspect of formal writing by using films as cultural texts—a Hollywood rendering of the Scopes Monkey Trials in *Inherit the Wind,* for example—that illustrate argument for their students while making visible the cultural and sometimes logical relativity of what counts as an argument in any given culture. They ask students to attend closely to the rhetorical dimensions of the film within the context of what an argument is within the predominant Anglo culture of the United States.

Chanock's students are predominantly rural Australian kids who need the extra help her lunchtime seminars on argument provide to be able to negotiate with their other college courses. She too is charged with teaching the basics of good academic writing, "argument," to her students. She uses a documentary film that presents a complex argument about biblical interpretation in light of the Dead Sea Scrolls. This enables her students to see how the verbal and visual aspects of the film work together to create its author's argument.

In addition to being nonnative Americans, many of Salmon's students are also from "at risk" and marginalized sectors of American culture. Many of her students attend community college as a last hope for getting an education after miserable experiences in the public schools, impoverished broken families and neighborhoods, and difficult menial jobs. Salmon teaches a class for beginning writers that includes many ESL students, some of whom are senior citizens, and a few of whom already have four-year degrees but are changing careers. Salmon's work raises the sometimes critically unpopular realities xif "starting where your students are," which often means allowing them consciously to construct the very forms and categories of thought that the culture most conservatively (re)produces in its canonized texts (and that cultural theorists most often want to critique). She asks students to read the film *Educating*

*Rita* and to compare Rita's experience in the film to their own academic lives. Like Dunbar-Odom she focuses the class on the topic of education, and like Schmertz and Trefzer she uses empathy as a pedagogical tool, asking her students initially to identify with Rita. However, she complicates this agenda by opening up the classroom to students' critiques of both the film's politics made visible rhetorically and in its formal structures, and the links between those politics and structures and the socioeconomic realities of getting a college education today. She also acknowledges and values the diversity of her students by providing a space for students from different cultures to compare the politics of the film as it represents, perhaps, an Anglo ideal, with the political realities of their own homelands.

The final section of this book, "From the Film Studies Perspective," consists of two essays by authors who see themselves as primarily film scholars who are also committed to the integrated classroom where film and writing interact in complex ways. John Heyda, in "Challenging Antiwriting Biases in the Teaching of Film," begins with an instructive review of the major undergraduate Introduction to Film textbooks currently in use in American universities and colleges. He carefully critiques what he calls the "antiwriting biases" within the larger economic realities of the large, budget-saving lecture courses they are used in. Focusing on the film textbooks' assertions that film is art, he takes this claim to task, demonstrating how it becomes the argument that prevents a more culturally situated examination of the production and reception of film texts—the place where students' writing about films and film viewing, in particular, and the larger connections between writing and film, in general, would be most relevant. He then goes on to offer practical advice for teachers of film courses on how to redesign these courses in ways that enable students to become active and aware participants in the production of knowledge of and about film.

Finally, Lucy Fischer draws on the work of Marshal McLuhan, whose ideas still permeate our cultural understanding of film in relation to writing, in "Apocalypse Yesterday: Writing, Literacy, and the 'Threat' of 'Electric Technology.'" Fischer presents a brief overview of the difficult relation between print and electric mediums (TV and film) since the advent of film. She argues that the anxiety about electric technologies both taking over and debasing American literacy is ridiculous. Then, drawing on an enormous array of world films, she offers advice and examples of how writing and film can be integrated in the composition classroom and how, in fact, filmmakers have long been commenting in their own medium on this complicated and interesting relationship.

All of the essays in this anthology take the relation of film and writing seriously within the larger cultural studies framework that has come to dominate English departments since the 1970s. They share a commitment to producing students as critical thinkers who can both responsibly speak to and read their media-saturated world, and who can identify and work with the "questions posed by language," as literacy has been succinctly defined (Pattison 1982, 14).

Understanding film and other visual media is as significant as understanding the printed text and the endless complexity of language, Marshal McLuhan's fears notwithstanding. The authors in this anthology acknowledge this with the careful classroom and course designs they have developed and represented here.

## Works Cited

Bartholomae, David. 1985. "Inventing the Unviversity." In *When a Writer Can't Write: Studies in Writer's Block and Other Composing-Process Problems,* edited by Mike Rose. New York: The Guilford Press.

Pattison, Robert. 1982. *On Literacy.* Oxford, England: Oxford University Press.

### *Films*

*A Dry, White Season.* 1987. Directed by Euzan Palcy.

*Cry Freedom.* 1989. Directed by Richard Attenborough.

*Do the Right Thing.* 1989. Directed by Spike Lee.

*Educating Rita.* 1983. Directed by Lewis Gilbert.

*Higher Learning.* 1995. Directed by John Singleton.

*Inherit the Wind.* 1960. Directed by Stanley Kramer.

*Pretty Woman.* 1990. Directed by Garry Marshall.

*Rear Window.* 1954. Directed by Alfred Hitchcock.

*12 Monkeys.* 1996. Directed by Terry Gilliam.

# 1

## Interpreting the Personal

### *The Ordering of the Narrative of Their/Our Own Reality*

Patricia Caillé

Even though I have been using film regularly in literature and composition classes, I have always found it excessively difficult even to begin to chart a territory, a space, in which I can reflect on my own pedagogical practice. My difficulty as well as my reluctance to do so have been heightened by the awareness that to use film in the composition class is to find oneself caught up on one side or the other of a debate that divides the proponents of film studies and composition specialists. The former emphasize the need to derive the conditions of the study of film from theoretical and historical frameworks, that is from an investigation of the properties of the medium, of its specificity, and of the historical developments of the relationship between film and culture which produced this specificity, while the latter feel that these frameworks may provide an introduction for film studies but remain inadequate for developing a reflection on writing.[1] Even though this polarization of the debate may seem overly reductive, I do believe it is at the core of the ambiguous status of film in the composition classroom.

The purpose of this essay is to argue for the need to move away both from film imagined as a vaguely defined and under theorized category within composition, on the one hand, and film as a self-enclosed cultural medium, on the other, in order to develop instead local projects which can generate sophisticated understandings of some of the issues at stake in visual culture, issues which can then generate a reflection on writing. I will first examine some of the assumptions, as well as some of the contradictions, which inform the use of film in the composition class and, more particularly, which govern teachers' attention to students' responses to film. Having provided a frame for my reflection, I will then explore how classroom work centered on contemporary film documentaries has enabled me to bring to the fore an investigation of the description of the forms and functions that the "personal" takes in interpretive strategies.

# I. The Pitfalls of Using Film in the Composition Class

### a) Some teachers' assumptions in relation to film

Even though approaches to film and composition have not yet been widely theorized, the use of film in the composition class constitutes a popular pedagogical practice operating around certain sets of choices which, due to the absence of theory, are not always self-conscious ones. Under such circumstances, I find it useful to clarify some of the assumptions which underlie the uses of film, assumptions which find themselves reproduced in most classroom discussions of film because of a lack of attention to the preconceptions that teachers and students bring to film in this context.

In a film and composition class, film almost automatically means fiction film, fiction films which are then put into different categories roughly borrowed from film studies courses or popular culture courses and which condition and predetermine the responses to the films themselves. Teachers also tend to favor contemporary feature films examining them in the light of their commentaries on culture. In the absence of a language to talk about the mechanisms of meaning-making at work in the perception of a particular cultural production, films are often equated with the representation of the culture they carry, and these representations end up bypassing the film altogether. Films are assumed either to contain the seeds of a cultural critique *(Do the Right Thing)* or to construct the worst possible ideological scenario which then needs to be exposed *(Forrest Gump),* leading to countless discussions about the story told by the film, and about what is not explicitly brought up in the film. In other words, film does not just say what it claims to be saying. In both cases, these conversations lose sight of the film as a construct within the larger discussion of the social issues it is assumed to be about. However, the discrepancy between *Forrest Gump'*s huge popularity and the scornful response it received from the intellectual elite, for example, a debate which finds itself reenacted in the classroom, is rarely acknowledged as being already at play in the discussion and interpretation of the film itself. In the same way, even though Spike Lee's signature is inherent in the status of the film as cultural critique, it does not often enter into the discussion except as the mark of intentionality which brings to bear unexamined assumptions about authorship in film. In other words, the ambiguous status of film in the composition class often leads to an unreflective understanding of what film is, what film does, and the types of work which are required for bringing film into the composition class. In particular, the privileged focus on representation squeezes out the material conditions of production and reception of film as a cultural artifact with its own shifting relationship to culture and to the viewers themselves. Film becomes instead a self-contained and autonomous rebus waiting to be deciphered.

This leads to an unselfconscious deployment of interpretive practices which reproduce the hierarchies, values, and frameworks present either in film studies, cultural studies, or elsewhere, rather than leading to an investigation of the film's specific relationship to "culture." Students are then expected to reproduce these interpretive practices without having been provided with the tools or the disciplinary frameworks which may enable them to make this type of work relevant. As a result, textual interpretations become the ultimate purpose of the course, even though they can only be inferior to those produced in a film course. They remain peripheral, supplementary to, and independent from the film as a cultural production as it has been conceived in particular disciplines. This process uncannily reproduces the awkward status of film in the composition class; it postpones the question of writing in relation to film interpretation by making writing solely the means by which the student can record and craft an already sanctioned interpretation; and by doing so, it fuels the controversy about the use of film in the composition class. In this all-too-familiar scenario, the student is positioned at the bottom of the two hierarchies, that of the interpretation of film and that of the reflection on writing.

### b) The student's assumed relationship to film

In the same way, students tend to sign up for a film class, instead of a composition class, for what the teacher often regards as "the wrong reasons": because they do not like to read, because they like film so much, or because they thought it would be "more interesting" than a regular composition class. Writing about film makes composition less painful, an assumption that carries with it certain expectations about how one should write about film. Students come with a multifaceted and undisguised affective relationship to film, most of them claiming that they love film. Film is both very close in the immediacy of the pleasure it provides and very removed in the difficulty of exploring the forms of this pleasure. Working with film can only become a means to address and name the pleasure of watching film and to develop a knowledge which can make students experts about film. In the absence of any other model commonly available, to become an expert is understood as acquiring the tools and developing the criteria necessary for the evaluation of film, evaluation becoming a means of mastering the medium, a means to move from "I like the film" to "it is a good film because. . . ." And, while this approach can be useful, it too often prevents further critical thought on the student's part; once a judgment is made, the work is done.

Even though students are eager to learn about film, bringing film into the classroom also appeals to a certain curiosity, a sense that film does not belong to the classroom—some teachers would say that the students perceive the use of film in the composition classroom as "transgression."[2] Paradoxically, the recognition of this affective relation to film on the part of the students carries with it the implicit defense of this pleasure. Intellectual critical work constitutes a threat to that pleasure, and students often regard it as unconvincing, as reading too deeply into what is mere entertainment, a feeling which generates some frustration for both the student and the teacher. Students feel that they are not learning as much as they would like about film—they are not being provided with the tools to become experts—whereas teachers complain that they should not need to waste so much time persuading the students that they should look more deeply into the presuppositions that watching film carry with it. Here again, the unexamined relationship between film and culture often creates a gray area which confuses the students as to the goal of the course. Is it about film? Is it about representations of culture(s)? How does composition fit into this?

What I saw in this approach on the part of both teachers and students was the automatic perpetuation of the oppositions between teachers and students, learned and ignorant, work and pleasure. However, the opposition between high and low culture is maintained in the teacher/students relationship in the class (the response to *Forrest Gump*), while it disappears in the relationship between film and culture. Culture becomes what can be represented in film, again reinforcing a loaded assumption about the properties of the film medium and its privileged relation to culture. In such a context, how can we foster a reflection about film which contributes to a reflection about writing? Do we need to, and could we consider Film and Composition as a Film Analysis 101 class? Obviously not. Do we need to introduce some of the language of film analysis? Not necessarily. However, if we do, we need to ask ourselves about the effects that the introduction of such a language carries with it, including the theoretical frameworks it brings to bear on our work with film. If we do not, we also have to remain aware of the ways in which it may leave our understanding of the relationship between film and culture under theorized.

At this point, I believe little is available by way of theoretical frameworks that might enable us to think about the relationship between film and culture in the composition class. I do not aim here to provide such an overarching framework, and in many ways, my work here is simply *bricolage*. However, I want to foreground this kind of approach which is the result of various experiments with film in the composition class.


### c) Delineating a local project

As I mentioned earlier, my endeavors to have my students explore their responses to film remained at the very best only partially successful because I could never persuade them of the relevance of the task at hand. Students acknowledged instead a response to the films and engaged in the production of powerful critiques, "ways of seeing" film loosely borrowed from unacknowledged disciplinary inquiries and most often tied to the texts we were reading in parallel to the main focus of the films themselves. The appropriation of these "ways of seeing" remained fairly rigid, mechanical, and more or less well-crafted interpretations, i.e., they were the outcome of interpretative strategies which somehow remained external to the students' experiences of the film and tended instead to disavow this experience.[3] Sometimes students internalized the critique; in other words, these interpretations which provided them with useful tools to [re]think their approach to film ultimately became an authoritative way to talk about film, substituted themselves for, and subsumed the students' initial emotional, or visceral responses to the films. Besides perpetuating wrongly, or at least inadequately, the opposition between emotional and intellectual responses to the films, it became quite clear that even though I begged my students to write personal responses, the interpretative strategies they were applying to the films did not authorize such responses. I realized fairly quickly that my pedagogical approach was torn between two apparently irreconcilable goals. On the one hand, I felt impelled to focus on both representations and their conditions of production and reception, an approach that inscribes the film in a network of material relations of which the composition classroom forms one part with its own specificity. It is a teacher/student relationship with a tradition, a set of self-representations, and more or less widely shared objectives. On the other hand, even though I believed that eliciting the students' personal responses in order to examine and possibly critique the viewer's position very often implied in the films may have provided the class with the means to write back to the disciplinary models which the essays provided, I could not successfully manage the interplay between the personal and the academic. Within this particular context, it became necessary for me to look into the issue of writing: it seemed to me quite clear that the question of the personal did not go beyond a reflection about the position of the viewer which inherently deflected the power of any interpretation produced by students in a composition classroom.

It became increasingly clear that the set of issues I was trying to address intersected with concerns widely discussed among compositionists: the return to the personal. I was also traveling what Richard Miller describes as "an increasingly well-worn path" and felt I was trapped in arguing one more time for "a return to the 'personal' or 'non-academic' writing as a way to reclaim an expression that really matters" (267). Even though I could empathize with Miller's longing for an expression "that matters," I remained very suspicious of the opposition between academic (i.e., theoretical, institutional, coercive, disembodied, and masculinist) and personal (authentic, feminist, empowering) which he himself was trying to rethink in his desire "to produce an idea with which we can think anew about writing as a place where the personal and the academic, the private and the public, the individual and the institutional, are always inextricably woven" (267).[4] However, I was all the more suspicious of this distinction as I could not relate to the pervasive perception that academic theoretical discursive formations had stifled the personal in composition, as many academics have lamented. Like Joel Haefner, I felt, on the contrary, that "the personal essays [were] too deeply embedded in [American] educational institutions and the publishing industry to be easily extricated" (132), and that this presence was ideologically loaded with assumptions about "individualism" (Miller 1996, 267) and "democracy," i.e., the personal stood as "resistance" to "system and dogma" (Haefner 1992, 130). Even though I understood Gordon Harvey's claim that the personal had been a way for feminists to challenge the universalism of "traditional academic analysis," I also agreed with his remark that these narratives were coming "out of academic life" and that the students did not have such narratives at their disposals (1996, 643–44).[5] In other words, the discussions over the place of the personal in academia and the battles to challenge hegemonic practices were and still are being fought in fairly clearly delineated institutional spaces; they are inter- or intra-departmental debates involving colleagues working under the pressure of a certain set of professional constraints within a more or less legible hierarchical structure. To bring such a "personal" perspective to bear on the debate within composition is to promote, and not always self-consciously enough, a story of success with liberatory and progressive overtones, a story whose success remains to be assessed.

Part of the problem with dealing with the personal in these terms may be tied to a misleading tendency to regard the personal as functioning in the same way in classroom interaction as in departmental and institutional relationships of power, what I could describe as a propensity to consider the problems encountered by student writers in relation to the personal as identical to those we encounter as professional writers in the academy. Obviously, I do not wish to deny that our work as writers is informed by our work as teachers of writing, nor do I mean to deny the relationships of power at work in the composition classroom, but we need to examine the specificity of these relationships. If one focuses on the role of the personal in composition, it becomes necessary to take into account a much less clearly delineated and less homogenous institutional space than a department; the composition class is a space involving the vast majority of students, i.e., groups from very varied backgrounds, for a period of intensive work but one that lasts only one or two terms. Their adherence to and participation in the work at hand may need to be nothing more than perfunctory, no matter how much we wish them to engage with the work. And, sometimes, they do get very involved. Within this particular structure, I want to emphasize what Harvey describes as the "conflict" within the community of writing teachers "between the demands for rigor and empathy" (642), a conflict which needs to be examined in the light of the roles that composition teachers have assigned themselves and/or have been assigned in the university. And even though there is more to Harvey's contention than I can account for within the scope of this essay, I would like just to keep in mind that the project to honor the personal, from the teacher's standpoint, may at times be fraught with the benevolent desire in the academy to give voices to those who may not normally be heard, a desire which carries some unexamined assumptions about the teacher/student relationship as a relationship of power and about the power of the personal in American culture. Here again, I do not wish to question the claim that the personal may be liberatory, may be a form of empowerment, because I believe it can be. However, simply to assume that it is liberatory discounts the ways in which students also use the personal as a means to resist both teaching practices and teaching materials, moves which in and of themselves can also be liberatory. What is more troubling to me is a lack of attention to the effects of the power of students' interpretations. Reed Way Dasenbrock contends that "writing instruction seems utterly impossible unless one assumes that student texts are authored and thus that students are authors in control of (or capable of being taught to take control of) the texts they produce" (277). However, to focus exclusively on the relationship between the student-as-author and his text limits the work of the teacher to making the students aware of and confident in the power of their own interpretations without having to reinscribe the effects of this power within a larger network of relationships. One of the side-effects of considering the "personal" as inherently liberatory and empowering, before examining its forms and its structuring power in an interpretative strategy, has been to dismiss the violent interpretations that sometimes lead to aggressive exchanges in the classroom. Even though these exchanges may be productive, they can also become nightmarish and bring the class to a standstill; but in most cases these violent eruptions of the personal find themselves minimized, or if explored at all, it is in the privacy of departmental workshops as a marginal phenomenon regarded within the larger scope of social and institutional transformations.

> If interpretation is the violent or surreptitious appropriation of a system of rules, which in itself has no essential meaning, in order to impose a direction, to bend it to a new will, to force its participation in a different game, and to subject it to secondary rules, then the development of humanity is a series of interpretations. (151)

I find Michel Foucault's definition useful here in that it forces us to conceive of interpretation as a means to impose a direction, an act of power and subjection, which compels us to ask ourselves about the directions which the intrusion or the omnipresence of the personal impose on interpretations. Even though this reflection on the personal as it encounters the relationships of power within the composition classroom may appear to be taking me away from a reflection on the uses of film in composition, I find it essential. We need to take into account these relations as well as the status of the texts we bring to the classroom—a status which exceeds the limits of an academic environment—as they have an impact on the process of appropriation and interpretation by both teacher and students.

I would like to recover these questions and bring them to bear on the interactions and the work being produced in the space of the composition classroom. My concern here does not lie with the personal essay—which I would qualify as a specific kind of assignment—but rather with the ways in which the personal is at work in interpretive strategies. Thus, I understand the "personal" as a term loose enough to subsume notions as diverse as personal experience, [auto]biographical data, testimonies, confessional voices, informal writing, moments of self-realization, affirmations of one's identity, conversion and coming out narratives, the presence of the "I" in essays, etc. Indeed, part of the work in the classroom should be the description of the forms that the "personal" takes and their effects in the process of appropriation of texts.

In order to make visible, if only artificially, and to scrutinize the forms and functions the personal has fulfilled within student writing, I thought it might be useful initially to make the distinction between personal response understood as [auto]biographical narrative and personal response understood as interpretation. What led me to such a distinction was the realization that in the class discussions and in my comments on student papers I had consistently subordinated the personal [auto]biographical narrative of the pleasure or displeasure which watching film produced to interpretation, instead of focusing on the relationship between the two. As a result, my students carefully learned to minimize the biographical, as they felt it could not belong in a discourse which disowned it. By doing so, I had perpetuated a certain order of narratives, a certain order of tasks in dealing with these narratives, and a certain order of positions. How could I bring my students to reflect on and to draw a link between their own experience of the image, their understanding of the relationship between image and culture, and scholarly responses which were in their own right driven by a narrative exposing the students' "wrong" responses to the film? I decided to turn to documentary—and the ways in which it calls on the personal—in order to explore these [re]presentations of the personal, to problematize the relationship between the interpretative and the [auto]biographical, and to focus on the ways in which these documentaries weave a complex and hierarchical network of personal narratives, both autobiographical and interpretative, at the level of their production and of their reception. Even though I let the class work on the description and distinction between biography and interpretation, I would describe the relationship between them as the interplay between moments of life which the writer sees as shaping his understanding of culture and moments of reflection on certain aspects of culture which compels the writer to revise his own sense of himself in culture. More specifically, I wanted to investigate the ways in which the meshing of autobiography and interpretation not only produces knowledge but also establishes power and authority.

## II. Personal Response as Experience

In her essay, "Experience," Joan W. Scott sharply criticizes the perception that "knowledge is gained through vision; vision as a direct, unmediated apprehension of a world of transparent objects. In this conceptualization of it, the visible is privileged, and writing is then put in its service. Seeing is the origin of knowing. Writing is reproduction, transmission—the communication of knowledge gained through (visual, visceral) experience" (24). She contends that "When experience is taken as the origin of knowledge, the vision of the individual subject (the person who had the experience or the historian who recounts it) becomes the bedrock of evidence upon which the explanation is

built. . . . The project of making experience visible precludes analysis of the
workings of this system and of its historicity; instead it reproduces its terms"
(25). Even though this observation may seem redundant, I find Scott's under-
mining of the self-evident relationship between writing and experience very
useful here. "Writing that matters" can never be the expression of a personal
response understood as personal experience; it cannot be satisfied by simply
acknowledging this response but must also explore the ways in which a learned
response finds itself inscribed in a natural, sometimes even bodily, reaction to
a visual experience.[6] Scott reminds us that our visual or visceral perception of
the real does not produce a more reliable knowledge than the long-decried de-
ceitful reality of the film image. Even though this may seem like the mundane
reiteration of a commonplace, my purpose in bringing film to the classroom is
not to create a space to expose the deceit of the film image. It is to foster an exploration of our own experience of watching a film within the workings of this
specific film, within the conventions which we bring to the consumption of cultural productions, while keeping in mind that the context of the class also affects the conventions we normally bring to bear on a particular experience of
film. There is no essential meaning to be recovered from the interpretation of
the film, let alone a truth, about film or about one's self watching film, only a
better understanding of the workings of film within a specific cultural context,
the personal response being inherent in these workings. We need to explore the
claim that "it is not individuals who have experience, but subjects who are constituted by experience" (26). In the production of interpretation, we have to pay
attention to the context and the language in which experience is being produced
and subjects constituted.

## III. The "Aural Image": A Reflection on the Conditions of the Production of the Personal

### a) Documentary as construction of the personal

In my exploration of the forms and functions of the personal in interpretive
strategies, I was intrigued by a slew of documentaries released fairly recently
about "marginal" experiences—in and of itself an even more problematic category than that of the documentary—which have succeeded quite unexpectedly
in reaching a fairly broad audience: *Roger and Me* by Michael Moore, *Thin
Blue Line* by Errol Morris, *Paris Is Burning* by Jennie Livingston, *Brother's
Keeper* and *Paradise Lost* by Joe Berlinger and Bruce Sinofsky, and *Hoop
Dreams* by Steve James, etc. To work with this genre, which in some ways
could be described reductively as the anthropological tradition returned home,
does not constitute a reflection on the nature of documentary based on a historical or theoretical understanding of this category. I find this remark necessary as a means to underscore the conjectural nature of this return to the personal to which a certain type of contemporary documentary production has
contributed. Besides temporarily bypassing the problems of the conventions

customarily associated with the experience of watching films, i.e., fiction films, starting from this particular documentary image, combined with a focus on the production of the personal, enabled my students and myself to make connections with a wide array of images with which my students were familiar but which did not fit into standard film studies categories: commercials, television news, educational documentaries. It even enabled us eventually to return to fiction films from a new vantage point.

These documentaries function at the intersection of various categories in that they can be pleasurable, entertaining while claiming to produce a certain knowledge. Furthermore, they appropriate certain traits and rituals from the feature film: they are the same length as feature films and they are often narrative driven; they are exhibited in film theaters, etc. Unlike fiction films, however, they foreground their relationship to culture and the independent, low-budget character of their production, bringing to the surface certain assumptions about authorship and individual responsibility. They flaunt their sense of commitment, even though it is useful to investigate the ways in which this commitment is made visible, its object, and its effects on the viewers' responses. I am aware that it would be fairly easy to produce a scathing critique of such documentary productions, and Trinh Minh-ha's analysis of the anthropological documentary tradition in "The Totalizing Quest of Meaning" is perfectly relevant here. However, this sweeping generalization does not take into account a film genre's ability to transform itself in a dialectical relationship to its changing audiences. This critique also dismisses the documentaries' fairly broad appeal as well as my students' strong personal responses which is precisely what I want them to investigate. What is interesting for my purpose here is that they provide what I would call a *mise en scène* of the personal. These documentaries rely extensively on interviews which imply a double move: the camera crew moves to marginalized communities, while the members of these communities are positioned in front of the camera, relating their own experience, an experience which would not normally be heard, bringing it from the margins to the center. I often find it useful to talk about the process of "translation," understood as a process by means of which the documentaries both affirm and contain difference. In order to do so, it is important to emphasize the relationship between the voice of the experience and the image which is never neutral and which may support, undermine, ignore, discredit, or exoticize the "experience." I will refer to the production of the personal in this particular documentary tradition as the "aural image," because it foregrounds the voice of the experience. The aural image emphasizes the discursive nature of this experience and problematizes the relationship between discourse, image, and time in the production of the personal through a questioning of the mechanisms of its reception.[7] Focusing on this *mise en scène* of the personal—which mixes a wide variety of forms: interviews leading to confessions, autobiographical narratives, interpretation of these narratives, personal views, expression of desires, in both private and public moments—we try to discern the ways in which the personal produces difference or sameness, that is to say, we try to examine the model(s), or background against which this personal experience is being described, and the effects on the viewer's response to these experiences. In this preliminary stage, the experience is appropriated and objectified; we discuss the forms it takes and its effects within the overall *mise en scène,* a process which is never neutral or objective. We then try to examine the ways in which the viewers' responses weave themselves into the production of the personal and the effects of these responses.

Focusing on the sophisticated semiotic system which informs the aural image compels us to go beyond the standard critique of the manipulation of reality in the documentary image to examine instead the complex network of relationships which weaves together various layers of personal narratives and provides us with the material to think about the interconnections between the personal as biographical and the personal as interpretative: the aural image foregrounds the personal narrative as self-representation which is always in contradistinction to other unnamed models and which participates in a particular ordering of culture. It is then the task of the writer to examine the ways in which the aural image engages the viewers as well as the forms which this engagement takes. It is within this network of relationships between personal narratives and images that I find it productive to work on the [re]presentation of the personal and the workings that generate it as they collide with other narratives which comment on the relationships between documentary image and culture.

Even though this may seem controversial, and even though there may be much to criticize about the ways these documentaries do so, what I find useful is their varying and paradoxical self-consciousness in relation to evidence and to the power of the image.[8] These personal narratives are embedded in the film's signaling, in a more or less overt way, its own intervention in the production of its narrative.[9] For instance, most obviously, we may or may not hear questions being asked of the protagonists; we may or may not see film crews and their equipment. *Paris Is Burning* signals the presence of an interlocutor by filming Pepper Labeija at the very beginning of the documentary as he asks what he should say, his "name and everything?" But then the viewer does not hear any other question. Students are prompt to point out that *Paris Is Burning* is dedicated to the memory of another Livingston, which brings the personal to the fore in the production. Michael Moore, the director of *Roger and Me,* becomes a protagonist in his investigation of the effects of industrial restructuring in Flint, Michigan. *Hoop Dreams* extends to a web page which four years after the release of the documentary keeps the viewers informed of the progress of Arthur Agee and William Gates in their basketball careers, to mention only a few marks of the intervention of a documentary practice. Through the marks of this intervention, the documentary inscribes a sense of purpose, the forms of a relationship with a community, and the possible effect of this intervention on the reality of this community. These documentaries tend to foreground the question of authorship which constitutes a singular reversal of the power of the image as it is commonly described, discussed, and criticized.[10] As part of its immanent critique of the image—a critique which may nevertheless be very problematic—the aural image raises not only the question of the intervention of the film crew into the production of the personal, of its effect on the production of the personal, it also puts the question of the author and of authorial intent to the test.

To raise the questions of authorship and personal interpretation as inextricably linked in the investigation of the forms of the personal narratives in documentaries and in composition is to make visible the relationships of power at work in the production of interpretation as well as to raise the question of the forms and status of the knowledge being produced. More precisely, authorship comments on how power and authority can be derived from the production and appropriation of personal narratives, and it does so in two different ways—at the level of the production of the documentary, as well as at the level of its reception by the class. Thus, we need to address the ways in which the writer's attribution of authorship affects his own ordering of the world. At this point, reviews of the films may be a useful starting point for the discussion, as they often highlight, more or less deliberately, this network of relationships. If the aural image functions within an implicit understanding of the relationship between the subject, the documentary maker, and the viewer, then we need to examine the workings that govern this relationship, as well as the hierarchies that these personal responses establish among them, between oral and written narratives, naive and scholarly ones, peripheral and central ones. It is in the tension between interpretation and biography that one can strive to understand how a dominant sense of the relationships of power weaves itself into a particular documentary practice as well as into the composition writer's affirmation of power and authority to make these particular personal narratives meaningful. All the same, I find it useful to postpone the process of examining the making of meaning in order to highlight instead the structuring power at work in any interpretative practice while remaining aware that the two are inextricably linked.

## IV. The Text Not Only as a Way of Seeing and But Also as a Way of Affirming Authority

*Ways of Reading: An Anthology for Writers* highlights the network of relationships which run across the production of experience. About reading, David Bartholomae and Anthony Petrosky contend that, "you begin to see the author's project, the patterns and rhythms of that particular way of seeing and interpreting the world" (2). By becoming a "way of seeing," the text foregrounds an intention: it is "what the author said," (2) albeit an *a posteriori* construction. In a Foucauldian move, the text seems to "point to this figure who is outside and precedes it" (115), a figure delineated in the text, and with whom the student writer enters into conversation. She is a figure whose authority, founded on her ability to alter our ways of seeing culture, can be challenged. And, it is this authority, this strategy of defining a position, which is itself rooted in an understanding of the workings which have produced experience, that we hope our students will emulate by taking on responsibility for making the essay meaningful (8), that is to say, by making it relevant to their own experience. Such an understanding presupposes a certain relationship between text, author, and student writer. It is the necessity in the interpretative process to imagine an author which I would like to highlight here in order to have writers reflect on the need for an author, the uses of authorship, and the effects of the attribution of authorship in relation to the production of the personal.

*Ways of Reading* empowers the writer, providing her with an opportunity to raise herself to the level of the author and to explore his ways of seeing as a means to engage with her own. By pointing to a figure which precedes and is delineated in the text, a way of seeing maintains the personal narrative, which is itself autobiographical, in a tension with the personal narrative that constitutes interpretation, and reveals the ways in which the two often need to be combined to ensure the authority of the writer.[11] The value of a particular understanding of culture depends to a large extent on the writer's ability and willingness to define her position in relation to that culture.

In Foucault's "What Is an Author?," the author is also a "function" which can be described as "an effect of discursive practices and cultural institutions" (Dasenbrock 1994, 262), and it is precisely this effect which I seek to investigate in the particular context of a reflection on the personal. A focus on the aural image enables us to raise a somewhat different set of questions: who in the process of producing "personal experience" can be given the status of author? What are the implications of granting and denying access to authorship? What are the ways in which the appropriation of certain narratives, their interpretation and confrontation with other personal narratives constitute a [re]ordering of culture? In relation to this particular question, we need to address the issue of the specificity of a documentary practice, and of the ways in which it may give power to the interviewee, the documentary production, the viewer, or take it away from them. We need to expose the ways in which the viewer's appropriation of personal narratives also grants a different power to the viewer from that which is traditionally awarded to the reader of an anthology: the pervasiveness of the "reality" image in American culture as well as the relative marginality of these documentaries have an impact on our experience of these particular films, and so does the status generally attributed to film in the humanities. This is the place where the effects of interpretation can be brought to the fore in this [re]ordering of culture.

An examination of the aural image in the composition class compels us to question the ways in which any particular way of seeing marks the distinction between "us" and "them," between common and foreign, etc. And writing—understood as a reflexive examination of the tension between biographical narratives and their interpretations—effectively materializes the hierarchies which make experience meaningful as well as their role in the constitution of the subject. If writing constitutes the ordering of the personal narratives between the documentary maker, the interviewee, the viewer, the scholar, it also becomes the means by which we can understand the process through which we impose this ordering. In her critique of the anthropological documentary tradition which can be extended to this new wave of documentaries, Trinh Minh-ha contends:

> The common people. . . . They are the fundamental referent of the social; hence, it suffices to point the camera at them, to show their (industrialized) poverty, or to contextualize and package their unfamiliar life-styles for the everbuying and donating general audience "back here," in order to enter the sanctified realm of the morally right, or the social. In other words, when the so-called "social" reigns, how these people (/we) come to visibility in the media, how meaning is given to their (/our) lives, how their (/our) truth is construed or how truth is laid down for them (/us) and despite them (/us), how representation relates to or *is* ideology, how media hegemony continues its relentless course is simply not at issue. (97)

I find this moment a useful point to start exploring my students' experiences of the documentary. Trinh Minh-ha's authoritative voice, which may in part be attributed to a sweeping generalization, nevertheless invalidates the position of the compassionate viewer, certainly one of the most readily available ones. It forces the viewer, if only temporarily, to question her own response. It establishes an us/them relationship which automatically inscribes an incommensurable distance between the interviewee and the viewer, but it also enables the viewer to establish a distance with her own experience: it is not only about "how their truth is construed," it is also about "how our truth is construed." Although Trinh Minh-ha swiftly disavows one form of personal response, the personal cannot be as readily eradicated from the interpretative strategies for documentary as it is for most fiction films because this documentary practice relies on the personal as a means to establish authority in an attempt at a reordering of culture. A focus on the aural image exacerbates the haunting question of the personal not only as an academic debate in composition but also as a strategy always and already at work in the relationship between the biographical and the interpretative in the writer's affirmation of a position in relation to the appropriation of the personal. And we can start addressing this question in the composition class by examining the effects of the writer's personal narrative as it inserts itself into this process of giving meaning.

## V. The Power of Interpretation: Claiming Authority over Experience

Even though at times my students felt discouraged by the difficulty of the essay, they were also seduced by the strength of Trinh Minh-ha's argument which exposes quite convincingly the hierarchies at work in documentaries, as well as the limits of the access to reality as it is presented in this genre. She debunks the "technologies of truth" and their claims to promote a less mediated access to the real, and exposes instead the relationships of power at work between documentary maker, the individuals being interviewed, and the audience. Looking more closely at the strategies at work in one of my student papers, a paper whose purpose was to assess Trinh Minh-ha's critique of the technologies of truth in *Paris Is Burning,* it is possible to trace the ways in which certain configurations of the relationship between author, text, and students work to give a particular and familiar ordering of culture. In a general commentary about this documentary practice, one of my students, whom I shall call Ann, affirms that she does not believe a documentary maker can produce a "complete picture" of reality; what we get instead is a "personal vision" or a "truthful account" on a particular subject. This understanding of documentary conveys a clear sense of the mediation at work in the production of experience, a mediation which Ann recognizes and authorizes. This attribution of authorship to the documentary maker, however, reduces the subjects to "subject matter" and bypasses the authority of other narratives. In other words, self-representations become a matter of representation, a move which in itself deserves further inquiry.

In the longing for a resolution to the question of the power of the documentary image, Ann's comment subsumes a critique of the documentary image— of its inability to capture the real—into an authorial control that neutralizes it. She reduces a documentary practice to the expression of a personal vision which she applies then to Jennie Livingston's *Paris Is Burning.*[12] All that the viewer can do is trust or distrust this personal vision, and even though Ann does not define the criteria by which this trust can be granted, it was implicit that Livingston had not lived up to the standards expected from a documentary maker. In effect, Ann had embraced Trinh's critique. Quoting directly from "The Totalizing Quest of Meaning," she concludes her paper with the statement that she has "entered the sanctified realm of the morally right, or the social" (97), that she is only a "spectator," and that nothing more is expected from her. Ann is not just decrying the power of the documentary maker contained in an authorial intention, she is also claiming that the viewer cannot have any viable power of her own. Situating authorship in a single individual, the documentary maker, makes the documentary nothing more than a personal vision that also denies any authority to the viewer who can only remain the passive recipient of this authorized vision. The strength of Ann's statement lies in its embracing Trinh Minh-ha's argument, as she comes to occupy the undesirable position of the spectator which Trinh denounces, thus dispensing Ann from dealing with the relationship between the technologies of truth in the documentary. This interpretation makes use of Trinh's critique and ultimately gags the image.

My class then tried to examine the interpretative strategies at work in this particular paper and their effects, only to realize that the paper foregrounded the personal narrative. Ann recognized that her appropriation of Trinh Minh-ha's critique dovetailed with her own experience: Ann felt she was "in here" while the documentary was "out there" (97). Retracing the argument backwards, however, led us to discover a fundamental discrepancy between Trinh Minh-ha's and Ann's arguments: it was the personal narrative that Ann brought to the experience which led her to feel removed from it. She could find nothing in the documentary to "identify with"; she felt hindered by her "heterosexual preconceptions," preconceptions that it would have been necessary to overcome in order to get an "understanding" of a gay lifestyle in New York City. In its acknowledgment of a real unease, of a conflict at work between an awareness of what ought to be done and what cannot be done, the personal narrative stands as the marker of the distinction of an "in here" and an "out there" which in and of itself does not deserve further interpretation, even though it rules over the possibility of interpretation. The adoption of such a subject position, which I believe most teachers encounter, directly raises the question of how a pedagogical practice can address the issue of the personal. This represents a point of collapse in the discussion. Instead of avoiding such passages which I have often done, letting silence speak, I found it useful to engage very cautiously with the categories brought to bear on personal narratives.

Following the path of the paper, I encouraged my students to explore the forms of the personal in the documentary, those that could be subsumed within the documentary maker's controlling "personal vision" and those that could not be reduced to it. I had my students explore the extent to which they believed the image could be the product of a "personal vision." By exploring the forms which the personal takes and the ways in which they affirm sameness and difference in relation to preexisting models, we then tried to develop a reflection on the strategies of interpretation we bring to the experience of film in such terms as "preconception," "youth," "understanding," "identification." What I hoped to achieve with such an approach was the rupture, the temporary detachment between the affirmation of a position, of an identity, and the discussion of the forms of the personal, not so much to dismiss the position as to work on the circulation of the personal, on the relationship between the personal as biography and as interpretation. I tried to have a discussion which reinscribed the personal in a system of relations in language which establishes power, identity, and authority while deflecting the tensions which are inherent in the affirmation of one's identity. Such a reflection enabled us, I believe, to go back to the ball in *Paris Is Burning* as a performance, that is as a play with identities which extends beyond language.

Trinh Minh-ha provides a frame for Ann to think about documentaries. She in turn, appropriates Trinh's argument to produce a powerful critique of the conditions of production which ultimately bypasses the experience. However, in her condemnation *with* Trinh Minh-ha of the technologies of truth, personal testimony being one of them, Ann throws the baby out with the bath water. Thus, we may want to address the issue of the effects of her argument that establishes the author in order to make her bear the blame for gagging the experience and validates Ann's interpretation as it is grounded in a personal biographical narrative. In this particular context, I found it useful to examine the interconnection between two strategies, the attribution of authorship and the reliance on the personal, strategies which our students often bring more or less consciously with them to the composition class and which have become constitutive of interpretation. Making visible the forms of the personal and of its circulation, giving them a linguistic materiality, i.e., considering them as words to which we not only attach an understanding of ourselves in response to the experience of a particular film but also our relationship with culture, provided me with the material to trace an interpretative strategy rooted in the personal. From there, it became important to redirect our work as a class and among other things to refocus the class on the critique of the technologies of truth which made possible an investigation of the power of the personal, both biographical and interpretative, as it can be expressed within and contained by a documentary image. Ultimately, moving away from the voices of experience and language, we explored the forms of the personal that extend beyond language in the performance and in the silences of the image. In this respect, I find *Paris Is Burning*'s emphasis on language very useful as a starting point for a discussion of a community's identity as it is constructed both within community and in relation to dominant perceptions of American culture. This emphasis on language, however, does not necessarily entail a relegation of the image because the intertitles call attention to the construction of the documentary; in other words, it problematizes the image's privileged relationship to reality.

It is quite clear that the documentary here proposes a *mise en scène* of relations which engages Ann's argument dramatically. Ann refuses to occupy a self-righteous but powerless spectator position *and* blames the documentary maker for the failure of the mediation between subject matter and viewers. Such a strategy foregrounds authorship and interpretation while exposing the discrepancy in the argument which, on one hand, grants total power to the documentary maker, but, on the other, renders the documentary powerless with regard to the "experience" the viewer brings to the documentary. It leaves the whole process of interpretation in limbo while justifying its collapse. I found it useful to start from a student writer's reliance on the personal in order to go back to the image, that is to retrace from the writer's argument a network of relations between the writer, the production of the documentary as she imagined it, and Trinh Minh-ha's critique. Having explored the strategies which the writer had brought to bear on interpretation enabled us to go back to the personal narratives in the documentary which the writer had bypassed in order to examine the models against which these narratives set themselves up; we tried to imagine the strategies at work in the production of these personal narratives, the gesture these narratives make toward an audience. While acknowledging the fundamentally personal character of our visceral responses to images which in turn propel or cut short interpretation, I hope that this approach provided my students with a glimpse into the circulation of the personal narratives as a strategy at work in a particular documentary practice as well as in their responses to it. My objective in this process was to foster a reflection on the forms—and the

authority that can derived from these forms—of the personal as it meshes together biography and interpretation in the process of transforming a reality by
way of a documentary image.

In his desire to "think anew about writing as a place where the personal
and the academic . . . are always inextricably woven" (267), Miller looks back
at the event in light of which any hermeneutic system breaks down, his father's
suicide attempt, as it collides head-on with that which motivates the deployment of a whole hermeneutic system, the television show *Rescue 911*. Miller
brings to the fore the question of how the personal biographical narrative can
break with interpretation. My approach here is different, less powerful: and exploration of the aural image with its powerful and sometimes excessive appeal
to the personal encourages an investigation of the conditions of its production
and of its effects. It enables us to question the personal biographical narrative—
which is always "moistened with meaning"—as it inserts the writer in a network
of material relations which determines the form, the extent, and the effects of
interpretation, of the production of a knowledge subjected to the definition of
the position of the writer.[13] An exploration of the personal narrative in the aural image can problematize the moments when the biographical narrative precludes interpretation and the moments when, on the contrary, it authorizes or
lends itself to interpretation. It begs for an understanding of the system which
governs the responses to a documentary practice. We may agree with Miller that:

> To think of culture as not only present in a series of intellectual debates car-
> ried out in the academy but also as the varying registers of taste and distaste
> physically experienced in the body is to take down the cordon separating the
> public and the private and to recognize that all intellectual projects are always,
> inevitably, also autobiographies. (285)

However, my project here is less ambitious because, before returning to the
body, we also need to examine with our students in the composition classroom
the ways in which the personal inserts itself into certain theoretical, historical,
and cultural frames in order to thrive on their legitimacy and/or to subvert
them. The point in doing so is not to track it and to eradicate it but to understand its power. This is because taste is primarily an affirmation of one's position, i.e., one's difference, in relation to those who do not have the same taste,
in a logic which is independent from the actual cultural commodities to which
these various registers of taste or distaste are being applied.

In this particular essay, I have not dealt with sequencing, although I believe
that it would be a necessary follow-up to this preliminary study. I chose instead
to privilege a specific moment in my exploration of the potential relationship
between a specific set of texts and a concern with composition. Doing so has
enabled me to bracket, at least temporarily, some assumptions which are current in composition; I have been wary of the liberatory overtones inherent in
some discussions of the personal in Freshman composition, and of the assimilation of liberation to power. Even though I believe that teaching writing should
be a means to empower students—indeed, such an ambition is included in the

very definition of most Freshman courses that are intended to give students the tools to write in the academy—it is also necessary to begin with an exploration of where and how the personal inserts itself within the interpretative frameworks that we lay out for the class, knowing that every new text, every new document we bring to it implies a reordering of the relationships at work in the production of experience. Without wanting to confine the personal to a working definition which it would always exceed, I find instead that it is more productive to make the looseness of "the personal" the subject matter of the class, that is to provide a space to describe and discuss its forms, its functions, and its effects in clearly defined contexts. If bringing in the personal is liberatory, it seems important to discuss the kind of liberation it brings about as well as the consequences of this liberation. From there, it becomes possible for us and our students in the class to assess the effects of adopting certain subject positions, the authority which can be derived from them as well as the limitations they may impose on interpretations. I find the question of the relationships of power at work in the production of the personal and the forms of its appropriation very useful, in that it makes the exploration of the personal an integral part of the production of knowledge understood as an ordering of culture.

# Notes

1. I also tend to resist using film in terms of metaphors about writing which would make it at best an inadequate analogy. These metaphors subordinate film to writing and, even more problematically, they make of film and writing formal constructs without taking into account the material relations and the hermeneutic systems which produce and make these constructs meaningful. See, for instance, William Costanzo in "Film as Composition" who claims that "Instead of using media from time to time as 'visual aids,' or as mere diversions from the process of writing, we can use them more directly and more productively by treating film, television, and writing as analogous forms of composition." p. 79.

2. Daniel Wild's presentation about the uses of film in the Composition classroom at a workshop on Visual Culture in April 1997 at the University of Pittsburgh. This notion of "transgression" deserves further exploration, but I find it intriguing because it points us to the use of film in the composition class as signaling a shift in the students' perceptions of the teacher/student relation.

3. Here, I am using this term in the sense of David Bartholomae and Anthony Petrosky's understanding of the relationship between reading and writing in the composition class. See Part IV.

4. This is the opposition at the core of Wendell V. Harris's argument in "Reflections on the Peculiar Status of the Personal Essay" and of Gordon Harvey's in "Presence in the Essay." Both arguments also converge on and define one of the problems encountered when dealing with the "personal" in academia as being the absence of a definition to work with; Harris describes it as "looseness of terminology" while Harvey introduces "presence" in the essay as a means to track the personal and its effects.

5. Ruth Spack turning the gaze on the teachers in "The (In)Visibility of the Person(al) in Academe" attributes the focus on the personal in the classroom to "feminist

challenges to the Western academy's traditional privileging of objectivity." Crediting Kathleen Weiler's work she traces the "liberatory pedagogy's notion of transforming the teacher from lecturer to participant" back to its "leading proponent," Paulo Freire. p. 10. Here again, Spack focuses on the personal as liberatory, and even though she seeks to draw attention to teachers' subject positions and visible or invisible identities, she does not explore the violence of the teacher/student interaction which she describes as personal experience. What is striking, however, is the violence of the incident which took place in her classroom as well as the inhibiting impact it had on her teaching. pp. 21–25.

6. Here, I find Miller's reintroduction of the body insightful in his reading of Pierre Bourdieu's *Distinction*. Referring to Bourdieu's description of "distastes" as "visceral intolerance," Miller then remarks that taste "involves . . . a way of feeling that is scored into and emanates out from the body. And this way of feeling is . . . experienced as natural." p. 272.

7. We may want to address the ways in which the documentary production is self-reflexive in both acknowledging its presence as a foreign element in the environment whose reality it is trying to capture, and in minimizing the interference of this presence. We may also want to interrogate the ways in which these documentaries emphasize their working on the long term, their bringing out the humane dimension of the shared experience between film crew and subject by making the whole documentary apparatus appear geared towards obtaining the maximum hearing for its subjects. It brings out the dimension of time (*Hoop Dreams* over more than four years, *Paris Is Burning* over more than two years, *Brother's Keeper* and *Paradise Lost,* each over the duration of a trial) and forces us to examine the relationship between the narrative and the image in relation to time.

8. For instance, although the voyeurism at work in *Brother's Keeper* might be considered objectionable: it becomes crucial to investigate the networks of relationships it promotes between interviewees, interviewers, the media, American culture (the Law), the community, and the viewers.

9. I am aware that I am dealing with generalities here, and that various documentaries do so to varying degrees. However, I feel authorized to say so, if only by the care which these documentaries take in highlighting the artisanal character of their production, the intimacy or, at least, the congeniality between film crew and interviewees, with the exception of *Thin Blue Line* which deflects the conflation between documentary and reality in other ways, see footnote 10.

10. In spite of Trinh Minh-ha's claims that "the filmmaker's perception may readily be admitted as being unavoidably personal, the objectiveness of the reality of what is seen and represented remains unchallenged," some documentaries alert the viewer to the construction of their argument. For instance, *Thin Blue Line*'s blue motif, its music, its recurring close-ups of key elements in the murder, its reconstruction of the murder from various points of view highlights the social construction of the murderer while constantly deflecting the truth of the documentary to give it instead a thriller, almost film-noir like, quality. p. 95.

11. In this respect, the introduction to *Ways of Reading* and its examination of Richard Rodriguez's "The Achievement of Desire" is eloquent: "The power and value of Rodriguez's reading . . . are represented by what he was able to *do* with what he read, and what he was able to do was not record information or summarize main ideas but, as he says, 'frame the meaning of my academic success.' Hoggart provided a frame, a way

for Rodriguez to think and talk about his own history as a student." In the same way, *Ways of Reading*'s attention to the presentation of each writer at the beginning of each essay is also revealing. p. 3.

12. *Paris Is Burning* is a documentary which in a centripetal movement explores a certain gay lifestyle in Harlem through a significant event, the ball. While paying close attention to the language through which this community defines itself and to history, the documentary intercuts live recordings of the balls themselves and interviews of drag queens which provide first-hand accounts of how meaningful the balls are, and extend to more general accounts about the interviewees' lives and desire.

13. Quoting Barthes, Trinh T. Minh-ha writes that the "West moistens everything with meaning." p. 107.

# Works Cited

Bartholomae, David, and Anthony Petrosky. 1993. Introduction. *Ways of Reading: An Anthology for Writers*. 3d ed. Boston: Bedford Books.

Berlinger, Joe, and Bruce Sinofsky, dir. 1992. *Brother's Keeper*.

Berlinger, Joe, and Bruce Sinofsky, dir. 1996. *Paradise Lost*.

Costanzo, William. 1986. "Film as Composition." *College Composition and Communication* 37 (1): 79–86.

Dasenbrock, Reed Way. 1994. "Taking in Personally: Reading Derrida's Responses." *College English* 56 (3): 261–79.

Foucault, Michel. 1977. *Language, Counter-Memory, Practice*. Edited and translated by Donald F. Bouchard. Ithaca, NY: Cornell University Press.

Haefner, Joel. 1992. "Democracy, Pedagogy, and the Personal Essay." *College English* 54 (2): 127–37.

Harris, Wendell V. 1996. "Reflections on the Peculiar Status of the Personal Essay." *College English* 58 (1): 934–53.

Harvey, Gordon. 1996. "Presence in the Essay." *College English* 56 (6): 642–54.

James, Steve, dir. 1994. *Hoop Dreams*. Katemquin Films / KTCA-TV.

Lee, Spike, dir. 1989. *Do the Right Thing*. 40 Acres and a Mule.

Livingston, Jennie, dir. 1990. *Paris Is Burning*. Video Miramax.

Miller, Richard. 1996. "The Nervous System." *College English* 58 (3): 265–86.

Moore, Michael, dir. 1989. *Roger and Me*.

Morris, Errol, dir. 1988. *The Thin Blue Line*. Video Miramax.

Scott, Joan W. 1992. "Experience." In *Feminists Theorize the Political,* edited by Joan Scott and Judith Butler, 22–40. New York: Routledge.

Spack, Ruth. 1997. "The (In)Visibility of the Person(al) in Academe." *College English* 59 (1): 9–31.

Trinh T. Minh-ha. 1993. "The Totalizing Quest of Meaning." In *Theorizing Documentary,* edited by Michael Renov, 90–107. London and New York: Routledge.

Zemeckis, Robert, dir. 1994. *Forrest Gump*. Paramount.

# 2

## Writing Images

### *Some Notes on Film in the Composition Classroom*

### Daniel H. Wild

While the leap from text to images is something very intimate and familiar to good readers, as words might conjure up imaginary landscapes in the solitude of the act of reading, the move from images to words remains much more difficult to achieve than we are wont to imagine. No doubt the difficulty of such a transition has been obscured by the abundance of writing on films: Movie reviewers evaluate the merits of any given film and grade it on a more or less subjective point- or star-scale, films are reduced to plot summaries on the back of video boxes, replete with bold-faced words, sentence fragments, and exclamation marks as the written equivalent of sound bites, and TV guides offer us a phrase, a description, or a sentence or two to tell us what the listed film is about. Such is the state of writing on film, the written discourse around film with which incoming university students are mostly acquainted. Composition teachers might recognize in my description also a more general approximation of the writing quality in first-year students' essays on any subject matter: a description of similar texts or commonplaces that are produced when students write themselves into the university, when they have to participate in a debate that has begun long before them and for which they have not yet acquired the necessary skills to speak forcefully (Bartholomae 1985, 135).

It is the task of the composition teacher to offer a space in the classroom for participation in such debates and to introduce students to the complexities of serious intellectual work. Broadly speaking, then, the aims of a composition class should extend and move beyond the honing of already acquired rhetorical writing skills or perfecting the awareness of prescriptive standards of grammar. The primary focus thus becomes the production of writing that moves toward a self-reflexive understanding of its discursive functions, an understanding of the student writers' role within this discourse and an emerging sense of the scope of intellectual practices in writing. Formal concerns notwithstanding, drafts, developments of ideas, and revisions become crucial on this level. The process of revision allows room for correcting sentence-level errors, but the emphasis in the development of critical thinking skills lies in the act of revision, of reseeing one's written work, illuminated by assertions, commentary, and classroom debates. The project of this composition pedagogy thus becomes the question "[b]y what method can students learn to think differently?" (Spellmeyer 1989, 715). In brief, if a composition class is to serve as an introduction to academic thinking, our pedagogy must always return to an understanding of how difficult this kind of thinking differently is for students. Revision, the act of seeing again and anew and to subsequently integrate one's insights into (re-)writing, might serve as a basis. But it is the very act of seeing or of vision itself here that film in a composition class can illuminate, if the class is dedicated to the articulation of different thinking in writing, rather than different articulations of the same. I would like to sketch out, then, some theoretical and practical questions that arise in a composition pedagogy with the medium film as its central textual basis in order to reflect on the difficulties we and our students must face when we begin to attempt to translate filmic images into words.

I take as the starting point a necessary connection between the activity of reading and acts of writing. As such, reading becomes a hermeneutic process, where readers "generate critical questions that enable them to reflect on the meaning of knowledge and on different processes of knowledge formation" (Salvatori 1996, 440). In other words, the emphasis here is to shift away from a restrictive writing framework that asks the students to produce text versions of what they as readers already know towards an epistemological investigation of the question "how do we know what we know?" Composition as a pedagogy is involved, then, in the production of texts by investigating the compositional aspects of the manner in which a text is created and to understand or rethink the intellectual framework that informs the creation of these texts. This approach sees a composition course as grounded in the correlative conjunction between writing and reading, between "the constructedness of a method of reading through enacting translations and interpretations in writing, that is, textual work itself" (Bartholomae and Petrosky 1996, vi). This structural relation, however, becomes more difficult to sustain when we introduce film as a text because the very notion of reading does not easily extend to the complexities of the film viewing experience.

How does one read film? Ostensibly, our skills as composition teachers allow us to pay close attention to the workings of language and to recognize layers of allusion or divergent movements within texts. Yet, even for those of us who, as readers, have become amazingly adept at detecting subtle registers of irony or minute nuances of tone, the filmic text can constitute a limit point.

Here we tend to resort to symbolism of the crudest kind when it comes to the materiality of filmic images. A white dress, then, symbolizes purity or virginity and a killer in a black car stands for death and evil. It is this very understanding of film as a representative or symbolic text that we first and foremost need to take into account because it hinders rather than enables a productive use of film. Any composition teacher interested in working with film must be very careful not to impose a mode of analysis, or reading, that reduces the field of visual images in film to a reference text merely pointing to an interpretive text of a higher order. To understand film solely on such (literary) terms means to ignore the complexities that the act of seeing film entails, for it assumes a simplistic signifier/signified relation that cannot do justice to the kind of thinking that is already in place on the level of visual images themselves. Here I am following the work of the French philosopher Gilles Deleuze who, at the end of his daunting two-volume work on the cinema, concludes that "cinema itself is a new practice of images and signs," a philosophical practice which requires a corresponding "conceptual practice" on our part (Deleuze 1994, 280).[1] Rather than eroding film then, the act of reading which we bring to the cinema is already an interference inscribed in or given rise to by the cinema, but, as Deleuze argues, it is precisely at the level of the interference of many practices that things happen or, in other words, that cinema makes happen "beings, images, concepts, all the kind of events" (280).

If to make things happen on an intellectual level in writing is programmatic for a composition class, then the initial part of the class needs to focus on the interferences at work (or in play) in our understanding of film. For incoming university students and composition teachers this generally means first of all a large set of expectations that does not necessarily see the filmic text as a field of images. In accordance with the conventional discursive writing around film, a composition class with the medium film will usually be expected to constitute a form of screenwriting or an occasion for movie reviews.[2] Here, the task of the teacher must be to foster the imagination of what writing on film might be or become. Nonetheless, while the introduction of film might pay attention to the material from cultural artifacts and discursive realms with which our students are very familiar in order to generate a kind of cultural literacy to use an over-determined term here, it can also be considered an act of transgression by teachers on the students' part. Despite the general interest and predilection students might show for a writing class with a focus on film, this enthusiasm can easily turn to hostility when composition teachers are seen as transgressing into the terrain of their popular culture to dissect and desecrate the experience of film. This is especially the case when film is used only as classroom material in service of something else, that is, as supplementary audio-visual material which might complement or make accessible some other pedagogical project.

I am constantly amazed by the level of sensitivity towards the visual experience of film that students display when they sense a kind of reductionism on the teacher's part. This is not to say, however, that, within the context of a class-room, such reductionism is absent in the students' work. Part of the difficulty in beginning to work with the material of film, then, is to problematize pre-cisely our tendency to reduce film to a legible text, which excludes more elu-sive concepts such as, for example, affective responses to film through specta-tor positioning, the experience of time through the duration of images, or our immersion into the visuality of images and the play of light. Lest this be seen as a lack of critical distance in relation to the medium film which celebrates a form of sensationism, I want to stress that, in order to understand the profound and pervasive influence that visual images impose on us, it would be fallacious to leave aside this integral aspect of film in favor of a clinical detachment that merely focuses on the narrative or textual skeleton of film. The affective expe-rience of film is very much part and parcel of our relation to visual images and renders film as an area of private and subjective pleasure, which effectively re-sists any attempts to transfer it into the broad daylight of the classroom, so to speak. Moreover, our students themselves are very much inclined to forget the affective power of film when films are made the subject of scholarly inquiry. That is, they are well aware of certain conventions of discussing texts and bring in a considerable theoretical apparatus that is supposedly appropriate for an analysis of film within a classroom environment.

In this theoretical framework I have frequently encountered an astonishing ability to unravel or strip a filmic text down to the level of statements like it's just entertainment or the film is about believing in yourself, in simultaneous combination with a stunning interpretive relativism, which postulates that, even though we all see the same images, anyone can read anything into the film. While film certainly is a profit-based form of entertainment, such an utterance can be productively used to investigate the nature of what constitutes entertain-ment, especially when it is in the service of profit maximization. The cinema as a spectacle of attractions then becomes the most volatile commodity, the experience of which is restricted by the time-frame it offers us, so as to render us ready to repeat this experience over and over again. Conversely, to reduce a film to what it might be about attests to an analogously widespread reading practice, which Mariolina Salvatori describes as "immobilized within text-books" and reduced to "sets of disparate simplifying practices that, separated from the various theories that motivate them, turn into meaningless and arbi-trary exercises" (Salvatori 1996, 442). In this sense, it is precisely a habituated way of reading or a way of talking about the act of reading that the student who offers the interpretation of *Forrest Gump* as a film about believing in yourself has acquired. Such statements, however, should not baffle the teacher of litera-ture, who can expect to find a similar mode of reading in place when "The Lovesong of J. Alfred Prufrock" is reduced to a poem about loneliness. To counter a rampant interpretive relativism that a discussion of texts reduced to their about-ness can easily generate is a challenge we must face frequently, but one way of beginning a more sustained and rigorous analysis for film would be to offer for discussion the limitations of a statement which proclaims that *Titanic* is a film about oceans.

These kinds of approaches towards film, to be sure, should not be dismissed as more evidence for the decline of the humanities in our students' high school education, but rather as sophisticated and habituated textual practices that interfere when film is made the focus of a university classroom. Students are well aware of actual or assumed teacher expectations and will readily offer what they presume the teacher wants to hear. The tendency, for example, to discuss a film's message can thus serve as evidence for their willingness to see the social implications of a film, to already understand it as part of a social intervention. Here the difficulty lies in moving towards an analysis of how a film might be said to participate in social and political debates, rather than merely recognizing its status as a political text. Likewise, we can expect our students to have at their disposal a certain rudimentary understanding of a film as a text itself: frequently students show a familiarity with subtexts or intertextual references and will possess an awareness of audiences as an integral part for the actualization of a filmic text. That this awareness might, at the same time, take shape as the claim that audiences in Hawaii will not be able to relate to the film *Fargo* because it is so cold in North Dakota should alert us to the fact that a lot depends on the analytical framework through which we ask our students to write on film. Finally, students are generally more attuned to formal qualities of the filmic structure than we tend to assume. Expectations of closure and resolution allow them to hypothesize plot developments, they already understand a film like *Pulp Fiction* to violate conventions of linear narratives, and they will easily distinguish between dream sequences and diagetic reality, acknowledge scenes as flashbacks within the time-frame of the film, or explain close-ups as foreshadowing.[3] Such meta- or proleptic leaps in the sequence of images demonstrate the facility of understanding the filmic language, as well as the pervasiveness of the visual system with which anyone who views films is familiar.

It is at this point that we can understand why the concept of legibility has so easily been extended to include the filmic text, since it appears to operate within a linguistic system of meaning production through editing or montage techniques. The possibilities of envisioning the question of language as a mode of representation via the help of a linguistic system of a different order can facilitate an awareness of the way language functions in texts. The formulation of thoughts in relation to a different linguistic structure is helpful in establishing the ability of thinking across intersemiotic lines, a fundamental difficulty that is often identified by student writers as their primary problem in the composition of texts: "the inability or difficulty to put thoughts from my head into writing." Thus, the *bricolage* of images that comprise the filmic experience make visible, in all senses of the word, the difficult interpretive strategies that film in general or a film in particular demand of their audiences. As such, films make visible the notion of a text as a virtual work, something that is in flux as an event unfolding in its temporality rather than spatially on the page. This emphasis on temporality can illuminate the status of any text as an event to be reenacted by hermeneutic interpretation. Moreover, the temporal, that is, textual, structure of the class itself can be made an object of interpretation by relating it to filmic temporality. The recourse to a literary vocabulary such as plot as the unfolding of events in a time sequence and story as the mental reconstruction of the significance and meaning of the events, then, can allow students to articulate and locate moments in which classroom discussions become too difficult to follow as lines of thought, corresponding to the difficulties that complex written texts demand of their readers. At the same time, such an analytical framework can be brought to bear on the discursive structures of student essays, e.g., as the question "how does the story this writer wants to tell differ from the plot of the essay?"

Paradoxically, however, the facility with which films can be approached on such conventional textual levels occludes the materiality of images as images, since the hermeneutic interpretation of images rests on a shift from the understanding of the image as being what it is, to the image-idea, or *eidos,* seen as present only within its representational functions of the text. This double-bind results from our reluctance to abandon the notion of film as a purely representational text and manifests itself in our and our students' willingness to read films only symbolically in a classroom context, that is, to rely on varying literary levels of familiar representational codes, while our general experience of visual images might already be much more complex and advanced than this approach might suggest. Rather, through the filmic power of visibility, our students may already have obtained a more profound understanding of images in film, an understanding they may be willing to relinquish in order to accommodate a composition teacher's predilection towards representation or textual translation, which then results in more or less inept discussions on the symbolism at work in film. Instead, cinema, as Deleuze argues, "brings to light an intelligible content which is like a presupposition, a condition, a necessary correlate through which language constructs its own 'objects'" (Deleuze 1994, 262). "This correlate," he continues, "consists of movements and thought-processes (pre-linguistic images), and of points of view on these movements and processes (pre-signifying signs)" (262). The recovery of these thought-processes in and through the language of our students is the fundamental difficulty a composition teacher faces when working with filmic images. This is the moment in which filmic understanding becomes knowledge, not merely of the content of meaning, but a knowledge of the form of inquiry that makes the meaning of meaning itself become possible.

To be precise, this philosophical digression exceeds by far the scope of an introductory composition class devoted to the development of intellectual thinking in relation to filmic images, but it is the linguistic construction of objects, or ideas generated through film, that should concern a teacher of composition. In other words, we do not need to make programmatic for our students the complexity of cinema itself, so long as we are able to show that the students' textual work does not deviate from or violate the cinema but rather constitutes a fundamental part of the interferences that film constructs for us. Let me illustrate this with two examples. A student analysis of understanding film tends to oscillate within the polarity of film as a work of art, which permits a supposedly free and subjective range of interpretations, and directorial intention, which categorically reduces film to one specific meaning. This contradictory understanding calls attention to the very question of the "author function" that is attributed to a text and might form the basis of a discussion where this polarity is not presented in either/or categories but as a difficulty that constitutes the filmic text or the student text itself (Foucault 1979, 13). In other words, the question becomes not an occasion of determining one's position, of the familiar territory of taking a stand on the pro or con divide, but rather becomes an invitation to partake in an act of intellectual imagination, that is, to enable thinking which moves from a familiar dialectical framework towards thinking the impossible, towards imagining what it means to think paradoxically.

Certainly this might sound presumptuous for those of us who are used to working in an academic environment where students are likely to ask for the definition of the word ambiguous. But it is precisely at this level of convergence between ideas and their translation into words that the difficulty of serious intellectual work begins or has begun for all of us. In this sense, let me point to an excerpt of a student essay that exemplifies both a willingness to think the concepts that cinema gives rise to and at the same time demonstrates the intellectual difficulty of giving meaning to these thoughts in language. Here, then, is a discussion of the temporal structure of the film *12 Monkeys:*

Before reaching the airport Dr. Railly and James Cole put disguises on. James Cole recognized Railly from his dream because she now had on the blond wig. Kathlyn Railly said that she recognized James Cole in this form also. This just proves my point of life being a continuous cycle. She knew who he was with the disguise on because she had already been in the airport with him. The airport scene was always happening. When James Cole was sent to 1990, Dr. Railly said that she recognized him from somewhere, but she did not know where. Later in the film, James Cole was sent to World War I and he was shot in the leg. Next he is in 1996 and he kidnaps Dr. Railly. After kidnapping her, he tells her about his wound. When she is returned home she had the bullet analyzed and found out that it was fired before 1920. Railly then remembers that she had seen James Cole in her World War I pictures. James Cole remembers being in the airport on December 13 and he remembered the shooting. In his flashbacks he recalls being there as an eight year old boy and also as an adult. This proves the fact that James Cole has already been there from the future. This trip was not his first and will not be the last. He is living the same life over and over again. This reminds me of the movie *Ground Hog Day,* in this movie Bill Murry became stuck in one day. Everyday he would

> wake up and it would be the same day as it had been yesterday. The difference
> would be that Bill Murry could change what he did in that day but James Cole
> cannot. James Cole is stuck in the same set life and keeps living it over and
> over again. (Grabowski 1998)

What amazes me about this analysis is the grammatical understanding of tense shifts that approximates the difficulty of temporal levels that this film postulates. This excerpt attempts to render in the linguistic recourse of tenses available, from past tense continuous via past perfect to future and conditional, a filmic experience that unfolds in linear time but needs to be reconstructed as images of time in writing. Moreover, the writer constructs a textual field through her own filmic memory that does not see film as a symbolic system of representation. Rather, she locates an idea of time at which both films converge and is, at the same time, able to recognize the interference between two divergent thought-processes in relation to time. The difference, she states not quite yet, is that Bill Murray is endowed with the agency to change his own position, that is, to see history as progressive, while Bruce Willis (James Cole) has become part of an understanding of history as ineluctable, repetitive, and cyclical. Yet, for all its formal lack in grace and style, this writing already reflects ideas generated by film and makes visible the thoughts within the images. To enable students to find adequate words for these image-ideas as an act of representational translation through writing, then, means to take seriously our position as composition teachers.

In conclusion, let me offer some practical considerations on how to structure a composition class that attempts to work with film as an intellectual field of inquiry. I find it useful to supplement classroom discussions and writing assignments with some (excerpted) film studies texts. Such texts, however, should not be seen as tools to be applied to films in order to serve merely as exemplary modes of analysis, but rather as grounds for the formulation of necessary and important questions that illuminate the study of film.

Conversely, the assignment sequence for essays needs to build on ideas and terms that are generated through the films and the student essays discussed in class. For example, opening assignments might ask students to introduce themselves in filmic terms, that is, to present visual scenes as representative of their lives. A writer who is able to construct an image of herself here through fragmented close-ups of her dorm-room furniture and its objects demonstrates a more advanced understanding of film than the writer who begins by writing that "we see a girl who has led a happy life, ready to experience the adventures of college-life." Subsequent assignments can build on and work with a connection between cinematic form and the formal structures of student essays. Some of the most interesting and challenging essays I have read resulted from an assignment sequence that used circular filmic narratives as the basis for a description of images or experiences in a circular manner. The conceptual difficulty here notwithstanding, many students were able to produce writing that keeps returning to its original premises, yet at the same time builds a text around the foundations of their premises.[4]

This brings me to the question of what filmic texts to select. Teachers who have used materials from popular culture in their classrooms will know that the shelf-life of these texts is remarkably short, a problem that is evident in our own inability to remember last year's summer movies. For this reason, we need to constantly pay attention to the films that circulate, not as a way of catering to the topicality or capriciousness of our students' tastes, but as a way of keeping up with the intellectual possibilities that films give rise to. Some of the films that I have found useful for course work include *Pump up the Volume* (USA 1991), *Reflecting Skin* (Canada/GB 1990), *Zentropa* (Denmark 1991), *Barton Fink* (USA 1992), *Forrest Gump* (USA 1994), *Before the Rain* (Macedonia 1994), and *12 Monkeys* (USA 1996).

While technological inventions such as the VCR have enabled us to over- come the "mourning of the lost image," something which film studies used to call le deuil cinematique, it might be important to remind ourselves that, as composition teachers, we usually tend to work with future forgotten texts. That is, even the most intellectually engaging classroom will generally produce student essays written not for posterity but for the moment, and even the most stimulating films will soon be replaced by the experience of other, more immediate films, as images recede into our collective memory banks. All the more profound, then, are the questions that should illuminate our pedagogy. The experience of film will continue for our students long after the memories of one classroom among many others have faded. But for film in a composition class the fleeting memories of a particular film are not as important as remembering the general intellectual work that writing in light of film might initiate. As teachers, we can then take solace in the fact that our students have begun to see thinking reflected by film and we may hope that film will continue to illuminate their thought.


# Notes

1. For all its difficulties, Deleuze's conclusion can nonetheless be useful as an introduction to a composition and film calls. That is, students are much less reluctant to discuss and follow the implications Deleuze's writing represents than it might seem from the level of difficulty it invokes.

2. I am basing my descriptions here on various courses at the University of Pittsburgh entitled "General Writing: Film," an option among the composition classes that freshman or sophomore students in the College of Arts and Sciences are required to take. The writing abilities of the students on this level are beyond "basic writing," although there is usually significant discrepancy and variation in regard to writing proficiency.

3. In fact, "flashbacks" constitute a highly sophisticated temporal dimension in the experience of film, where the linear and subsequent temporal unfolding of filmic time is marked by our understanding of the time-frame in which the plot unfolds. The emphasis on "plot," then, obscures the various temporal relations that are embedded within the images. Conversely, "foreshadowing" can only be recognized temporally *after* the fact, as it were, unless it is an educated guess or hypothesis, determined by a proficiency or "literacy" in formal filmic conventions.

4. The student essay excerpted above was written in response to a preliminary assignment for the work with circular narratives.

# Works Cited

Bartholomae, David. 1985. "Inventing the University." In *When a Writer Can't Write: Studies in Writer's Block and Other Composing-Process Problems,* edited by Mike Rose. New York: The Guilford Press.

Bartholomae, David, and Anthony Petrosky. 1996. Preface. *Ways of Reading: An Anthology for Writers.* 4th ed. Boston: Bedford Books.

Deleuze, Gilles. 1994. *Cinema 2: The Time-Image,* translated by Hugh Tomlinson and Robert Galeta. Minneapolis: University of Minnesota Press.

Michel Foucault. 1979. "What Is an Author?" *Screen* 20 (1): 13–29.

Grabowski, Jennifer. 1998. Film Essay on *12 Monkeys.* Unpublished paper for General Writing and Film, University of Pittsburgh, June.

Salvatori, Mariolina. 1996. "Conversation with Texts: Reading in the Teaching of Composition." *College English* 58 (4): 440–54.

Spellmeyer, Kurt. 1989. "Foucault and the Freshman Writer: Considering the Self in Discourse." *College English* 51 (7): 715–29.

# 3

## *Rear Window*

### *Looking at Film Theory*
### *Through Pedagogy*

## Edward Maloney and Paul Miller

Early in composition's brief history as a discipline there was an extended discussion about the use of film in the teaching of writing, the highlights of which are reviewed by Joseph Comprone in his 1976 bibliographic essay "The Uses of Media in Teaching Composition." Comprone's essay reflects the tendency of composition's adaptation of film theory in the 1960s and '70s to foreground composition studies' interest in formalistic and universalistic elements of written texts. Claims for universal and formal standards in composition naturally led to an emphasis of those aspects—the formal, visual structure—in the uses of film in composition courses. Thus, there was a good deal of interest, as Comprone notes, in the visual "grammar, punctuation, and syntax of film" and in comparing such elements to their analogous elements in writing (170). This emphasis on formal matters in the work that he reviews is also often accompanied by a greater interest in art films rather than popular films, and in one telling section Comprone is dismissive of—and only cursorily treats—the "conventional, sometimes even tiresome tendency to claim a place for media in the writing course merely because students are exposed to a great deal of media in their everyday lives" (171).

Though many in composition, and certainly we as authors, look more favorably now on employing texts familiar to students, we want to go beyond claiming a role for media such as film *merely* because students are extensively exposed to such things. Nevertheless, there are reasons for advancing a role for popular culture and media in composition that hinge on students' extensive ex-

32

posure to them. By and large, the emphasis on film as a formal medium or as a content driven text has ignored some of the significant ways in which film has become what we might call a "naturalized text" for students. By naturalized text we mean an object that has become so familiar to students that the mechanisms by which that object produces meaning and value for students are often obscured by students' relative familiarity with the object. As a naturalized text, film is a valuable object for the study of writing. Students' familiarity with film allows for a common discursive text for the entire class—something that is harder to attain with what we might call 'high literature' since many students are often resistant to written texts[1]—and thus makes it easier on one level to focus on students' writing rather than spending a disproportionate amount of struggling with students' resistance.

As a naturalized text, then, film works with the desire to illustrate the practice of writing by reference to texts and contexts familiar to students, a desire which has been one of the more significant developments in composition studies since the 1976 publication of Comprone's essay. Over the last twenty years composition studies has developed a notion of the inherent value of energizing the purpose and content of writing by having students write about texts, ideas, issues, values, and experiences familiar to them, while it has questioned a focus on basic composition structures or rules of grammar at the expense of such content. If we consider composition as having moved historically from an emphasis on the text (grammar, modes, etc.), to the writer (cognitivist approaches), to the context of writing (social construction, cultural studies), then the shift in emphasis is not surprising: indeed, it might be thought surprising how much interest film generated in composition given the more formalistic, product-oriented attention to the text prior to 1976. But the shift to an emphasis on the context of writing is certainly not reducible to—and not even most importantly—an interest in studying texts that students are familiar with. Several related shifts have attended this new emphasis. Foremost among these was a movement away from a universalistic and formalistic approach to texts that emphasize the contingent, nonuniversal world of culture, value, ethics, and politics, a movement which has been accompanied by a corollary interest in the critical thinking that attends any analysis of such matters.

These shifts have brought a renewed interest in the contexts of writing themselves—previously the charge of literature, cultural studies, and gender studies programs—which has led to the increasing influence of a cultural studies paradigm within composition courses. This interest in context has required that composition instructors balance the teaching of writing with the critical analysis of the contexts for that writing, or more specifically a critical analysis of students' perceptions of and experiences within a given culture or discourse community.[2] Interest in discussing such cultures and communities has led to a desire to find texts that offer a meeting place for teachers and students to talk about shared experiences while still being able to produce critiques of the larger socioeconomic issues at stake in the course. One text that fulfills these interests, of course, is film.

When we first set out to design a composition syllabus that used film as a primary source, we did not, however, wish to ignore the formal aspects of film. Using film as a cultural text enables teachers and students to gain quick access to different perspectives on our culture, but it does not highlight the unique experiences of the medium of film. Our experiences with film are often different than our experiences with literature, television, or advertisements, and these differences are a direct effect of the conventions of film. These differences lead to a second, formal approach, which sees film as a separate and distinct medium that requires its own hermeneutic structure of investigation. A formal approach closely mirrors the direction of the discipline of traditional film studies, and much of the critical work done on film (and the adaptation of film to the composition classroom) tries to suggest methods for reading the formal aspects of film. The fact that film's conventions and narrative techniques often parallel traditional literary techniques has led to an overlap between film theory and literary or narrative theory. As with a cultural studies approach to teaching film, formal approaches to film have both advantages and disadvantages. In addition to recognizing and accounting for the effects of the specific filmic experience, the formal aspects of film can be used as a model of the composing process, of the rhetorical elements of both organization and style, and—as Comprone notes—of aspects of "grammar, punctuation, and syntax."[3] We would argue, however, that a narrow, formal treatment of film often ignores larger cultural issues, issues that we have seen increase in value for composition studies. In addition, the constraints of the focus of a composition course means that a discussion solely of the formal aspects of film might take away from the focus on students' writing.

Given these considerations, we decided that it was important to integrate, as much as possible, formal and context driven readings into our syllabus, while we also recognized the need to compensate for the problems that both would bring to the course. In addition, we felt it was necessary to make it clear to our students how our reading of film worked within the larger structure of a composition course. In order to make this claim, we needed to show two things: that our reading strategy worked within the current emphases of composition studies, and that the models we were developing for the analysis of film were helpful tools for students who were learning writing. This meant showing how the critical analysis of film paralleled the writing process, both as a formal study and as a cultural reading practice. Ultimately, we were trying to get our students to recognize the effect that film—and other cultural productions—had on their lives and their attempts to write successful critical analyses. Our approach, then, was threefold: to give students tools to analyze film; to facilitate students recognition of the value of film as a cultural text that has something to say about the society in which we live; and to help students see film as model for, or at the very least a parallel of, the writing process.

Implementing this threefold approach presented logistical hurdles. We realized that not all films would be useful in emphasizing all three aspects. Rather, we decided we would have to alternately emphasize one aspect over the other two, with the hope that by the time we got to the last films on our list we would be able to bring the three things together in a meaningful way. As with any course that uses extensive outside materials, one of the most difficult challenges was to balance the logistics of incorporating film into the classroom. We decided that we would show films at specific nonclass times and place films that were available through the library on reserve so that they could then be viewed by students at their leisure. When the library did not own a film on the syllabus and students could not attend the scheduled viewing, it was their responsibility to rent the film (all our students had access to video stores and players, either on campus or at home, and we confirmed that all the films we were viewing were available to all students). Film was thus treated as homework, just as reading a novel would be. An interesting effect of the familiarity issue we have been discussing, is that most university students, even those in their first year, are unused to treating film as a homework assignment, and therefore expect all films to be shown in the classroom during the scheduled time. One of the problems that instructors might face, then, is finding ways of making films available without wasting half of the scheduled meeting times showing them. This will be less and less a problem once film is used more widely in composition courses.

After a couple of weeks of introductory material on composition and film we showed our first movie. Since this was a first-year composition course, we felt that it was important to begin by making students aware of some of the ways film can work both formally and thematically to stress the structures of composition. Initially, we wanted to focus on the ways film makes meaning through visual cues. Also, since the remaining films on the syllabus were contemporary, we chose an older movie, partly to give students a broader range of experience with film and partly to ask students to look at a movie that did not rely on many of the conventions of narrative film making they were familiar with, such as special effects or a contemporary soundtrack. We chose the 1954 Alfred Hitchcock film *Rear Window.*

Because *Rear Window*—even as it is a murder mystery—is fundamentally a metaphor for film, we felt that it would be a good movie to start the course. *Rear Window* is the story of L. B. Jeffries (played by Jimmy Stewart), a magazine photographer who, at the beginning of the film, is in his sixth and final week in a wheelchair after having broken his leg while taking a risky picture of a crashing race car. During the six weeks he was in his wheelchair he was confined to his apartment, and he spent this time—in between visits by his down-to-Earth nurse, Stella, and his high society fiancé, Lisa Fremont— looking out his rear window. His rear window looks out onto a courtyard and into the apartments of the different complexes that all share the same courtyard. The first moment of the film is a camera pan up from the stairs leading into the courtyard, around the courtyard to the various apartments, then into Jeffries' apartment, around the main room, and finally resting on Jeffries, who is asleep. The sweeping of the camera around the courtyard and into Jeffries' apartment is a concise, visual analeptic narrative of Jeffries' life for the past six weeks, which consisted of little more than watching the lives of the various people in the other apartments. This narrative is told solely by the camera, with no voice over or textual clues students might be more familiar with. Many of the items that we see in the camera pan, such as a picture of Lisa, do not make sense until the film progresses and we are introduced (a second time) to these things. However, one of the things we were able to get students to recognize in this scene is the way the camera works to tell the story. For example, the movement of the camera from the photography equipment on Jeffries' shelf to the picture of a crashing race car to the closeup of the cast on Jeffries' leg, works to tell us how Jeffries came to be in a wheelchair. In addition, since Hitchcock made Jeffries a photographer, the emphasis on the visual gaze of camera makes more and more sense.

From the beginning of our analysis of the film in the classroom, then, we asked our students to pay attention to how visual cues could make meaning in fairly complicated ways. There are certainly many instances of this in *Rear Window*. As Jeffries watches the goings on of the people he sees in his rear window, we as audience members come to see how his actions parallel ours. As he watches, we watch. Our sense of similarity with Jeffries is heightened towards the end of film as the murder plot plays itself out. While playing the peeping tom, Jeffries believes he sees evidence that one of his neighbors has killed his wife. He does not actually see a murder take place, which is what creates tension between himself and the friends that visit him in his apartment; his friends do not believe that murder has taken place, and each in turn, like Jeffries, must spend time looking out his rear window to the 'screen' of the courtyard to be convinced that a murder might have been committed. As the murder plot works itself through, the metaphor of the film as film continues to develop as well. In order to understand the murder narrative, Jeffries' friends Lisa and Stella must watch. They become part of the audience; the audience that makes up Jeffries' apartment. This becomes important for the tension we feel as real audience members, especially since at certain points in the film we see things through Jeffries' eyes (or binoculars or camera lense) and we see things that Jeffries does not. For example, we see Thorwald, the suspected murderer, returning home while Jeffries is asleep. Jeffries never sees this, and this lack of information supports his theory of murder. There is a tension created because we are asked to identify with Jeffries' view and see the 'film' of his neighbors' lives as he does, but we are also one step removed because we are watching Jeffries just as he is watching others. In other words, as audience members we are watching essentially two films: the first is the events that take place in Jeffries' apartment. His relationships with Lisa and Stella take place here for the most part. We will call these events the first order film or text. The second order is made up of the events that take place in the courtyard and other apartments. We see these events primarily through Jeffries' eyes, and our visual experience is affected by this perspective, a perspective we would not have if we were watching through Lisa's eyes, for example. We will call these events the second order film or text. Instead of relieving some of the tension created by the plot, this double-watching heightens that tension. At different points in the film we move from watching Jeffries to watching his neighbors to watching both. Our interpretation of the film is filtered through these different lenses. These movements of perspective work to stress the formal constructions of the film that are used to create tension for us as audience members, and one of the things we worked on as instructors was to get students comfortable analyzing the moves of the film.

As we've discussed, we were not solely interested in the formal aspects of the film. Our close reading of the movie was used to help us see how the film makes meaning, and what the film might have to say about what we have been calling larger cultural issues. There are two separate strands at work here, each related to the first and second order films. A motivating subplot of *Rear Window* is Jeffries' struggle with his own insecurities about marrying Lisa, who is played by Grace Kelly. The film portrays this insecurity by offering a cultural comment on marriage in the second order film. It does this by connecting each one of the stories that Jeffries sees through his rear window to the idea of marriage, and this is what we try to get our students to recognize and analyze first. From the flirtatious young woman, Miss Torso, to Miss Lonely Hearts and the songwriter, each representing models of loneliness for Lisa and Jeffries, to the newlyweds, who start out on their honeymoon only to fall into stereotypical patterns of married life by the end of the film, to the happily married couple sleeping on their fire escape to escape the heat, to Thorwald, a husband so fed up with his "nagging" wife that he murders her, Hitchcock sets up cultural text within the second order film that portrays what are the perceived views on marriage at the time. Jeffries' decision, then, is helped along by what he sees in/out his rear window. In other words, Jeffries' choices about marriage are at the very least reflected in the second order film, but in more complicated ways they are arguably affected by the texts he views. The murder plot, then, complements the larger cultural text within the film, and the successes and failures of the various second order plots help Jeffries make his decision to finally marry Lisa, or so we are led to believe by the end of the film.

The second order film as cultural text is not the only cultural text in the movie. Just as we watch the film of the courtyard through Jeffries' eyes, we are also watching Jeffries and the events that take place in his apartment and his life. We are twice removed. At this point, we ran into our first resistance from our students. While they were inclined to recognize the cultural comments Hitchcock was making about marriage in the subplots played out in the second order text, it was more difficult to get them to recognize the cultural values and issues at stake in the first order text. The relationship between Jeffries and Lisa, for example, as well as the relationship the film constructs for the viewer with Jeffries and Lisa, can both be read as cultural comments not entirely under the controlling gaze of Hitchcock. There are, in short, moments in the film, just as there are moments in the scenes Jeffries is watching—where he sees either more or less and differently than the other characters and the viewing audience, and builds his own interpretations from what he sees and doesn't see—where the film viewers can see more (and possibly less) and differently than he sees or than Hitchcock saw and build interpretations from those views. The viewer can see what Hitchcock directed their attention to, critically, that is from their own different perspectives that locate him and the film in the broader cultural context.

We therefore tried to get our students to recognize the multiple layers of the film, and the tension that is created between the different levels of viewing—we feel tension for Lisa, as we see her through Jeffries' eyes, when she is caught in Thorwald's apartment, just as we feel tension for Jeffries when Thorwald enters his apartment. The reading process is similar to asking students to do cultural analysis in composition classes, where we ask students to recognize both the meaning of events and the meaning of the structures in which those events take place. *Rear Window* is a great case in point, because the visual emphasis of the film begs the question of who is looking (and from where). We tried to get our students to see how the visual cues made meaning, as Laura Mulvey argues in "Visual Pleasure and Narrative Cinema," but this time meaning that may not have been meant within the context of the film, rather meaning that might have been generated by the film's place in the larger cultural context of mid 1950s mainstream America. We emphasized the issues of the gaze and who controls the action; like the subplots of the courtyard scenes, the gaze and the action are tied to the issue of marriage and ultimately to the issue of gender.

As a model, Lisa represents the visual in a very different way from Jeffries. She represents high society and money, and her relationship to the visual is as the object of the gaze. For example, our first image of Lisa is a full close-up of her face that fills the entire screen, while our first image of Jeffries is of him asleep, an inactive action, as it were—even though Jeffries is inactive here, we know he'll wake up; we can't be so sure about Lisa. Jeffries, on the other hand, is a photographer, and an action photographer at that. He travels the world in search of wars or sporting events to photograph. His relationship to photography is active rather than passive. The film makes the connection between activity, passivity, and the visual very clear, and our students were willing to see this. Jeffries' power, in a sense, comes from his ability to look, to photograph, to see. When he is incapacitated by his accident, all he can do is look, which is similar to our situation as audience members. Jeffries' viewing allows the murder plot to develop, and it allows us to feel his tension when he is unable to save Lisa (other than by calling on the help of the police) or to defend himself from Thorwald.

The issues at stake in the first order film or cultural text are more complicated because they are less visible. For example, Jeffries' relationship to Lisa throughout most of the movie is lukewarm. He makes it very clear that he feels threatened by her, or rather by the idea that she will make him become a fashion photographer and thus take away his power and his freedom. During the movie, he maintains his distance and constantly keeps her advances at bay—until the moment she enters Thorwald's apartment and endangers herself. There are two things going on here: Jeffries fears for Lisa's life when Thorwald returns home and finds Lisa snooping around his apartment; and, more importantly, Jeffries' attraction to Lisa as soon as she enters the second order film. In other words, as soon as Lisa becomes part of Jeffries' gaze—rather than a member of the audience watching the courtyard with Jeffries—his interest in her is renewed. Lisa cannot watch anymore; she must be watched. Just as the thematic aspects of the Lisa character—as model, as future wife—affect Jeffries' relationship with her, the position that Lisa occupies within the filmic metaphor affects his, and ultimately our, relationship to her. As Mulvey notes, as an object of the visual gaze, Lisa no longer represents a threat to Jeffries' ability to see, and thus his ability to control. The film ends with the promise of marriage, and it does so because Jeffries is finally able to see Lisa as we, in the audience, do. What we tried to show in the classroom, then, is that the relationship between visual imagery and power is caught up with issues of gender and ultimately with cultural contexts of the film.

As we've said, our goal in introducing the formal aspects was to help students see how film makes meaning within larger cultural value systems. Primarily, what we were hoping to show, is that film, as a cultural text, can both reflect and affect the cultural value systems in which it exists. We were successful in getting students to recognize the cultural contexts of the second order film in *Rear Window;* we had a harder time getting them to recognize the cultural contexts of the first order film, however. Students were willing to see how the second order film could reflect and even affect Jeffries' decisions about marriage. They were also willing to analyze the ways both the first and second order texts reflected the larger cultural views of the time about gender and marriage. But even though we were able to get them to see how our perspective, as audience members, meshed with Jeffries', they were much more resistant to the idea that the cultural values in the film could in some way affect the cultural values of the people watching the movie, or them in particular. This was, in part, because we were asking them to critically analyze structures—particularly of the cinematic gaze—that they all took for granted. It was also because we were asking them to comment on a film that was made forty years ago and that had little, at least from their perspective, to say about present day culture. We recognized that we could only take the idea of how films affected our perspective on cultural issues so far with *Rear Window.* In the next part of the course, we originally chose a more contemporary film—*Pretty Woman*—that worked within narrative structures that our students were all familiar with, namely fairy tales.

Our goal with *Pretty Woman* was to focus on the broad range of ways in which film reflects and affects culture. One of the primary values film brings to a social constructivist syllabus is its richness as a text which operates simultaneously as a medium of education,[4] entertainment, and commentary. Our experience with *Rear Window* and other films had convinced us that film (and, of course, television), like literature in the late nineteenth century, has come to occupy the position of what we might loosely parallel to Louis Althusser's concept of an Ideological State Apparatus (ISA). Thus, although film often provides insights into the cultural values and beliefs of the time, and though it has the power to influence the popular perception of the culture, it is also like Althusser's ISAs in that its influence often goes unperceived and unexamined. In this regard, there is an ethical motivation for the use of film and popular texts in general: to the extent that students are unaware of the power of popular texts such as news, film, television and advertising, they can be influenced by such texts without their conscious choice. We would argue, indeed, that facilitating an understanding of the ways in which popular texts shape issues, sell products, and promote values is as or more important than any other form of civic/humane education within the state.

When we initially team-taught a first-year writing course that focused on film—before teaching either *Rear Window* or *Pretty Woman*—we were immediately surprised by our students' reluctance to consider film as anything more than escapist entertainment, and certainly as nothing approaching an Althusserian ISA. We were prepared to debate the extent to which film reflects and affects society, but we were surprised by the predominant view of our students that popular film did neither. Given our students' attitudes and after emphasizing the formal aspects of film in *Rear Window,* we attempted to address the issue of culture in *Silence of the Lambs* before we moved on to *Pretty Woman.* Because of the background given by our discussion of *Rear Window,* students were very willing to talk both about the making of meaning through visual cues and the role of gender in the film. However, they were less comfortable talking about psychoanalytic readings of the visual—as we had planned to explicate this way of reading in relation to gender in *Silence of the Lambs*—partly because these readings asked students to add a completely new context to their reading practice. In the end our students remained unconvinced that the film affected the values of American society, let alone themselves, in any interesting way. Film for our students was the ethical equivalent of ice cream: some people liked it, some didn't; it could be made better or worse, but it was largely a matter of taste; and it certainly didn't have the power to shape or mirror worldviews. And many of our students were deeply committed to this view—a view which seriously undermined the relevance of our course by making any discussion of the cultural issues we intended to address a hollow, academic game.

In hindsight, our students' position is understandable. Purveyors of popular culture—unlike parents, religion, and friends—are often interested in denying (or at least soft-pedaling) their bias and degree of influence. Cigarette advertisers, for instance, claim that they only influence choices among brands of cigarettes, and for decades Hollywood has been concerned with camouflaging the political content of both the form and content of its films (see Mulvey 1988). Furthermore, first-year students are often at a point of heavy identity stress: at Ohio State they are often away from home for the first time, trying to decide on a major or career, deciding whether to join Greek societies, trying to live with roommates who are under similar stress, attempting to find new friends, and trying to understand a new academic system and whether or not they should identify with it. In the midst of all this pressure on how they define themselves, popular culture is often a means of escape. The last thing that a person in such a position would want to hear is that their means of escape is actually another source of formative pressure.

In our discussion with students about what they felt influenced them, it became clear that they felt that their childhoods were particularly impressionable, and that in addition to the influence of parents, school, and friends they felt affected—at least in their youth—by stories and fairy tales. And indeed in one class none of our students had seen *Casablanca,* but all knew the story of Cinderella either through children's books or through the Disney movie. Moreover, Cinderella was the only text that we could identify that everyone in the class felt familiar with. The following quarter we decided to discuss fairy tales—Cinderella in particular—and use them as a springboard for an analysis of *Pretty Woman* in place of the heavier introduction to psychoanalytic theory and *Silence of the Lambs.*

Our first goal was to use the Cinderella tale as a means of illustrating the variety of ways in which cultures can adapt and augment a story, which provides an entree into the broader question of how stories can reflect a society's values. This seemed to us most expeditious, because in general students were less resistant to the claim that movies reflect a culture than they were to the claim that movies affect a culture. Particularly useful in this regard were Marcia K. Lieberman's "'Some Day My Prince Will Come': Female Acculturation Through the Fairy Tale" (1972) and Louise Bernikow's "Cinderella: Saturday Afternoon at the Movies" (1980). These essays demonstrate the plasticity of fairy tales through time and culture and show both that Disney's version was not the first Cinderella story, and that it was significantly altered for its American audience.

Lieberman analyzes the various values reflected by the tale: the importance for women of beauty, of passivity, of obedience, and of marriage as a defining moment of social and economic success. However, women who are both powerful and good are rarely human: those who are human and have power (or seek it) are almost always repulsive. Bernikow's essay focuses on the competition and enmity between women that the tale reflects. Both authors introduce the idea of a master narrative, a broad narrative structure such as the

Cinderella tale that maintains a recognizable structure in its hundreds of muta-
tions across cultures, genres, and media. The essays laid the groundwork for a
consideration of *Pretty Woman* by not only showing how fairy tales are adapted
by cultures, but also by leading many students—especially women—to seriously question the image of women portrayed by the Cinderella tale.

After the essays, and in conjunction with the showing of *Pretty Woman,* we
had groups of students give presentations responding to six analyses of *Pretty
Woman* that developed the themes introduced by Lieberman and Bernikow.[5]
Particularly useful in regard to the fairy tale theme was Leda Cooks' "The
Fairy Tale Theme in Popular Culture: A Semiotic Analysis of *Pretty Woman*"
(1993), which outlines structuralist "codes" in the Cinderella tale (the Prince
code, the Princess code, the Godmother/father code, the Ball code, and so on).
She then explicates the ways in which these codes operate in *Pretty Woman,*
outlining parallels between the Cinderella tale and the film (e.g., Cinderella/
Vivian, The Prince/Edward Lewis, The Ball/The Opera Scene, The Gift of the
Dress/The Shopping Scene, The Godmother [father]/Barnard [the hotel man-
ager]). Thus, for example, students were able to see that in Cinderella the
Prince is not just a prince, but that he functions as a symbol for the apex of
power, prestige, and wealth in the society at the time of the fairy tale. When we
asked students who they felt represented the apex of power, prestige, and
wealth in American society, we got responses ranging from super athletes like
Michael Jordan to music stars like Garth Brooks. Students conceded, however,
that a maestro of corporate takeovers like Edward Lewis was certainly in the
running—especially given the film's release in 1990—and they understood
why such a character would work well as a "prince" in a film like *Pretty Woman.*
Likewise, they saw why a prostitute would work well as a "Cinderella" in the
film (though we had a long discussion about whether or not the Cinderella of
the source fairy tale could have been a prostitute instead of a poor girl with
mean older sisters).

Once this algorithm of comparing Cinderella and *Pretty Woman* was
grasped, the discussion became serious, lively, and contentious. Most of the
class, especially those who had previously decided that the Cinderella tale
didn't do women justice, had also very much liked *Pretty Woman* when they
had viewed it prior to our class. They now recognized that the film incorporated
the same characterizations of women as the Cinderella tale, and they weren't
sure that they should like the movie. In the process of the debate several wider,
useful issues surfaced. First, students began to seriously entertain the possibility that film could affect their values as well as reflect them. It became clear to
many students that their "impressionable" years as children had latent effects
and resonances that popular culture could appeal to in systematic ways, and
that such appeals couldn't always be relegated to a nonethical realm of "just
entertainment." Second, it became clear to many students that although they
had an extensive, innate understanding of film, they might not be fully aware of
how and why a film appealed to them. Because many students now seriously

entertained these issues, they were able to meaningfully engage the wide variety of reviews and commentary that addressed *Pretty Woman,* an engagement which in turn gave purpose to the writing in their journals and formal papers.

Though time and space do not permit an extended discussion of the use of film as a model for composition, it is important to recognize the value that film can bring to a composition course as both a formal and cultural text. It is clear that integrating film into composition courses requires an understanding of the inherent conventions of film as well as the value of film as a product of cultural values and perspectives. In his review of the role of popular culture in the classroom, Comprone summarizes John H. Clarke's argument against the use of popular media as presented in "One Minute of Hate: Multi-Media Misuse Pre-1984." Clarke, Comprone notes, fears that film and other popular media are "too often used as mere entertaining fillers in writing classes and create, as a result of this misuse, passive students and teachers who, rather than learning to criticize what they see and hear, become passive receivers, completely under the control of the media-makers" (Comprone 1976, 172). Certainly these dangers exist if film and other media are treated merely as naturalized texts in the classroom. Indeed, student resistance to treating popular film as anything more than "just entertainment" would lead quickly down the path Clarke fears, unless that resistance is addressed directly and immediately. When we worked to denaturalize both the form and content of popular film we found that students were less passive and more critical than they had been with any other material. They were able to develop their own critical skills in conjunction with the discussion/writing/revisison process at the heart of the course. As students become familiar with the tools of critical analysis, their relationship to writing becomes richer and more complicated. The value of film for the composition course, then, is in part because students' predefined familiarity with film enables connections, while our ability to denaturalize film without destroying its allure enables critical thinking and writing.

## Notes

1. It is surprising how little scholarship there is in composition on film given the recent emphasis on cultural studies and student-centered pedagogies. Between 1970 and the 1976 publication of Comprone's essay, in *College Composition and Communication,* for instance, there were three articles published that were devoted to the issue of using film in composition. In the 22 years since Comprone's article we found only one comparable article in *College Composition and Communication,* William Constanzo's 1986 "Film as Composition."

2. This shift toward a interest in social constructivism has been primarily a North American phenomenon, but the shift has implications for students from a variety of socioeconomic backgrounds.

3. See Jeske and Costanzo for extended treatments of film as a model for composition.

4. Documentaries, of course, are the primary sources of education in the most narrow sense of the term, but we would also suggest that film acts as a more subtle form of cultural education. See Mulvey and Althusser.

5. See Caputi, Cooks, Greenberg, Kelley, Lapsley, and Miner.

# Works Cited


Althusser, Louis. 1971. "Ideology and the Ideological State Apparatus." In *Lenin and Philosophy and Other Essays,* translated by Ben Bewster, 127–86. New York: Monthly Review Press.

Bernikow, Louise. 1980. "Cinderella: Saturday Afternoon at the Movies." In *Among Women,* 17–37. New York: Crown.

Caputi, Jane. 1991. "Sleeping with the Enemy as Pretty Woman, Part II? Or, What Happened After the Princess Woke Up." *Journal of Popular Film and Television* 19 (1): 2–8.

Comprone, Joseph J. 1976. "The Uses of Media in Teaching Composition." In *Teaching Composition,* edited by Gary Tate. Fort Worth: Texas Christian University Press.

Cooks, Leda, et al. 1993. "The Fairy Tale Theme in Popular Culture: A Semiotic Analysis of *Pretty Woman.*" *Women's Studies in Communication* 16 (2): 86–104.

Costanzo, William. 1986. "Film as Composition." *College Composition and Communication* 37 (1): 79–86.

Greenberg, Harvey Roy. 1991. "Rescrewed: *Pretty Woman*'s Co-opted Feminism." *Journal of Popular Film and Television* 19 (1): 9–13.

Jeske, Jeffrey M. 1984. "Using the Short Art Film as Model." *Writing Instructor* 4 (1): 7–23.

Kelley, Karol. 1994. "A Modern Cinderella." *Journal of American Culture* 17 (1): 87–92.

Lapsley, Robert, and Michael Westlake. 1992. "From *Casablanca* to *Pretty Woman:* The Politics of Romance." *Screen* 33 (1): 27–49.

Lieberman, Marcia K. 1972. "'Someday My Prince Will Come': Female Acculturation Through the Fairy Tale." *College English* 34: 383–95.

Miner, Madonne. 1992. "No Matter What They Say, It's All About Money." *Journal of Popular Film and Television* 20 (1): 8–14.

Mulvey, Laura. 1988. "Visual Pleasure and Narrative Cinema." In *Feminism and Film Theory,* edited by Constance Penley, 57–68. New York: Routledge. First published in *Screen* 16 (3), 1975.

# 4

## Representing Student Culture

### Field Research and John Singleton's Higher Learning *in* the Composition Classroom

Donna Dunbar-Odom

As director of a first-year composition program at a medium-small state university, I am responsible for the two-semester sequence of composition classes. The catalog and the department's curriculum and composition committees have determined that the first semester will be devoted to the writing of essays, the second to library-based research and the structures of argument. For the first course, I designed a sequence of reading and writing assignments which lead students to explore, develop, and question their "idea of a university." The second course, however, proved more of a frustration and a challenge, as I struggled to continue to find ways to get students to grapple with intellectual complexity and to move beyond the production of "canned" research papers.

The problem seemed to me primarily to be how to offer them a taste of the experience of "real" research, research one feels one has a stake in and is committed to, rather than the production of yet another version of the always-already-written, one-side-or-the-other research paper. Even when I avoided the clichéd topics—i.e., abortion, capital punishment, lowering the legal drinking age—the form was generally the same with the writer serving the form rather than the form serving the writer. There seemed to be little connection made between the writer and the thing being written. How does one begin to forge a connection where there is no "authentic" connection? How does a writer become a researcher when she knows little about the focus of her research? How does she begin to negotiate that terrain when it is, for her, unknown territory? In her article, "Ethnography and Composition: Studying Language at Home,"

45

Beverly J. Moss (1992) describes in much the same way her own difficulties making a connection with and developing a dissertation project: "I realized that much of the research I had read seemed to have no real connection to me and where I came from, that a large gap existed between the people I knew and the people being described in that research" (153). Moss goes on to explain her own sense of "otherness" as an African American female researcher in a field which tends to describe African American writers as the ones with "problems": "Much research in composition studies focused on novice and expert writers and on how one group (usually people from backgrounds similar to mine) didn't measure up to another group (expert writers, usually white, middle-class students)" (153).

In her efforts to forge a connection between her experience and her research, Moss turned to ethnography. While I certainly do not mean to imply that Moss is a "beginning" researcher in the same way my first-year students are "beginning" researchers, what occurred to me as I reread Moss' words is that the "gap" can be said to exist similarly between my students and the people with whom and the problems with which they tried to connect in their own attempts at research. Further, it seemed to me that, as it did for Moss' research, ethnography—or, more accurately, field research—also offered possibilities for introducing first-year students to what research is as well as why any sane person would want to do it. What I have since found is that ethnographic methods of research have a great deal to offer the composition teacher and student.

A sense of expertise lies at the heart of what motivates research, and to bank on that I have focused my sequences of assignments on the culture of schooling—more specifically, on the culture of higher education. Every student in every classroom is, in a certain sense, an "expert" at being a student. He may not be the most gifted student on campus, but he still is certainly the "star" of his own student story. All assignments offer representations of higher education and/or of student experience, and the written assignments ask students to respond in increasingly complex ways to those representations, with students ultimately responsible for an extended project for which they research an issue relating to the student experience that has, for whatever reason, struck them as particularly true, false, or significant.

Students read from Cardinal Newman's "The Idea of a University" or Allan Bloom's *The Closing of the American Mind* or Mike Rose's *Lives on the Boundary,* but the medium that has proven most engaging on a number of levels has been film. While it strikes me as odd that, given how much box office money comes from the pockets of college-aged patrons, Hollywood's attempts to represent student culture frequently feature broad, parodic cartoons of student life, even such representations have served the purpose to get students to begin to look at their own experiences as if through a camera's lens. Films such as *National Lampoon's Animal House* (1978) or *Back to School* (1986) offer slapstick, larger-than-life versions of campus experience (e.g., the food fight, the fraternity party, cheating, etc.) that supersede the much more mundane routine that makes up most of college life. But bringing together film literacy and field research methods enables students to find significance in the mundane as well as to begin to notice and to question what is missing from these films—i.e., the real difficulties inherent in the transition from high school to college and the issues that the first-year student often must confront as a result, issues of race, sexual identity, sexual freedom, alcohol use and abuse, privacy, and so on.

A film that has proved more provocative and more productive in the classroom has been an interesting and ambitious exception to more stereotypical representations of college life, John Singleton's *Higher Learning,* a 1995 film that introduces and follows several first-year college students through their difficult adjustments to life at a large, public research university, fictional Columbus University. Every college teacher and college student knows what a pressure cooker the campus can be for some students, and the film ably shows both the small irritations and the huge explosions that can occur when so many people from so many diverse backgrounds are brought together with immediate expectations that they will get along with each other and will perform successfully at tasks they have never been exposed to before.

*Higher Learning*'s main characters—Malik (Omar Epps), an African American athlete; Kristen (Kristy Swanson), a white California liberal; and Remy (Michael Rapaport), a confused son of an Idaho survivalist—each respond to their first days at college with bewilderment. Malik, a former high school track star, quickly finds his assumptions about himself and his goals challenged. He assumes his speed and reputation will allow him to get away with skipping track practice and copping an attitude, perhaps as he was able to do in high school, but his coach responds by kicking him off the field and changing Malik's full scholarship to a partial one. Kristen is a nice California girl who has, so far, taken much in her short life for granted. In college, however, she must face a reduced standard of living (her father lost his job in the aerospace industry the year before but only now is she apparently feeling the effects), she must face her own prejudices (her roommate is African American), and she must take precautions to assure her personal safety (her subsequent "date rape" is foreshadowed by a discussion of the blue security lights lining sections of campus sidewalks and leading to emergency phones). In other words, her safe and secure world lined with safe and secure assumptions is not quite as safe and secure as she had once thought. Remy came to school to be an engineer and to get away from his father, but, perhaps shaped by his survivalist father's isolation, he cannot connect with any of the other students in the dorm around him; he wants to, but he's just too weird and too desperate. All three find the reality of college experience far different from the reality they had imagined.

Malik comes to college to run track and pave the way a better, more financially secure life after college, but he's challenged to question those assumptions by a radical Afrocentrist student Fudge (Ice Cube) and by his introductory economics professor Maurice Phipps (Laurence Fishburne). Both push

Malik to begin to think of himself and to act as an intellectual, to become a '90s version of DuBois' "Talented Tenth." Displaying the anger of the newly converted, Malik fixes on the injustices of American society and, temporarily at least, has difficulty finding balance and perspective. Helping him find that perspective is his girlfriend Deja (Tyra Banks), also a track athlete, who wants him to push himself academically and to reject violence as a viable response to injustice. Her death, at the hands of Remy, provides Malik's trial by fire from which he emerges politicized but balanced.

Kristen arrives at Columbus University a little bewildered to find herself with a hip African American roommate and in a place where things she thought she knew are not necessarily true. For example, in a quick early scene long before they actually meet, Kristen and Malik are together, alone, in an elevator. Kristen, reflecting her white suburban upbringing, places her hand over her purse, thinking herself at risk from an African American man. Later, we see, however, that she has sensed danger in the wrong place. With a group of "friends," she allows herself to get drunk on shots of tequila and then allows Billy, a cute, clean-cut, white fraternity boy, to take her back to his room. She seems perfectly willing to go along with such a crude "seduction" until Billy refuses to stop long enough to make use of a condom. It is at this point that the their sexual act becomes rape as Kristin screams and struggles to get Billy to stop and Billy, thrusting away, keeps telling her to wait. This act serves as the catalyst that moves Kristen toward feminism, brief exploration of lesbianism, and political activism as she is the one who, at the film's climax, instigates the peace rally to protest acts of violence directed toward African Americans and gays but which, ironically, offers Remy his prime opportunity for very public acts of murder.

Remy, in many ways the least satisfying and most cliché-ridden character in the film, wants passionately to fit in but is rejected by the "normal" people around him. He's tall and gawky, and banter doesn't come easily for him. After Billy stumbles downstairs with his pants around his knees, trying to catch up to a sobbing Kristen, Remy, who has crashed the fraternity party, makes a pathetic attempt to "bond" with him by making reference to the sexual encounter. Remy is utterly unable to read the situation—i.e., that Billy is not viewing the experience as a successful sexual conquest and is in no mood to joke about it— and his behavior is inappropriate and alienating. Ultimately, the group that not only wants him but seeks him out is a freaky group of white supremacists, complete with shaved heads and Nazi paraphernalia. In scenes paralleling Malik's politicization and identification with Fudge and his followers, Remy becomes increasingly aware of what he sees as signs of whites' loss of power and increasingly identifies with his neo-Nazi buddies. In a pivotal scene, Remy looks up from his studying to see students of all races and colors sitting near him, seemingly surrounding him in the library, and, as a sign of his complete conversion, whips off his baseball cap to reveal a newly shaved head. It is Remy's sad eagerness to belong, to show that he's willing to fit in, that leads him finally to agree to commit murder for his group. Reminiscent of Charles Lincoln Whitman at the University of Texas in the '60s, Remy fires a high-powered rifle from the roof of a campus building, killing two students attending Kristen's peace rally, one of them Deja. In a final scene of heavy-handed irony, Malik is restrained by the consistently and stolidly racist campus police from subduing (and perhaps beating to death) Remy. Trapped by campus security, who still seem blithely unaware they have the murderer in front of them, Remy shoots himself with the pistol his father had given him and taught him to use.

The three characters begin as separate stories with separate plot lines, coming together only by chance as Malik and Kristen sharing an elevator near the beginning of the film and as Malik and Remy living in the same dorm. They are brought together, finally, by a slow escalation of violence. Singleton begins the violent chain of events with Kristen's experience of date rape at a fraternity party. So common it's practically become a horrible cliché, the combination of fraternity parties, alcohol, and date rape is a frequent occurrence on any college campus with campus housing or fraternity houses. Campus violence is no anomaly either. In *Bright College Years: Inside the American Campus Today,* Anne Matthews (1997) points out that the vast majority—80 percent—of campus violence is student against student. She writes:

> Gay or minority students are favorite targets—flyers pushed under a door, yells in the night, spray paint on a car, beatings behind the gym. Weapons offenses on campus are rising, too. A 1995 survey of seventy-three institutions revealed that 7.5 percent of college students had carried guns, knives, or other weapons to school in the last thirty days. Some armed undergraduates are gang members (an increasing worry for campus security staff) and some students who do not wish to become a statistic while walking to the college library parking lot after dark. (93)

Just recently on my campus, a female student was suspended when her handgun accidentally went off in her book bag when she dropped it on the floor of our Writing Center; she claimed that as a single mother, she had a right to protect herself and her children—even, one supposed, in the Writing Center.

Violence serves as the engine that moves *Higher Learning*'s plot, but the film ends with a sweetly contrived scene that brings together Kristen and Malik at the statue of Christopher Columbus, the spot where Deja died, the memorial site for students trying to come to terms with the tragedy. Personifying white liberal guilt, Kristen tells Malik, "I feel like it was all my fault." Edgily, Malik absolves her of guilt, and they effect a shaky introduction since, even though they've been in the same economics class (and on the same elevator), they've never really met.

Singleton takes the first-year college student experience as an opportunity to foreground issues he has explored in previous films—*Boyz N the Hood* (1991) (for which Singleton received an Oscar nomination for Best Director) and *Poetic Justice* (1993)—particularly the issues of race, violence, and youth culture. As Roger Ebert writes in a review of the film, "The college campus in John Singleton's new film is a racial and ideological war zone where students rarely talk to other students who are not more or less exactly like themselves." Anyone who teaches on the college level can testify to the fact that this description is not just true of Singleton's fictive campus. In every college I've taught, students have tended—with some exceptions, of course—to seat themselves in class, in the library, in the cafeteria, and in other public spaces with members of their own ethnic groups. This past semester, in fact, a Latino student in a teaching assistant's class called for segregated dorms to the TA's horror but apparently to his classmates' approbation. Singleton's representation of campus life is not far off the mark, in other words.

Clifford Geertz in "Thick Description: Toward an Interpretive Theory of Culture" (1973) writes:

> Understanding a people's culture exposes their normalness without reducing their particularity. . . . It renders them accessible: setting them in the frame of their own banalities, it dissolves their opacity. (14)

In a certain sense, this is what Singleton is attempting to do as he places his young characters in situations and locations where they are confronted by racism, date rape, sexual politics, alcohol abuse, neo-Nazism, the exploitation of black athletes, and so on. At the same time, he forces them to consider what role the life of the mind should play in their college life. Singleton attempts to represent the lives of these students as complex, yet at the same time they too are caught up in the larger than life representations of Issues—i.e., they come to represent types more than rounded characters. The most obvious example is Remy as the goofy white kid from Idaho who becomes a white supremacist. We also know that Kristen is only "dabbling" in lesbianism and that Malik will triumph over adversity and that Fudge will most likely graduate. The film fronts important issues but ultimately is unable to "expose their normalness without reducing their particularity."

As a teacher working at another public university with students who could be "read" in many of the same ways as Singleton's characters as well as with many nontraditional students who were in no way represented in his film, I found myself wondering how my own first-year writing students—students who were immersed in ongoing ethnographic research of student culture—would respond to Singleton's representations of their experience. What interpretations would they provide? How might they respond to this characterization of their life in and out of the college classroom? What would they make of the ways the various threads of the plot were tied together and how would they compare them to the "stories" they told in their own ethnographic research? Most important, how might a greater knowledge of film literacy facilitate their abilities as researchers?

I have used the film in different ways as part of the "readings" for sequenced assignments leading toward a final research project which brings together the film with their own field and library research. The general pattern, however, is to begin with students writing about their initial expectations and impressions of college life, especially what they've found to be most startling or unsettling during their first year. Next we view *Higher Learning* to compare the issues it foregrounds to their observations. We follow with a variety of readings from a variety of sources and then move to field and library research. The film serves as the linchpin for the intellectual labor to follow.

While I expected students to be able to respond forcefully, I was surprised by their abilities to draw from their research in real, responsible ways, and I was struck by how their serious viewing of and work with the film productively complicated their abilities to question and problematize their observations and survey and interview results. Time and time again, my own assumptions about how my students would respond were overturned. For example, I knew a number of them had already seen *Higher Learning* (several owned their own copies, in fact), so I expected that viewing the film in class (for those few who hadn't seen it in the theatres or on their VCRs) would most likely be a less than satisfying film experience—i.e., I expected some problems with absenteeism, talking in class, etc.; however, I was surprised to find that attendance was unaffected (even better than normal in one class, I'm embarrassed to say) and the only talking largely came from students wanting to express pleasure or disgust or anger at something that had happened in the movie as when Remy threatens his roommate and Malik with a gun and Malik ends up being the one campus security forcibly detains. In each class with every viewing, also, a surprising number of students openly wept when at Deja's death.

I had also been concerned that commuting and/or older students, who make up a considerable percentage of our campus population, would be put off by the film's exclusion of them and their interests. But they reported in journal responses and in discussion that they felt connected enough to the issues dealt with in the film that they weren't put off. We also made the fact that commuters and nontraditional students played no part in the film a topic of discussion (and a topic for further research). Several students, traditional as well as nontraditional, reported that they were fascinated by the picture of the kind of "big" university that they had actively rejected when they were deciding where to go to college.

Of course, the film is entertaining, and most students would rather watch a film than pretty much any other classroom activity. But what *Higher Learning*'s real value has been its offering a "safe" way to begin to talk about difficult issues—issues that can quickly polarize a class if not handled carefully. For example, a tiny but important scene, a scene mentioned above, portrays the moment on the elevator between Kristen and Malik. Kristen puts a protective hand on her purse, a move Malik observes. It is not an overt act of racism, which perhaps makes it all the more powerful and telling because the scene offers effective evidence that racism is totally ingrained in the behavior of even those people who would never consider themselves racist. I ask students, "Is Kristen a bigot?" The answer so far has consistently been that she is not. I then ask, "Is this a racist act?" Here the responses get more complicated. I throw Malik's response into the mix and ask, "Is this the first time something like this has happened to Malik? How can you tell?" This scene is useful in that it allows us to talk about race and racism in ways that don't immediately devolve into a class that can be grossly characterized as white students on one side of the room saying that they know no racists and that everything is fine now and why don't African American students "get over it" while African American students sit silently and angrily on the other side of the room. Focusing only on Remy's extreme racism does not offer an avenue into serious discussion because (very rarely) will students identify with him (openly, at least), and, in fact, Remy's story lets them off the hook, so to speak, because he gets to stand as the definition of racism without further discussion. As long as they're not like him, they can congratulate themselves for not being racists. But Kristen's act complicates that way of seeing things and provides a place where more productive discussion can begin. This scene, however, also becomes emblematic of part of the field researcher's job in that it shows students how the smallest acts can be and often are highly significant—a valuable lesson for the beginning field researcher. As Clifford Geertz states, "Analysis, then, is sorting out the structures of signification . . . and determining their social ground and import" (1973, 9). This small scene, then, also made possible a larger discussion of the "social ground and import" of small acts in relation to culture.

Film literacy in addition offers a fruitful transition to field research in the form of a discussion and understanding of *"mise-en-scène,"* that is, the physical environment represented on the screen which informs the audience what to think and feel about a character or event. Early in the film, Singleton cuts back and forth among his three main characters as they decorate their dormitory rooms. Malik tapes up posters of luscious African American models, Kristen puts up photos of family and friends, and Remy displays a poster for heavy metal band Danzig. When we first meet Kristen's roommate, we see her staring, bemusedly and sardonically, at Kristen's sweet display. In my classes, I generally pause at this frame to introduce the ethnographic term "cultural artifacts." Elizabeth Chiseri-Strater and Bonnie Sunstein (1997) in their introduction to ethnography *Field Working* define "artifact" as "any material object that belongs to and represents a culture" (43). They go on to define culture as "the invisible web of behaviors, patterns, rules of a group of people who have contact with one another and share a common language" (43). With these definitions available for our use, I then ask students to tell me what Kristen's roommate is doing and how she is able to do it, rewinding the tape so that we can look again at Kristen's decorations and "read" them together.

The next step generally makes students less comfortable: I ask them to read the classroom and everyone in it—i.e., what can we tell from the way the room is arranged, what we're wearing, where we sit, and so on. In other words, things and arrangements that seem "natural" have import and are legible. The next step goes back to Kristen's roommate's response to those decorations so that I can introduce to students the problem of trying to see their own assumptions and how those assumptions can color their readings and research. Chiseri-Strater and Sunstein explain, "Fixed assumptions are the personal facts that might influence how you see your data—your age, gender, class, nationality, race—factors that will not change during the course of your study but are often taken for granted and unexamined in the research process" (57). Since I teach in a state university where few students come from out of state, most come from the northeast Texas region, and well over half identify themselves as Baptist, this is an important concept to introduce early. For example, one student, still smarting over rejection from one of the campus Greek organizations, proposed to research Greek organizations as exclusionary, biased, and harmful. The rest of the class quickly pointed out that rejection had resulted in assumptions that were coloring the research even before it was started. Another student, the son of a Baptist minister, used his project as a means of directly questioning assumptions he had never before considered—specifically, he had assumed that religious beliefs and fraternity membership were incompatible. He did an extensive project, observing and interviewing a number of fraternity members, and emerged with the knowledge that reality was far more complicated than his assumptions had allowed.

Because the focus of their ethnographies was "higher learning," students were also able to use issues raised in the film in their own research. For example, one important issue that emerged in our in-class and on-line (via the Daedalus program) discussions of the film and of their projects was the role the life of the mind plays in students' expectations and experiences of college. Some of the students wanted to argue that knowledge was power; the more one knows, the stronger and fairer and more just one will be. But in our on-line discussion, that position was quickly problematized: Vince Leibowitz pointed out, "knowing more about the problem will not solve it. In fact, I'd almost want to go out on a limb and say that it compounds the problem. For example, Malik was not so 'gung-ho' about racial issues until Fudge gave him 'more knowledge.' Remi did not feel that he was getting the short end or the stick until the neo-nazis told him that he was." Daniel Clayton responded, "I am reminded of Remmey's mentor who told him the most effective way to further the cause of white power was to become a lawyer or doctor. That statement didn't surprise me in the least. The best way to advance your beliefs is to become a person of power then to expose others to your now 'respected' opinion."

Seeing these issues made "real" on the screen helped students in my class frame them and develop questioning and observing strategies. One student observed that his experience of having a roommate of a different race from his had been much smoother than Malik's and focused his project on how others had experienced and made the transition (or not). Another, noting that he hadn't seen interracial romantic relationships represented in the film (except as victims of Remy's pals), focused his project on interviewing the six interracial couples he knew about their experiences. As part of the project, he also spent some time following behind one couple as they strolled across campus with the arms around each other, making notes about the reactions from passersby when they thought no one was watching, as well as interviewed African Americans, Latinos, and Anglos about their attitudes toward interracial relationships. Even for those students who made no connections between the film and their ethnographic projects, learning something of cinema literacy—i.e., "reading" scenes—helped them "read" and analyze behaviors of the people and situations they observed and helped them understand what I was talking about when I asked them to read body language and group dynamics and the *mise en scène* of the objects of their research.

The "distance" of film also allowed us a "neutral" place to begin discussions of difficult, potentially painful problems specific to our campus. In particular, members of an African American campus organization were the target of gunfire when they left the student center late one night. Fortunately, no one was hurt, but the whole campus was shaken, and African American students, those who had attended the event and those who hadn't, were profoundly angry and hurt. It was impossible to dismiss the violence in *Higher Learning* after the event, and it was impossible to dismiss African American students' rage after hearing of the violence on campus and seeing the violence on screen. In addition, virtually every student living in a dormitory had witnessed cases of campus security "hassling" African American or Chicano students but ignoring Anglo students doing the same things the others had been warned about (usually congregating around loud music). In other words, we could begin to broach hard subjects by means of discussion of the film and then move to more painful local experience. I won't say this made it "easier" for my students and me to hear each other, but it at least offered us a way to begin without it being immediately heard as recriminations and/or excuses.

Finally, I do not claim that combining film literacy with field research automatically produces a collection of brilliantly conceived and brilliantly executed ethnographies, but I will make two modest claims. The first is that it was virtually impossible for my students to plagiarize using papers purchased via the Internet or elsewhere or papers pulled from files maintained by various organizations on campus; the sequence of assignments produces a long-term project that cannot be produced fully formed at the last minute. The second, more significant claim is that beginning the research process in the role of participant/observer put my students in a position to understand research in more concrete terms. In other words, research was a much more complicated act than a quick dive into *The Reader's Guide to Periodical Literature.* They were responsible for telling their "side" of an argument (i.e., religious students are capable of being critical thinkers; body art is not necessarily a sign of social deviance or rebellion; and so on) and for telling their story within that argument as well. I might add, quite happily, that the papers my students produce—even the more poorly written ones—are genuinely interesting because all had offered something of their experiences and observations of higher learning as they had lived it so far. In other words, as was rarely the case when students wrote about capital punishment or gun control or animal rights, I was able to learn something about what they and their peers had experienced during their first year of college and how they had experienced and come to terms with it.

In this essay, I argue for the bringing together of ethnography and film to introduce composition students to research and analysis and to enable them to work from a position of authority from which to question and critique representations of our culture in the mass media. The role of participant/observer accorded them a kind of expertise, which, in turn, made them feel empowered to take part in an argument in which they felt that had something at stake. While John Singleton's *Higher Learning* provides a provocative means to a wider discussion of the problems and challenges of representation, ultimately, I want to argue that the possibilities of the film itself are less important than the possibilities enabled by juxtaposing film literacy and field research to move composition students toward a more sophisticated understanding of research, analysis, culture, and writing.

# Works Cited

Chiseri-Strater, Elizabeth, and Bonnie Sunstein. 1997. *Field Working: Reading and Writing Research.* Englewood Cliffs, NJ: Prentice Hall.

Ebert, Roger. 1995. "Issues of Race, Rape, Political Correctness Explode in 'Learning'." *Lexington Herald-Leader,* 13 January. <http://www.kentuckyconnect.com/heraldleader/movies/fl/higher.html> (22 May 1997).

Geertz, Clifford. 1973. *The Interpretation of Culture.* New York: Basic Books.

Matthews, Anne. 1997. *Bright College Years: Inside the American Campus Today.* New York: Simon & Schuster.

Moss, Beverly J. 1992. "Ethnography and Composition: Studying Language at Home." In *Methods and Methodology in Composition Research,* edited by Gesa Kirsch and Patricia A. Sullivan, 152–71. Carbondale and Edwardsville, IL: Southern Illinois University Press.

Singleton, John, dir. 1995. *Higher Learning.* Columbia Pictures.

# 5

# Reading Race in the Multicultural Classroom

Ellen Bishop

When Dave Bartholomae (1996) asks in a recent essay "What Is Composition and (if you know what it is) Why Do We Teach It?" he makes explicit the primary challenges composition teachers face every semester with every classroom of students. The university expects freshman composition to prepare students to write careful, grammatically correct, literate essays across the range of undergraduate courses. Yet students tend to resist and sometimes resent the course because it involves a fair amount of work and the assessment of their writing often seems vague and fuzzy. And composition teachers, feeling the pressures of contemporary literary theory and the growth of cultural studies, want to teach more than just grammar or standard argument or at least to teach those basic skills from an informed, critical perspective that does not ignore larger social and political issues. Finally, faculty from other fields often have very different ideas about what constitutes good writing and ask their students, who are also ours, to write within the bounds of the generic requirements of their particular fields. The result of this multiple and heterogeneous set of demands and expectations is a classroom that can be chaotic. The composition teacher's job, then, is to create order from this chaos. In this chapter I articulate, as explicitly as I can, what I think about this situation and how I create order by teaching writing and film together.

I generally teach several sections of freshman composition that include film. I choose to work with film partly because my students like it and partly because it is the mass entertainment medium of the world. The challenge for me is to integrate film and writing rather than to use film simply as a supplement to writing. I want to hold film and composition in a useful and interesting relation with a certain amount of tension between them, to integrate them rather than just to use one in service to the other.

Following the logic of philosophical theorists Deleuze and Guattari (1980), I want to situate my students and myself between film and writing without find-

56

ing some dialectical synthesis of the two that would erase the specificity of either medium, and without setting up an opposition that would beg for a value judgment with little consideration of the complexity of the texts in question and the issues they represent. I want to be in between, in the middle, enacting Deleuze and Guattari's thinking in difference. This thinking in difference entails the construction of pairs of terms or concepts that might at first look like the old familiar binarisms of traditional thought but that work differently. For example, I situate students between film and writing, not to ask which is better or to privilege one over the other in an opposition that requires closure and judgment between them, but as terms that exist in a complex conversation with each other. My questions to students, then, tend to be ones that ask them to listen to the conversation, to follow it, and to see where it leads them.

Given this form of thought about film and writing, I need to situate it within a specific context, a content area, and to define some "skills" that act as guidelines for my students' work. So, I use cultural studies as the field of play and "critical thinking" as the intellectual skill I want my students to develop. The choice of Deleuze and Guattari's difference as a model for my thinking about the course is, of course, itself an example of the critical thinking I want my students to begin to do. I further define critical thinking as Robert Pattison (1982) defines "literacy," as "a consciousness of the problems posed by language" (14), and as the ability to examine a text or group of texts—including student papers—in some of their complex rhetorical, political, and psychological differences both within and between themselves and all in relation to the reader and the cultural moments that produced them both. In short, I want to construct a classroom where my students find themselves between the rhetorical, political, and psychological dimensions of the texts we examine, so they can look at (1) how a story is told through a given medium, culture, and subject to discern what its politics might be, and (2) to decipher how those two aspects of the text work with and against each other to produce a particular story. I want them to examine, too, the significance of these stories for readers who are also always embedded in a particular cultural perspective.

With this critical thinking paradigm in mind, I go on to choose a topic of current cultural interest. One such topic is the issue of race in America. Bill Clinton's call for town meetings to discuss this issue, the recent O. J. Simpson trial, the Thomas-Hill hearings, prominent nationwide court battles over the alleged racism of police and other institutions, and the perplexing tensions between black and white students on university campuses all make this issue both timely, difficult, and volatile.

Unfortunately, my students tend to polarize around issues of race and racism in ways that can make productive classroom work almost impossible. I've had classes with students ready to fight defensively and uncomfortably about racist texts, words, ideas, and perspectives derived from "personal experiences" that are not seen by the students as open for examination, as well as classes in which students effected an elaborate disinterest in the topic that often masked a real fear of being erroneously (mis)read as racists for something they said in a conversation or a paper, especially in reference to a complex text like Spike Lee's film *Do the Right Thing* (1989), for example (see note at end of chapter). I have also encountered angry reactions from students to what seems to them to be a compulsive desire to "beat up on straight white males" on the part of the academic community with its new multicultural focus on difference. The local politics and racial tensions of the city that surrounds our campus often spill over into campus life, aggravating the situations the students must face. And, although it is part of my job to open up these difficult, affectively charged moments in the classroom to the issues of language, logic, perspective, and stereotype—the basic concepts-as-tools of critical thinking—it's often been nearly impossible to do so.

In response to this dilemma, I have chosen to create a distance between the topic and my students' lives by choosing texts that examine the problems of race in another culture, in this case in South Africa. I chose three texts (two films and one novel): *Cry Freedom,* an American film directed by Richard Attenborough and released in the United States in 1987; *A Dry, White Season,* another American film with a South African director—Euzan Palcy—released in 1989; and the novel, *A Dry, White Season,* written by Andre Brink and published in Great Britain in 1979 and in America in 1980. All three texts are powerful stories that demand an end to apartheid in South Africa during the latter half of the 1970s.

These texts also fulfill my requirements for encouraging my students' critical-thinking abilities. Taken together they produce a sophisticated meta-conversation that makes visible to the critical eye both the mechanisms and effects of storytelling strategies, rhetorics, in specific relation to the mediums they are constructed in and by, and the complex political conversation about the resistance to apartheid in South Africa in the second half of the 1970s: a discussion about racism somewhere else. The distance gives my students breathing room where they can become "conscious of the problems posed by language" herein represented by the different ways the three texts tell their stories and the different devices that each medium—film, literature, and students' and professional writer's essays—use to make their cases within a charged political atmosphere.

Distance also serves another more psychological and critical purpose. Dave Bartholomae (1996) tells a story about a freshman composition course in which his students productively struggled through Mary Louise Pratt's *Imperial Eyes* (1992). One of the writing assignments was for students to write a travel story of their own. He wanted to give them the opportunity to read their own stories in light of both Pratt's complex critical understanding of cultural imperialism as she uncovers it in the narrative forms of various travelogues, and in terms of their own complicity with an inherited narrative form—the missionary tale. He reproduces one student paper, which recounts the adventure of a student who went to a Caribbean country with his church group to help clean up after Hurricane Andrew.

The tale is unintentionally and so problematically a missionary narrative in its positioning of the student as coming from a superior culture. I asked Bartholomae if this student or any others in the class were able to see this after working with Pratt's text and seeming, at least, to get the gist of what she was saying. He said, "No." His students were too caught up in the assertions of reality and the truth vested in their true stories to make the complex move to a perspective that includes the rhetorical dimension and its psycho-politics—especially when it was their realities and truths that were being called into question. In short, for them the opposition between truth and falsity is so fixed and real that no one wanted to be judged a liar—the only position available from their points of view—if their stories were questioned. They were too threatened by the idea that the stories we often tell ourselves into and make our realities are complex cultural constructions rather than just simple, "true" tales about our lives.

This is a crucial but often overlooked issue in undergraduate classrooms, especially for younger students. We need to define reality for our students, I think, *as a concept,* a working hypothesis subject to complex cultural forces that are psychological, political, and rhetorical. This does not mean that there is no truth or no real discernible world, but that our grasp of that real world will always be partial and subject to shaping by the cultures' available story forms, no matter how useful or consistent and reassuring they prove to be. Using texts that tell the same "true" story differently, then, can enable students to begin to question for themselves the absoluteness of any one "truth" claim and to begin to juggle the complexities of multiple perspectives and story forms in relation to "truth." It might also loosen up their own needs to be "truthful" without (1) sending them into the nihilist abyss of "no truth"; or (2) confronting them with the simple-minded accusations of "liar" or "fool" that too easily arise in charged discussions of difficult issues involving personal experiences; or (3) allowing them to coast through their own work with clichés, that is, with story forms that remain unexamined givens. Instead of falling into the binary trap of truth or consequences, using multiple versions of a story can enable a thinking in difference that opens up the complexity of the problems posed by language in a very tense political world.

## Classroom Practice

What follows is the more practical application of these ideas in the form of writing assignments that are also the basis for class discussions on the three aforementioned texts. The emphasis is on encouraging my students to begin to do close analytical readings of the texts based on a theoretical perspective similar to the one previously outlined. These assignments are not absolute. I change, rewrite, and rearrange them constantly based on what actually happens in class discussions and in students' papers. Classes have personalities of their own and they take their own tacks, which are never completely predictable. The discussions of the assignments are gleaned from different classes' conversations as we moved through the texts. Obviously, these assignments don't cover the field completely. I want these assignments to remain a bit open-ended so that I can be surprised once in a while too. They do, however, open up the issues of race and racism by providing students with opportunities to see the complexity of the issues and the sometimes enlightening and sometimes blinding effects of language on our attempts to talk to each other.

## *Assignment 1*

Video boxes, like book covers, are designed to address you. They are designed to appeal to you, to get you to pick them up, look them over, and then buy or rent the text they represent. Writing these "blurbs," these advertisements, and designing the visual images *on* the covers and *as* the covers is a very specific task that is highly motivated. Video box and book cover blurbs have, we could say, a strong rhetorical dimension. They are meant to be highly specific in their appeals. The people who write them want, in a sense, to psych you out, to figure out what and how to appeal to YOU, the prospective, paying audience. They are, then, making assumptions about who you are and what you are interested in that appear in the appeals their blurbs make. This makes it possible, in turn, for you to read these blurbs analytically and ask yourself, "Who do they think I am, based on how they have structured their appeal to me?"

For this assignment, I'd like you to analyze the video box blurb and the book cover for *A Dry, White Season,* and the video box blurb for *Cry Freedom* as well, in terms of what the appeal to you is and how it defines you as the prospective audience for the text. Please look carefully and closely at the covers and take into consideration both the verbal and visual cues, as well as what is said about the texts and how it is said and how all of this is put together both to appeal to you and to represent how they think of you. Who are you to them? Who do they imagine you to be?

**Assignment 1 Commentary**     This assignment usually requires at least one substantial revision. Students have some difficulty with balancing descriptive summaries of the blurbs and the assignation of meaning to what they have described. They tend to do one or the other, but not both. So, revision assignments ask for the appropriate adjustments and give them another chance to think through their readings after class discussions and readings of a few students' drafts.

Also, and more germane to the critical ideas we are pursuing in the course, they need some guided class discussion on how to begin reading the blurbs from the perspective I have asked them to take. I am asking them to imagine, from "clues" in the blurbs that they identify, who the designers think they are. This is a sophisticated task that involves an implicit recognition of the rhetorical dimension of the texts.

We examine the video boxes in class first by describing reactions to it, and by simply describing in words what we see there. *Cry Freedom,* for example, features a Janus face. Denzel Washington's and Kevin Kline's faces look in opposite directions, and the words "Cry Freedom" are written in the blank space between the faces. Beneath these words are much smaller ones: "the true story of the friendship that shook South Africa and awakened the world." What possible significances are there to the double-faced design? Two men, one mind? What might that mean? Who would it appeal to and why? What about the statement beneath the title? True stories and significant friendships between black men and white men that presumably shake countries and "awaken" the world are all apparently thought to be significant to the prospective viewer. Who is such a viewer?

The cover of *A Dry, White Season* is split down the middle vertically into black and white. Across the top the title is written in red letters meant, perhaps, to signify an African style (although they are English words). Beneath these letters sits a naked Negro man facing us with his feet drawn up to his chest, his head raised, and his hands also raised, spread-fingered in front of his upturned eyes. His body is split by the colors of the box and colored oppositely, so that it takes on the quality of a black-and-white photograph and its negative. At the very top of the picture are enthusiastic comments about the film from the *New York Daily News* ("Electrifying"); *US Magazine* (". . . A scathing commentary on the barbarity of apartheid"); and *Rolling Stone* (". . . Brando is sensational"). Students are usually quick to begin to read the fragments of reviews in terms of the critical question I have set for them, seeing the prospective viewer as someone who thinks Marlon Brando is a great actor, for example, and as someone who reads and trusts Peter Travers' reviews in *Rolling Stone.* This often leads to a discussion of who the intended reader of *Rolling Stone* is and how and why that person might be connected to the film.

Interpreting the visual images, however, proves to be a more difficult task. What is the significance of a black African man represented in a patchwork of black and white? Does it signify differently to an African American audience than to an Anglo American audience? What about Americans who are neither African nor Anglo?

The book cover for our edition of *A Dry, White Season* is a drawing of a black man sitting in a chair in an empty room with a bare light bulb hanging from a wire in the middle of the ceiling and positioned so as to obscure his face. Is there a difference between book covers and video boxes by medium? Is the drawing different in significance from the enhanced photo on the film box?

All three covers, in short, provide ample material for interpretations of imagined prospective readers. While the verbal clues tend to be more easily read and interpreted by the students, the visual designs provoke many tentative and open-ended readings that refuse easy closures and monolithic agreements. This guided discussion enables the students to begin to do the work I have asked them to do in their papers and opens up the critical concept of "positions," social-political positions, that can be assigned to (and accepted and/or refused) by intended addressees. What I hope for in the discussion is an emerging sense that the addressee—the you—being appealed to is imaginary, is a position based in this instance particularly on racial, ethnic, national, and gendered affiliations that only ever approximately fit any real person in our class or anywhere else. This idea often surfaces as students begin to build the reader for the blurb. Who, for example, is likely to like the idea of a strong interracial friendship depicted by two faces and one mind? If the one mind interpretation is accepted (tentatively), who is likely to like this idea? Who might not? What might it signify?

One conversation that emerged from this question spiraled around the idea of a necessary racial separatism. Some African American students argued that this "one mind" image was just another appropriation of the black man by the white man and that this integration really meant the erasure of the specificity of being black or of African descent. Some Anglo American students agreed, and many women of various racial and ethnic backgrounds were willing to agree to this argument, basing their positions on the feminist need to separate men and women. This is, of course, an issue of some debate on university campuses these days as some students voice their desires for segregated dorms and student organizations. Given the assignment's exact language, however, the issue at hand is one of defining the possible positions that the box blurb's and book's images produce. This slightly decenters the focus of the discussion away from the too easy slippage into polarized positions around the campus issues and enables students to sort out both the reasoning that accompanies the constructions of such positions in relation to the box and book blurbs and the concept of positionality as a rhetorical effect. One class got around to a discussion of what it meant to be "black" and/or "white" given the box blurb's imagined viewers. We were able to discuss race as in some respects a culturally defined position rather than an absolute biological category.

It is also arguable that both of these films are set up to appeal to white middle-class American audiences. In *Cry Freedom,* Donald Wood, the main character, a white male South African journalist, talks about his manuscript, which is the story we are seeing in the film, as a work that he will use to appeal to the American middle class (predominantly white?) in order to bring pressure to bear on the South African government. Also, both films are about apartheid, but both focus on a middle-class white South African male as protagonist. Denzel Washington as Steven Biko has a decidedly smaller role than Kline as Wood in *Cry Freedom.* And it is Susan Sarandon, Marlon Brando, and Donald Sutherland whose pictures all appear on the back of the box to *A Dry, White Season.*

One of the critical issues at stake here, then, becomes the students reactions to their interpretations of who is being appealed to and how it affects their readings of the films. If the films are perceived as appealing to white middle-class Americans, how can this affect viewer's attitudes? Will some reject them because they only appeal to middle-class whites? A polarization and totalization can both begin to occur simultaneously here, but the question can be raised about how some people might watch a film that they feel has not imagined them as its ideal viewer. References to gendered films (e.g., romance vs. action flicks) help students sort out a grounded experience of watching a film not meant for them, as does the experience of watching a children's film with a younger sibling or a child they are caring for.

We also read a review of the film by bell hooks (1990) that argues for *A Dry, White Season* even though it has a white male protagonist; in hooks' view, the film shows us his coming to consciousness and the pain involved for him as well as for the black Africans who are abused. For Benjamin du Toit, waking up to the horrors of apartheid involves the loss of his job, his friends, his family, and eventually his life. As hooks points out, the film shows us how hard it is—politically, psychologically, and ethically—to stand against the system and what courage it takes. *Cry Freedom* also shows us the suffering of Woods and his family, but it is much less horrifying than in the other film. Woods and his family just do the right thing without much hesitation. They are classic heroes in a Western tale of heroism and good faith.

At any rate, this segue serves to open up a critical space for a discussion of the experience of watching a film that is, perhaps, not made to appeal directly to a particular viewer, and how students go about deciding—through critical insight into the film's ways of making meaning—that this is the case. This enables students to take up the language of positions and apply it to their own and each other's experience of the films. One further note here is that the fundamental displacement of all American viewers is also often brought into the discussion, since the films are about South Africa—not the United States.

## *Assignment 2*

For this assignment, please examine the opening scenes of the two films. Read them closely in terms of their appeals to their audiences (you). What rhetorical, political, and psychological devices or tricks do the films employ to capture your attention? What do the films, then, imagine interests you? Do these issues and appeals work? Are you interested by the opening sequences? Why or why not? Are you interested by one more than the other? Why? After you write this paper please make some notes about how you have chosen to make distinctions between the political, psychological, and rhetorical dimensions of the opening sequences of the films.

**Assignment 2 Commentary**    This assignment is a reiteration of the first one, asking the students to perform the same reading task on the openings of the films as they did on the box blurbs. Rather than asking them to keep their distance, however (as the first assignment does by asking them to critically assess the intended viewer), this assignment asks them for more direct personal engagement with the texts. I want to set up a contrast within their own work between the intended viewer that the texts could be said to define for them and the real individual viewers in the class as a way of furthering their understanding of the concept of positions.

Class discussions for this assignment introduce a few basic technical film terms (such as *cuts, shots, freeze frames*); the uses of diegetic and nondiegetic sound; and an awareness of camera positioning and editing. They are all meant to provide students with a language for sorting out what they see as the political, psychological, and rhetorical tricks of the texts.

The uses of sound, lighting, and framing are also discussed in a technical look at the sequences. Briefly, *Cry Freedom* opens with a look at a black township, Crossroads Settlement, outside Capetown at dawn. The poverty and crowding is immediately apparent, along with the slow pace of quiet, early morning life. The scenes are periodically stopped as we hear the sound of a camera shooting, turning the live, moving scenes in color into black-and-white photos. The crosshairs of a camera lens also appear over the scenes as they turn from moving to stills. The scenes we glimpse take on more meaning as we see armored trucks full of soldiers appear and one child running to tell everyone that they are coming. The scene explodes into violence as the soldiers attack the settlement, setting fires and chasing and beating the residents. All the while, small white print from perhaps a Teletype machine or a fast typewriter appears at the bottom of the screen, telling us both about the scene and listing the film's credits.

*A Dry, White Season* begins with two children, boys about twelve years old, one black and one blonde and blue-eyed, playing an informal and gigglefilled game of football in a beautiful green gardenlike setting that we eventually learn is the backyard of the white boy's house, where the black boy's father works as a gardener. The camera movement is fluid and follows the movement of the boys. The music is a fairly traditional African chorus singing in a language most Americans don't understand.

Class discussions involve both the explanation and use of the basic technical vocabulary of film, as well as students' interpretations of the significance of the film techniques. We talk, in other words, about the ways the two films make meanings for us. This is followed by a discussion of the students' expectations of the films, what they will be about or like, based on the blurbs and the opening scenes. This analysis is really useful because it draws out and makes visible the implicit knowledges of genres that the students already possess but have, perhaps, not reflected on consciously. Genre is, of course, loosely defined, encompassing such diverse fields as political films, documentaries, blockbuster or Academy Award films, Hollywood films, and the more traditional categories by story type—adventure, science fiction, romance, and so on.

*Cry Freedom* is a slick Hollywood production (in my opinion) geared from the start to Academy nomination, while *A Dry, White Season,* although produced by MGM, has a much grittier feel to it. It eschews some of the more blatant tricks that Hollywood usually uses. I often take this position actively in class, as most of my students usually like to defend *Cry Freedom* as the "better picture," while I maintain that they feel that way because they are being played or seduced more successfully by it. My desire is not to win the argument so much as to make the political dimension of genre conventions and Hollywood tricks visible, once the students have brought them to the fore in their own discussions.

Another aspect of this assignment that accompanies the class discussions is that of race and the use of race as a visual marker in films. The opening of *A Dry, White Season* is so heavily structured around the black boy/white boy pair that it is impossible to ignore. But here again we can talk about the use of the child actors and their looks as visual tricks and cues that work to make meaning and to seduce us into the film just as the photography overlay works in *Cry Freedom.* Students can talk about the use of race and racial markers as rhetorical devices with political and psychological significances while deflecting a more polarized argument about personally felt exploitation.

## *Assignment 3*

For this assignment I'd like you to pretend that you are a film director. Take up the opening sequence (chapter) of Brink's novel and describe in shot-by-shot detail how you would film it. Obviously, Palcy chose to change the opening scene for the film for reasons we will speculate about in class. Taking the opening of the novel as given, however, how would you film it and why would you do as you do? Who would you be appealing to and how?

***Assignment 3 Commentary***     This assignment is fun for students. The active engagement with the novel, turning it into a filmed sequence, teaches them a lot about both the incredible sophistication and work of film production, while also inviting them to be very critically aware of the novel, the images, the scene, the technical effects, and the meanings each contributes to the work. Brink's novel opens with a shadowy third-person narrator recalling what he knew of Benjamin du Toit, the main character in the novel and the film. He recalls him from their brief and fairly superficial acquaintance during college some twenty years before the present. He explains that he has received a manuscript and some documents in the mail and, because he is now a journalist himself, Ben has asked him to handle them discretely and to get them out of South Africa. The narrator seems hesitant to do this. He is unsure of what is at stake, exactly, although he tells us he is worried since Ben was recently killed in a "car accident."

How students go about handling this narrator along with film's demand for images is the focus of class discussions of drafts of this paper. The connections between spoken words and images are addressed, as well as how film editing enhances meaning making. Also, then, the subject of making meaning in the broader sociopolitical terms of the story is brought up, as is the construction of a spectator by students' visualizations of the scenes.

It's also fun and productive to discuss a student's paper (or two) in the terms we use to discuss the shot-by-shot analyses of the film openings. For example, I ask them to read the first paragraph, the traditional "topic sentence" paragraph, as an "establishing shot." Also, we discuss transitions from one paragraph to another in terms of cuts, and evidence for their arguments in terms of the visual images shown to the reader that support the narrative or plot. By applying this new and unfamiliar language and perspective to the "tired old issue" (as the students often see it) of critique of their papers, I can make the work of re-vision more interesting and engaging. For example, most films use establishing shots to set up the scene of some significant action that will unfold. The opening of *Cry Freedom* is a case in point. We are taken into Settlement Township for a glimpse of life there through a photojournalist's camera. The scene is set, and with it the abstraction of apartheid is given a local habitation and a name. How might this work in a printed text? Brink's novel, of course, is a good example, but it is useful to take this idea one step further and apply it to a nonfiction essay such as the kind my students are learning to write. Can students compose their papers with the same attention to the explication of their abstract ideas with particulars? How would they do this? How does it work in/with the films? This technique also works well with bell hooks' essay. We playfully examine her essay in terms of its filmic potential and take apart how she sets up her reader and text. This gives students a glimpse at least at how this type of analysis might apply directly to their papers, which are more like hers than the films and novel. Also, students often set up the novel opening as a kind of detective noir scene, the voice-over technique being very familiar to them. Asking for readings of the students' imagined scenarios also reengages the earlier discussion of story forms and genre and can provide the class with a glimpse at the ubiquitousness of our particular cultural forms in their ways of thinking.

Several of my students were able to follow this shift to thinking about papers in terms of films and guessed that my emphasis on revision was connected to it. It was possible, they said, to guess what a film was about by the title or the ads or the opening sequences, but it was the body of the film that filled in not only an argument, a line of thought or reasoning that helped them understand the abstract "truth" of it, but also the complexity of any given situation from which, perhaps, several truths could arise. Thus, revision as reseeing was what allowed them to see if their abstract idea—the topic sentence idea—had a line of thought that made sense or, conversely, to see what specific thoughts added up to overall as they produced an abstract main idea. Many of them commented on their habit of watching a "good film" again almost immediately in order to see how it worked as an indication of this type of critical thinking.

*Cry Freedom*'s use of the photojournalist's camera is also a useful focus for discussion. The issue of truth and its construction comes to the fore here as well, since that camera signifies truth and documentation, the gathering of evidence in most students' opinions. In the next scenes we see a woman we will learn is a doctor hearing the news reports of the events at Crossroads Settlement. The newscast is completely bland and full of lies. The clichéd narrative form of the news is highlighted in a way that students are quick to grasp and that I can then later usefully exploit indirectly in terms of talking about their papers and the problems of truth that Bartholomae's students and others of mine have had.

Some class discussion time is also then devoted to Palcy's treatment of the beginning of the story. We speculate as to why she changed it as she did in terms of audience appeal and the demands of film and its difference from the written word.

## Position Paper

Now that you have watched both films and read the novel, please give us your critical appraisal of the three stories. Which do you like best? Why? You can think of this as a position paper: a short—two-page maximum—focused argument for your personal opinion.

## Assignment 4

Please examine these three texts in terms of a topic that came up in our earlier discussions of genre expectations: the hero. Who is the hero in each text? How do you know this? What in the stories—what in their constructions, in other words—makes it apparent to you who the hero is? What if anything in the three texts complicates this view of the hero? Is your view of the hero connected to the texts' assessment of who its ideal viewer is and who you are? How so? Is your sense of who the hero is connected to who you are? How?

## Another Possible Position Paper

Both films and the novel mention Steven Biko, a black South African leader of the outcry against apartheid. *Cry Freedom* features Denzel Washington in this role, which is larger in this film than in the novel or the other movie. It was made just before Washington became a solid Hollywood star, although his face was familiar to most American moviegoers. How is Washington used in this film? You might want to think about this in terms of how the other film represents the black South Africans who are actively opposing apartheid. In *A Dry, White Season,* Biko is just a name, but others are full characters whom we get to see and know. These actors are not stars who are or were familiar to American moviegoers. What is the difference in the ways they are represented in the films and the difference, then, in their effects on you? You might more generally consider the effect of having a known actor in a role as opposed to having an unknown one.

***Assignment 4 Commentary***     This assignment pulls together the critical work the students have done so far—the concepts of positions and genre conventions, for instance—as well as the explorations of the technical aspects of film, and implicitly, of literature, that they have undertaken in previous papers. Both texts have an internal "oscillation" between white and black male characters that belie any easy assignation of the role of hero to one or the other. While Kline is both the easy superficial choice on one level and clearly the film's choice in *Cry Freedom,* Denzel Washington's presence as Steve Biko and the ways in which he is visually presented open up a space for more careful critical reasoning that falls back on the concept of hero, its definitions and functions in texts. For example, the viewer and Donald Woods first see Steve Biko in a garden with bright light behind him forming a momentary halo. His face is obscured by leafy branches as he speaks in quiet and measured tones. Similar arguments can be made for *A Dry, White Season.* Sutherland would be the conventional choice of hero, but Zake Mokae's character is read by bell hooks, for example, as a hero in the film. Joseph Campbell's (1990) essays on the hero are useful here to help students conceptualize the pattern of the hero across narratives.

Also, it is possible and interesting to argue that in *A Dry, White Season,* the *idea* of the ending of apartheid is the hero in an unconventional way. What lives beyond Ben du Toit's death is the ideal of equality for all South Africans: an ideal his son seems to hold along with Mokae's character. It is this idea that moves through and constructs the narrative thread of the film, unhampered by the Hollywood need for quite the conventional heroic story. The pedagogical point here is that I don't think the question is one that must have one right answer. It is an open-ended question that asks students to offer opinions based in critically aware thoughts about point of view and readers' positions and the texts' manipulations.

I usually select papers for class discussions that have different views on the hero question and different selections of "best text." I do this in order to emphasize the use of the ideas of positions, ideal viewers, and other viewers, and their strategies for reading films not directly addressed to them. This selection also allows me to emphasize genre conventions and expectations in a discussion that enables perspectives and opinions to be put on the table without the personal vulnerability being so overwhelming.

## Conclusion

After this type of work with these carefully displaced texts, I often move back to the American scene and take up John Singleton's *Higher Learning* and/or Spike Lee's *Do the Right Thing* to follow through on the discussion of race in America. I often work in one or two readings of Lee's film in particular to introduce more "professional" critical opinions because my students are ready to read them carefully and critique the critiques they offer. I find that the work they have done with the first three texts prepares them for interesting and complicated discussions that focus now on specifically American issues. Because we have talked enough about the rhetorical dimensions of films, literature, and essays; the idea of positions and strategies of positioning; and the idea of genre and genre conventions; and because they have had some experience working within the complex multiplicity of perspectives in the texts and in the classroom, they can maneuver through these films and their complicated and politically charged representations without the level of anxiety that otherwise shuts them down.

# Note

I have also had first-generation Asian American students who suffered from acute discomfort when the topic of race was mentioned. They wanted to be seen as full-fledged Americans and found any referencing to their national origins or their parents' embarrassing. "I had to put up with all that racial and ethnic jazz about being Korean in high school. Look, I was born here, I eat Froot Loops for breakfast. I'm American." (Of course, the implicit definition of "American" here, vested in the ritual eating of Froot Loops for breakfast is interesting in a whole other way . . .)

# Works Cited

Bartholomae, David. 1996. "What Is Composition and (if you know what it is) Why Do We Teach It?" In *Composition in the Twenty-First Century: Crisis and Change*, edited by Lynn Z. Bloom, Donald A. Daiker, and Edward M. White, 1–11. Carbondale and Edwardsville: Southern Illinois University Press.

Brink, Andre. 1984. *A Dry, White Season*. New York: Penguin.

Campbell, Joseph. 1990. *The Hero with a Thousand Faces*. Princeton, NJ: Princeton University Press.

Deleuze, Gilles, and Felix Guattari. 1980. *A Thousand Plateaus*. London: Verso.

hooks, bell. 1990. "A Call for Militant Resistance." In *Yearning: Race, Gender, and Cultural Politics*. Boston: South End Press.

Pattison, Robert. 1982. *On Literacy*. Oxford, England: Oxford University Press.

Pratt, Mary Louise. 1992. *Imperial Eyes: Travel Writing and Transculturalism*. New York: Routledge.

## *Films*

*A Dry, White Season*. 1989. Directed by Euzan Palcy.

*Cry Freedom*. 1987. Directed by Richard Attenborough.

*Do the Right Thing*. 1989. Directed by Spike Lee.

# 6

## Reading the Right Thing

### Joseph Harris

The question I want to take up here is how to teach critical reading. By this I of course mean something other than simply teaching students the approved or licensed interpretations of various texts—showing them how to get the "real" meaning of *Paradise Lost* or *Huckleberry Finn* or *Citizen Kane* or even the video for Madonna's "Vogue." But I also mean something other than helping them take on or imitate the methods of academic criticism—training them in scanning metric feet or finding ambiguities or deconstructing oppositions or critiquing ideologies or whatever else may then happen to be in fashion. And I surely don't mean by criticism a kind of discourse that is more negative, aggressive, or arcane than usual. Rather, as I want to use the term, a critical reading is one that draws on and responds to the comments of others, that is public rather than private, that is argued for rather than simply asserted. To write as a critic is to take a stance on a text or issue in relation to what others have had to say about it. It is to respond to the question: Why do you read it that way?

There are two main ways of ducking this question, and most students are adept at both. The first is simply to give in, to abandon your reading in favor of somebody else's, usually the teacher's. ("Oh, of course, now I see . . . ") The second is to claim that the grounds for all readings of a text are personal and idiosyncratic, a matter of taste and nothing more. ("Well, that's just my opinion . . . ") The task of the teacher, then, is to move students past such gestures of surrender or dismissal, and to help them instead to *use* the responses of other readers in defining and articulating what they have to say about a text.

My sense is that this is very hard to do when the only alternative readings students come across are ones posed by their teacher. Many students are only too well used to coming to class only to find out, in effect, that they've gotten it wrong once again, that the poem or story they've just read doesn't mean what they thought it did—or what's probably worse, that the poem or story they couldn't figure out at all last night seems perfectly clear to their teacher. So even when what we're trying to do is simply to pose an *other* way of looking at a text, many students are likely to take any reading of it that we offer as the *correct* one, to defer almost automatically to our authority as critics and teachers.

Students are often far more willing, though, to argue with the readings of their classmates. One of the strongest moves we can make as teachers, then, is to shift the kinds of talk that go on in our classrooms away from discussions that we lead and towards exchanges that our students have among themselves. The simplest way of doing this is of course to ask students if they agree with what's been said so far. Did everyone here read the passage that way? Tom, is that what you thought the writer was doing too? And so on. But there are two problems with this method. The first is that it tends to make talkative students become even more so and shy students want to hide. The second is that it rewards an ability to think on your feet, to come up with a quick answer, more than it does a capacity to form a considered response, a careful reading. To do this, students need time both to formulate what they think about a text and to speak on it at length.

The best way I know of giving them such time is to make the writings your students do a regular part of what they read and talk about together as a class.[1] This goes not only for teaching composition but literature too. A powerful way of teaching a poem or story is to look at it *through* what students in the class have written about it. That is, instead of having students first talk about a text and then go home to write on it, with the result that usually no one but you ever reads what they have to say, you can instead begin by having them write out their responses, and then talk about the poem or story by looking in class at what a number of them have written. (You can do this either by making copies of their writings or simply by having students read their work aloud.) The question such a class centers on is not: What does this text mean? but: How does this person add to or challenge our understanding of this text? That is, instead of encouraging students to think of a poem or story as something with a "hidden meaning" that needs somehow to be uncovered or decoded, we can look at the competing ways a text can be read—and thus offer a view of it as something a reader has to *make* sense out of (and not simply "get" or receive the meaning of). In doing so, we can then also ask what gets highlighted or obscured, accented or downplayed, by these various ways of reading, of making sense of texts—and thus what might be at stake in choosing among them.

To give you a sense of what such a teaching practice might look and feel like, of how it might actually play out in a classroom, I'd like to talk here about some of the work students and I did together at the start of an first-year composition course at the University of Pittsburgh on Writing About Film. By way of context, let me simply say that the goal of this course is not to introduce students to the academic study of the cinema, to equip them with a set of terms and methods they can use in later film classes, so much as it is to get them thinking and writing about the ways they *already* have of looking at and talking about movies and TV. As a way of beginning to surface these kinds of viewing strategies, one of the first things I ask students to do is to locate a point where their understanding of a film breaks down, to write about a scene or image in a movie that they have trouble making sense of—that confuses or disturbs them, or that they have trouble fitting in with the rest of the film, or that just makes them angry somehow. To make sure that the problem they write about is an *interpretive* one, and not simply the result of having missed something (as we all do) while watching a movie in a theater, I choose a film that is available on videotape, and ask students to re-view the scene they pick, taking notes as they do, until they are sure they can accurately describe what gets said and done in it. I then ask them to recreate the scene as well as they can in their writing and to define the problem it poses for them as viewers. After talking about some of their responses in class, and commenting in writing on all of them, I then ask them to revise their first reading of the movie—to add to, change, support, or qualify it as they now see fit.

It's a simple enough assignment but it works towards a number of ends. One goal, as I've said, is to make students aware, by having them look at a point where they have trouble doing so, that as movie viewers they are always *making* sense of what they see, and not simply receiving a set of preformed meanings. Another is to suggest what practicing critics already know, that a text that poses no difficulties for you also offers very little for you to write about, that criticism begins with seeing problems, gaps, or inconsistencies in a text. I also want students to get a sense of what it is like to go back to re-view a scene in a movie, to look at it once again not simply to relive the experience it offered you the first time around (as we all do when we watch TV reruns or get a copy of a favorite movie from the video store) but to try to see or understand it in a new way. And I want them to get a practical feel for how hard it is to switch media, to use writing to "quote" or describe what happens in a film. And, finally, I want them to see for themselves how viewers of the same scene can often describe and understand it in strikingly different ways, and, when that happens, to get a sense of what might be involved in arguing for one view or the other of it.

And so in the spring of 1991 I asked students to define a problem they had as viewers of Spike Lee's *Do the Right Thing*. Lee's movie is set in the Bed-Stuy neighborhood of Brooklyn and offers a picaresque series of glimpses into life on a city block on the hottest day of summer. Lee himself plays Mookie, a young black man who delivers pizzas for Sal (Danny Aiello), a likable Italian patriarch who owns and runs the neighborhood pizzeria, and who along with his two sons, both of whom work in his shop, are almost the only white characters we see. (City cops, a lost motorist, and a brownstoning yuppie are the only others.) Early on in the movie we see what seems a routine blow-up between Sal and one of his customers, Buggin' Out, another young black man who fancies himself something of a political activist, and who tries to organize a neighborhood boycott of the pizzeria until Sal replaces some of the pictures of Italians—Rocky Marciano, Frank Sinatra, Al Pacino—on his "Wall of

Fame" with photos of African Americans. The only support Buggin' Out is able to raise, though, comes from (even by the standards of this neighborhood) two fringe characters: Radio Raheem, a mean-looking hulk of a man with no visible occupation other than walking up and down the street blaring the rap music of Public Enemy from his giant boombox, and Smiley, a stuttering hawker of photographs of Malcolm X and Martin Luther King (which we see no one but Mookie buy). While tempers flare at a number of other points during the day, none of these exchanges come to much, and the overall mood of the film is comic and quick. So when near the end of the movie Sal decides to reopen his doors to give a few teenagers a late-night slice, it seems as if the boycott and whatever threat it might have posed to the routine peace of block are over, that the neighborhood has managed to get through the hottest day of the year without serious incident. This isn't the case, though, as Buggin' Out, Raheem, and Smiley also take this occasion to renew their threat to close Sal down, and Sal and Raheem find themselves in a fight that erupts quickly and ends tragically. Harsh words lead to a wrestling match that sends the two men crashing into the street. Raheem pins Sal to the sidewalk and seems on the verge of strangling him when a white policeman pulls him away and, as a crowd watches in horror, chokes Raheem to death with his nightstick. Panicked, the police throw Raheem's lifeless body into a squad car and escape, leaving the enraged crowd to loot and burn Sal's pizzeria in revenge.

About a third of the class that spring chose to write on this scene, and it's easy to see why, since it seems so unclear as to who if anyone "does the right thing" in it, and so I decided to start our talk about the movie by looking at three of their responses to it. I began by noting that all of them had pretty much the same concluding paragraph: a plea for greater openness and understanding among all people of all races—be they white, be they black, be they whatever. My sense was that these paragraphs had less to do with the ending of Lee's film than with how these students (and most of the others in the class) felt they were required to end a paper written for school: on a tone of moral uplift, showing that they had indeed learned a valuable lesson from this important work of art, and so on. I didn't push this point much; I simply said that I was interested less in what these writers agreed on than in how and why they differed in their views of the film—which meant that I wanted us to look more closely at what got said in the body of their pieces than in their official conclusions. It's like TV sitcoms, I argued, no matter what, they always end happily, with everybody loving and hugging everybody else, but if you pay attention to what goes on *before* they wrap everything up, you often find both a more tense and interesting view of work and family life. (I think most students took my point, since I read far fewer homilies at the end of their second drafts.)

And what interests me about these three readings, why I chose them to begin our talk in class, was how each writer defines the boundaries of the scene differently, so that in each of their accounts a different action gets emphasized, and different sort of blame or responsibility assessed. In "Radio Raheem's Death," for instance, Holly Affeltranger describes the strangling of Raheem in detail.[2]

> This scene starts out with a racial fight in the street between Radio Raheem, an African American youth who carries around an enormous boom box that symbolizes his power, and Sal, a white, middle-class restaurant owner. People gather around the scuttle as Raheem begins to strangle Sal. This is when the police show up at the scene. Two white policemen pull Raheem off Sal and drag him off into the street. Meanwhile, everyone is screaming in a riotous manner. The police officer, named Gary, with the fair hair and the moustache puts his nightstick around Raheem's neck. Gary then goes through some kind of racial rage and begins to put pressure on Raheem's neck. Everyone watches in terror as they see their friend and neighbor get strangled to death.

Before anyone can stop Gary (and perhaps before he fully knows what he is doing), Raheem falls dead to the ground. Then, as Holly recounts the scene:

> [The police] begin to kick him and tell him to get up. When they realized what they had done they picked up Raheem's dead body and put him in the back of a police car. Spike Lee's camera work focuses on Raheem and then out of the back window of the car at people left in the street. . . . They stare into the camera and yell murder and real names of people who were actual fatalities from police brutality cases. . . . That concludes the scene I have chosen.

From this Holly is led to conclude that the "problem . . . in my eyes, is the police brutality and how it is covered up." What bothers Samantha Regnier, though, in "Isolating One's Heritage," is the illogic of the riot that follows Raheem's death—since it is made clear throughout the film that Sal treats his customers with an affection and respect that the Korean grocer lacks entirely, and yet the mob destroys his pizzeria while they leave the grocery untouched. Samantha begins her account almost exactly where Holly leaves off:

> As Sal's pizzeria was burning down the crowd suddenly turned around and altered all there attention toward the Korean family across the street persistantely swinging a broom at the people signalling them to stay away from their market. The Korean man was screaming don't touch my store, leave us alone we are the same as you, we are black too. One of the older men in the crowd says he's right there the same as us leave them alone. Instantly the crowd agrees and turns away with aggression yet fatigue.

Samantha goes on to argue that while Sal is shown as "open-minded" through most of the film, in the end he proves "not willing to change, or 'go along' with the blacks, but the Koreans were." For Samantha, then, the real issue comes down to who gets to claim ownership of the neighborhood and thus to call the shots. "Whatever the case the blacks were still trying to make the point of saying this is our neighborhood, we have lived here for years and you think you can just come in and take over." Underlying the savagery of the riot, then, is the sort of ethnic pride that warrants the use of "violence to receive . . . social justice"— a phrasing that seems to obliquely criticize Malcolm X's claim, quoted by Lee at the end of the movie, that oppressed peoples have "the right to do what is necessary" in fighting for their freedom. And so while Holly's horror at the cops' brutality led her to see Lee as arguing against the racism of "the system" or "the man," Samantha read the movie instead as indicting the sort of ethnic or racial pride that can quickly devolve into simple racism and violence.

In "The Hard Truth," Jim Khury offered yet a third reading of the scene that focuses on the verbal duel between Sal and Raheem that leads up to the fight described by Holly and the riot discussed by Samantha. Looking at how Sal shifts suddenly from the role of friendly *pater familias* to screaming racist leads Jim to conclude that:

> Here you saw Sal's true, hidden feelings come out. Through the entire film you see how Sal gets along with the blacks, but when confronted, he explodes physically and verbally at the blacks.
>
> The Public Enemy song, "Fight the Power" is played throughout the movie in a number of different scenes. It seems to have the most meaning though in that particular scene in Sal's pizza shop. In their neighborhood, Sal's pizzeria is in a way, "powerful." When the angered youths try to boycott Sal's pizzeria, nobody else will go in it with them. Also, in Sal's restaurant, Sal was in charge. He was in power and they couldn't tell him what to do. Because Sal was in power, it seemed to be an appropriate song for that scene.
>
> I think that the whole theme of that film presented us with a sense of the reality of racism and the destruction that occurs as a result of it. Most importantly, though, the film illustrates how deep nested and inevitable racism is. Though Sal accepted the blacks and was thankful for their business, that was the extent of it. As people, he didn't really respect them. This is clearly shown by his reaction towards the three blacks who confronted him in his restaurant, referring to rap as "jungle music" and calling them "niggers."

And so while Jim agrees with Samantha and Holly in seeing the movie as an attack on racism, he differs with Samantha in viewing Lee's anger as directed largely against *white* racists, and unlike Holly he refuses to sharply distinguish the actions of Sal from those of the cops. (Incidentally, or perhaps not so, Holly, Samantha, and Jim are all themselves white.) In many ways, Jim gives the bleakest reading of the movie, since he sees its critique as directed at one of the most likable characters in it. If Sal is a racist, he seems to imply, then so are we all, and the inevitable result of this will be violence, either to defend "the power" or to fight it.

In leading our talk about these papers, I insisted that at first our goal would simply be to understand and describe (but not yet to evaluate) the readings of the film they offered. I thus cut off any attempts to show how one of the writers had got it wrong, or failed to see something, or missed its significance when they did. *Do the Right Thing* was the first movie we had looked at that term, so this sort of talk was new to most of the students in the class, and pretty soon several began to hint, in various ways, that they'd like to know which of these readings was the "correct" one. Since my aim was to suggest that while none of them was correct in the sense they were asking about, all three offered potentially useful ways of looking at the text, I asked students not to compare these three readings yet, to argue right off for one or the other, but instead to think about how you might go about making the best possible case for each. Where else might you go to in the film, for instance, to support Holly's sense that Lee's anger is directed more against the "system" (as represented by the cops) than against white people in general (as represented by Sal and his sons)? Or how might you strengthen Samantha's claim that the "ethnic pride" of blacks is also being critiqued in the film? To have them do this, I broke the class into three groups (of about six or seven students), with each assigned the task of coming up with more evidence for one of these ways of reading the film.

To my pleasure (and, I must admit, with some hinting and prodding from me as I walked about the classroom and eavesdropped on their talk), each of the groups was able to come up with a striking amount of support for the view of the film they had been asked to discuss. The group that talked about Jim's paper, for instance, noted several other scenes where Sal could be seen less as friendly than as patronizing; they then remarked that it was, after all, the director of the movie, Lee, who plays the character, Mookie, who starts the riot, which would seem to suggest that he has at least some sympathy for such action; and they also pointed to how the last words of the film literally belong to Malcolm X, in a printed passage that speaks of the possible need for violence in a struggle for justice. They also heard a disturbing echo of "do the right thing"—words that are originally spoken in the film by Da Mayor, a character who later ineffectually pleads for restraint before the riot—in "you do what you gotta do," the puzzling last words spoken by Sal right before his pizzeria is sacked. (I wonder if there isn't a further echo or corruption of the phrase in X's "the right to do what is necessary.") Finally, they pointed to an interesting formal shift: Near the end of the riot, as Smiley pins his pictures to the ruined wall of Sal's pizzeria, we hear Public Enemy rapping "Fight the Power" *on the soundtrack*—that is, while the audience of the film hears the music, the characters in it do not. Before this moment, "Fight the Power" has only been heard on Radio Raheem's boom box, as part of the ambient sound of the film, which led the group to suggest that Lee seems at this point to adopt Raheem's music as his own. (In response, a number of other students pointed out that it is not quite true that until then "Fight the Power" is only heard through Raheem's box. It is also heard over the opening credits—but this only seems to strengthen Lee's identification with the aggressive stance of the song.)

All of which adds up to a very strong reading of the film, but not one that the other groups were willing simply to give in to. The group that had been working with Holly's paper, for instance, pointed out that in the scenes that follow the riot we see Sal and Mookie come if not to a reconciliation then at least to an uneasy truce. They also noted that, in the closing shot of the film, as the camera pulls away from the block, we hear the voice of a local radio DJ, Mister Senor Lovedaddy—who has served as a kind of Greek chorus, commenting on and explaining the actions of the various characters on the block—bemoaning the violence that has just taken place and exhorting *political* action instead. ("Your Lovedaddy says: Register to Vote! The Election is Coming Up!") This allowed me to point out that when it was first released many viewers saw *Do the Right Thing* as a kind of agitprop for David Dinkins in his campaign against Ed Koch for mayor of New York. Similarly, the group dealing with Samantha's paper had a list of scenes that poked fun (sometimes gentle and sometimes not) at the black residents of the block—that could be seen as mocking, for instance, Buggin' Out's pretensions as an activist, Smiley's inarticulate obsessiveness, Mookie's irresponsibility (he has a wife and child whom he pays very little attention to), the laziness of the street corner men, the drunken sententiousness of Da Mayor, and so on. They also pointed to what, with the exception of the riot, is probably the most striking scene in the movie: a quick series of characters spitting out a stream of insults against one ethnic group or the other—Italian, African, Asian, Hispanic, Jew—which by its end casts each one of them as both victim and bigot. And they noted that the passage by Malcolm X at the end of the movie is preceded by one in which Martin Luther King argues *against* the use of violence. (Indeed many students had cited the King passage—and ignored the one by X—in their own first writings on the movie.)

Thus by the end of our talk (which took all of a three-hour class meeting), we had developed not a single consensus reading of the film but three competing views of it. When I was asked, then, if this meant that these were all "good" papers, many students were surprised when I said no. They had the makings of good papers, I suggested, but for now they were all weakened by their failure to imagine and thus respond to other views of the film. In revising their own work, then, I wanted everyone to try to show why they *chose* to see the film as they did, why this perspective on it struck as them as more useful or persuasive than others. As a way of putting still some more pressure on them to do so, I told my students that in their second drafts they were required to deal with the responses of at least two other viewers (either from this class or outside of it), and, in doing so, to show how these other viewers added to or contested their own readings of the movie. If they were now past searching for a single correct reading, I didn't want them to settle for an easy pluralism either. I wanted to see them argue out their sense of the film, but I wanted to see that argument take place in writing and not to be preempted by a too quick taking of sides in our classroom talk.

During the next week, as students worked on revising their first readings of the film, we looked at still some more ways of approaching it. Among them was for the first time a piece by an African American student, Oronde Sharif, who wrote, in "I Just Don't Know Why," of his disappointment at watching Mookie try to be friends with just about everybody—with the result that it seemed unclear in the end just who he really stood with. As an example, Oronde pointed to what struck him as the moral incongruity of Mookie returning to Sal the day after the riot to ask for his week's pay. This piece proved useful in showing that there wasn't any particular "black line" on the movie (since several of the other black students in the class disagreed with Oronde), and thus that everyone in the class had equal need to argue for their readings of it—that simply being African American offered you no privileged insight into the film. This point was made again when we read "What Is the Right Thing?"—a critical symposium in *Cineaste* magazine that showed several African American viewers in sharp disagreement over the meaning and worth of Lee's film. What many students began to realize, I think, in reading this conflicting set of comments, was that they could see *Do the Right Thing* as a powerful expression of a view they did not agree with, that they could take on an adversarial as well as appreciative stance toward the movie.

In *A Rhetoric of Motives,* Kenneth Burke compares the give and take of intellectual debate to a "somewhat formless parliamentary wrangle," a "horse-trading" of ideas in which individual critics try to grab support for their own positions through whatever deals, borrowings, and alliances they can strike up with some colleagues, and whatever raids or attacks they can make on the views of others (188). While I prefer this description of intellectual work to Burke's much more often quoted metaphor of an ongoing parlor conversation, I have to admit that there also seems something slightly disreputable about it, and Burke himself points to the temptation, especially among teachers, to give form to such wrangles by placing opposing views in dialectical tension with each other, so that their conflicts can then be resolved at some "higher" or "ultimate" level (188–89). The best example of this sort of dialectic can of course be found, as Burke points out, in the dialogues of Plato—which characteristically begin with Socrates facing a diverse set of opinions on a subject (what is piety? what is justice?) and then gradually leading his listeners to a consensus about what can or cannot be known about it. In a famous passage from Book I of *The Republic,* Socrates himself argues for the merit of this approach, saying:

> If we were to oppose him [Thrasymachus, a sophist who is his current foil in the dialogue] . . . with a parallel set speech on the blessings of the just life, then another speech from him in turn, then another from us, then we should have to count and measure the blessings mentioned on each side, and we should need some judges to decide the case. If on the other hand, we investigate the question, as we were doing, *by seeking agreement with each other,* then we ourselves can be both the judges and the advocates. (348b; Grube 1974, 21, my italics)

From opposing speeches to agreement, diversity to consensus, wrangle to dialogue—that is the usual progress of teaching. What I hope to show here (and I think Burke might approve though surely Plato would not) is the value of keeping things at the level of a wrangle, of setting up our classrooms so that a variety of views are laid out and the arguments for them made, but trying *not* to push for consensus, for an ultimate view that resolves or explains the various conflicts of stance and opinion that surface in such talk. One of the problems with much teaching, it seems to me, is that the teacher often serves only too well (though often far more surreptitiously than Socrates) as both judge and advocate of what gets said, pointing out the weaknesses of some positions or readings while accenting the strengths of others. I would much rather see a classroom in which student writings functioned something like the "set speeches" that Socrates derides, that serve as positions in an ongoing argument whose blessings we can count and measure together, but whose final merits we can leave students to judge for themselves. (I am assuming of course that students will also be given as many chances as they want to rethink and revise what they have to say, that no one will be committed to a position before they are willing to accept and defend it as their own.) I'd rather have a wrangle that even if it is somewhat formless (or perhaps because it is) gives students a set of chances to come to their own sense of a text or issue, than a dialogue that has been subtly shaped and ordered by their teacher.

I am not trying to argue that we should somehow abdicate our authority as teachers. I don't think we could even if we wanted to. In teaching you are always in some way shaping what can or cannot be said in your classroom—as can be seen clearly, for instance, in my decision to begin our work with papers that offered such contrasting readings of *Do the Right Thing,* as well as in the strict limits I set on the sorts of talk I would allow about them.

What I am arguing for, though, is a style of teaching that aims at holding competing views or readings in tension with one another, that tries to keep a certain kind of talk going rather than to lead it towards a certain end. In reading through their second drafts on *Do the Right Thing,* then, I looked to see how students had incorporated the comments of other viewers into their own work as writers. Some patterns soon became clear. First, predictably, there were a number of students who had somehow failed to note or remember my demand that they deal with the responses of other viewers, and who thus wrote second drafts that showed few or no traces of the reading and talk we had been engaged in for the past few weeks. (The worst of these turned in second drafts that were virtually reprints of their first ones—with at most a few typos fixed or words changed.) I told them that this was failing work, and all but one (a woman who withdrew from the course) submitted third drafts that showed more actual revision. Then there was what I started to call the "as my friend says" group, who simply scouted through the various readings until they found someone saying something close to what they already believed, and then added a line to their text beginning: "As Robert Sklar says" or "As Holly says." I told them that this was just barely cutting it, and most of the students who had tried it laughed when they heard me describe their method. A slightly more complex version of the "as my friend says" routine was the "I disagree with" strategy, since this usually needed to be followed by a "because. . . . " Still a little better were the "Hansels and Gretels," who scattered trails of "I disagree with"s and "As my friend says"s throughout their text, but usually without much changing the original path of their argument. They were trying, though, and I praised their efforts. What I chose to talk about in class, however, were a few texts whose writers seemed to me to be doing more than simply adding things on to what they had said already, who you could see trying both to argue with other viewers and to show how these competing readings had influenced their own.

A problem in talking about these texts was that many of the influences on them would have been invisible to readers outside the class. In her first draft, for instance, Sidney Cooper, an African American woman, had centered her writing on the anger she felt when watching the murder of Radio Raheem. But by the time she wrote her second draft, though, her response had become more complex and ambivalent. Early on in "Who Did the Wrong Thing" she writes:

> I am left wondering who was right in this situation; was Radio Raheem's death justifiable because he refused to respect Sal's establishment and turn his radio off? Then was Sal completely innocent and not responsible for his death? Were the police really forced to kill Raheem? Was the destruction of Sal's Pizzeria compensation for his death? The answers to all the above questions I feel are, absolutely not. . . .

> I found it very hard to accept Raheem's death without becoming furious. By no means was it necessary. . . . Would the cops have taken the same measures if it had been a white man strangling Sal? . . . But is Radio Raheem's death only the police's fault, or do Sal, and for that matter Raheem himself add as catalysts to the horrifying ending?

In the rest of her piece, Sidney talks about her growing reluctance to side with anyone at the end of the movie. She quotes the critic Jacquie Jones asking if "the destruction of Sal's . . . is a reasonable response to unreasonable circumstances," and she notes Spike Lee's claim that the riot expresses the "horror" of the "whole community" at the death of Raheem.[3] But Sidney seems less willing now to see one form of violence or horror as a reasonable response to another, and she brings her piece to a close by saying:

> When I watched this scene, in the back of my mind, I was with Mookie, cheering him on to burn Sal's down to the ground after what they did. But who is or are "they"? This now brings us back to the question of whose hands do we place the blame: on the police, on Sal or Raheem, and this we do not know. When we can pinpoint who actually was responsible for Raheem's death, then we can decide whether everyone's reactions are justifiable. Until this is determined, I feel no one did the "right thing.

I think that Sidney makes good use of Jones and Lee in her paper—and, of course, in doing so, meets my demand that she deal with the comments of at least two other viewers. But what I am more struck by is how her writing draws on our previous talk in class about the film. For instance, when Sidney asks about where we can place blame, "on the police, Sal or Raheem," she is using a kind of shorthand we had formed for referring to the positions represented by Holly, Jim, and Samantha's papers—for readings of the movie that see it as directed either against the system (the police), white racism (Sal), or aggressive ethnic pride (Raheem). Sidney is not able yet to push beyond or even choose among these three positions, but I am impressed by how her writing suggests that she is willing take such readings seriously, while still holding on to much of her original fury at the racial hatred that underlies Raheem's death.

In other cases you could see how the work of the class had given some students a new way of viewing the film—though one that was still very much their own. For instance, Keith Davis was an African American student who had failed to make his view of the film very clear in his first writing, but who in later drafts began to articulate a strong critique of the film as he worked with and through the comments of other viewers. In his final draft of "The Uninterpreted Director," Keith more or less flipped the approach taken by his classmate Oronde Sharif. Instead of writing on what the film had to say to black viewers, Keith looked at how *Do the Right Thing* offered a picture of African American life to a largely white movie audience. This shift in perspective allowed him to talk about some problems he had with the movie that he had not been able to get at before, as he argued, for instance, that

> Spike does not develop his characters enough to make his movies come alive. Irene Davis thinks that Smiley is a politically aware character. I don't see how she arrived at her conclusion from just watching Smiley walking around with a picture of Malcolm X and Martin King. . . . The character of Smiley should have encompassed him running for an elective office or running a campaign within the community, then my view of his political consciousness would be justifiable. . . . This over-generalization misinforms the general public about life in a Black community. Hence, this is the only Black community many whites will ever see, yet they are seeing a distorted picture of that community.

Sometimes the effects of our reading and talk were even less predictable. One student, Christine Tappe, was married to a policeman, and thus felt much less inclined than most others in the class to blame the cops for the death of Radio Raheem. As part of her second draft of "Does Anyone Do the Right Thing?," Christine ended up arguing:

> Along with this hatred, Lee expresses other human and not always color-specific emotions such as rage and frustration. One in class critic, Holly Affeltranger, placed the blame of *all* the underlying problems upon the police community. In Lee's portrayal, one overly excited police officer was responsible for the death of a troublesome black youth who, in a similar state of rage over the same radio issue, attempted and nearly succeeded in strangling Sal to death. In this case, the police officers were not responsible for the underlying issue of racism, although they were the vehicles through which the prejudice was being transported.

Perhaps more interesting than this argument over a specific point, though, is the reading of the film that it leads Christine to. Having committed herself to considering some of the "human and not always color-specific" aspects of the movie, Christine ended up with some useful things to say about its *sexual* politics. Her paper analyzes a scene near the middle of the film where Mookie angrily looks on as Sal dotes on one of his favorite customers, Jade, who happily flirts back with him. The problem is that Jade is Mookie's sister, and the scene ends with him pulling her out into the street for a heated lecture against black-white sex. For Christine, this is the scene where we see Mookie finally "choose his loyalties," and she argues that it reveals that he has some personal as well as political reasons for later throwing the trash can through Sal's window.

I like how these second drafts show their writers responding to other readings of the movie without simply adopting or rejecting them. Instead each forges a reading of the film under pressure, in tension with other views of the text. But a weakness of these writings is that they often fail to make it very clear just who they are responding to. If you didn't already know who had said what in class, that is, you'd be hard pressed to see how other readers had helped shape their work. As we continued through the term, I pressed students to document the influences on their writing more clearly, both in assignments that asked them to respond directly to the work of other critics and in one on the "process of viewing a movie" that asked them to trace some of the expectations and assumptions that shape their understanding of a film. I also expect that those students who go on to take advanced courses in film or literature will get the chance to experiment with various critical methods that have been self-consciously defined as such—to learn what is now meant by, say, feminist or deconstructionist or new historical approaches to reading, and to gain a sense of the uses and limits of each. But I am aware that many will not go on to such study, and so I am happy at this point simply to help students gain a sense of what it is like to be part of an ongoing critical conversation (or wrangle)—to learn what it means to view a reading as something other than "just an opinion" or "just the facts," and to see how other readers can help them articulate their own understanding of a text. Teaching the conventions of citation before students have a sense of *why* they might want to deal with other readings in the first place, of what they can gain from listening to and arguing with what other readers have to say, strikes me as little more than drilling them in the forms of an empty ritual.

There is also of course much to argue with in all of these readings of *Do the Right Thing*. Again, though, my aim was not to lead students to what I believed was a superior understanding of the film but to involve them in arguing for a view of it that they had formed and chosen. Similarly, while *Do the Right Thing* led students to some very interesting talk and writing (a number of them said that they had never thought before that you could talk about any movie for three weeks), I want to make it clear that I don't think it is any better or worse a text to teach than most others. In the last few years, there has been a bitter public argument over what students most need to read—with defenders of the canon battling the advocates of multiculturalism, Virgil and Dante pitted against Franz Fanon and Alice Walker. (Or at least that's how it sometimes comes out in the more cartoonish versions of the media.) What troubles me about how this controversy has been framed so far is that both sides of it tend to be represented by reading lists and little else. The question of what students are supposed to do with the texts on these lists is rarely addressed. Instead, as Katha Pollitt has pointed out, all parties to the debate simply seem to assume that reading will have a kind of *medicinal* effect, that the right dose of the right thing will have the desired effects (whatever those may be) on students. And so Pollitt argues that "the canon debate is really an argument about what books to cram down the resistant throats of a resentful populace of students" (1991, 330)—when what we really want are better ways of showing them the uses and pleasures of reading.

The real question, then, is not if students are reading the right thing but what they get to do with what they read—the kinds of talk they are encouraged to have together and the sorts of writing they are asked to do. And I can't imagine how you can get students very excited about talking about movies and books so long as the conclusions they are expected to come to are clear from the start—so long as they can see, for instance, that in one class they are expected to admire Shakespeare because he was a genius and humanist, while in another they are supposed to critique him for being a white imperialist, while in still others they are to identify with the poetry of Adrienne Rich because it is woman-centered, or to respect the work of Nadine Gordimer because it is anti-racist, or to dig the novels of Don DeLillo because they are hip and postmodern, and so on. Such classes are set up as if the meanings of the texts being taught in them are already clear—and thus that the politics of a course can be gauged from a quick glance at its reading list. It seems to me, though, that for talk about a text to become at all lively, critical, or engaging, its possible meanings and value have to be left open to question. It is now fashionable to deride the old New Critics for their conservative politics and their preoccupation with the close reading of a select number of canonical texts—and for the most part I agree with such criticisms. But I also remember studying as an undergraduate in a New Critical department where I was given the (for me, exhilarating) sense that nobody really was quite sure exactly what Donne or Hardy or Lawrence or Eliot were up to, and that if I could argue out my readings of them well enough, that I would be listened to. I don't teach those sorts of books very often now, but how I teach still owes much to that early experience of being taken seriously as a reader. Perhaps my teachers gave me their respect before I had really earned it, but in offering it they also gave me something to build on in forming a sense of myself as a writer and intellectual. I've tried here to show some of the ways I've worked to take the talk and writings of my students just as seriously.

## Notes

1. In this and in all that follows, I am drawing on an approach to teaching reading and writing forged at the University of Pittsburgh by, among many others, William Coles, David Bartholomae, Anthony Petrosky, Mariolina Salvatori, and Paul Kameen. Without such colleagues I would never have begun to think about teaching in the ways I describe here. My thanks go to them all.

2. My thanks also go to my students for granting me permission to quote from their work, which I have reproduced here as exactly as possible, without editorial corrections.

3. See Sklar et al., "What Is the Right Thing?" pp. 34–35 for the sources of these quotations.

## Works Cited


Affeltranger, Holly. 1991. Radio Raheem's Death. Unpublished essay, University of Pittsburgh.

Burke, Kenneth. 1969. *A Rhetoric of Motives.* Berkeley: University of California Press.

Cooper, Sidney. 1991. Who Does the Wrong Thing? Unpublished essay, University of Pittsburgh.

Davis, Keith. 1991. The Uninterpreted Director. Unpublished essay, University of Pittsburgh.

Lee, Spike, dir. 1989. *Do the Right Thing.* Universal.

Khury, Jim. 1991. The Hard Truth. Unpublished essay, University of Pittsburgh.

Plato. 1974. *The Republic.* Translated by G. M. A. Grube. Indianapolis: Hackett.

Pollitt, Katha. 1991. "Canon to the Right of Me . . . ." *The Nation,* 23 September, 328–31.

Regnier, Samantha. 1991. Isolating One's Heritage. Unpublished essay, University of Pittsburgh.

Sharif, Oronde. 1991. I Just Don't Know Why. Unpublished essay, University of Pittsburgh.

Sklar, Robert, Jacquie Jones, Salim Mauwakkll, Zeinabu Irene Davis, Charles Musser, and Lisa Kennedy. 1990. "What Is the Right Thing?" *Cineaste* 37 (4): 32–39.

Tappe, Christine. 1991. Does Anyone Do the Right Thing? Unpublished essay, University of Pittsburgh.

# 7

## Reading Multiculturally and Rhetorically

### Higher Learning *in the*
### *Composition Classroom*

### Johanna Schmertz and Annette Trefzer

> Your assignment for this semester is as follows: to formulate your
> own political ideology. This will be dictated by your sex. Your back-
> ground. Your social, economic status. Personal experience. Et cetera,
> et cetera.
>
> —Professor Phipps,
> *Higher Learning*

Recently, many multicultural educators have been exploring ways to acknowledge cultural difference in the classroom—the "et cetera, et cetera" Phipps
somewhat dismissively refers to in our epigraph. As bell hooks says in *Teaching to Transgress* (1994), "there is not nearly enough practical discussion of
ways classroom settings can be transformed so that learning experience is inclusive" (35). We would like to address this lack of practical methodology by
talking about ways to transform teaching and the classroom so that multicultural education may be possible. John Singleton's *Higher Learning,* we discov-
ered, is an excellent vehicle for this purpose.

Challenging the approach of some cultural studies pedagogies that front
the political and ideological dimensions of texts, Ellen Bishop (1997) suggests that "teaching film as a medium with certain conventions and meaning . . .
(often vested in what I'm loosely calling 'framing') . . . is a way to give students the insights and concepts and vocabulary they need, so that they can get
at sophisticated readings of the texts and their socio-political dimensions for

themselves" (29). Bishop teaches a set of contemporary satirical film texts that always already refer to the sociopolitical contexts of their production. She does this in order to reimagine cultural studies as locating students as critical thinkers between the sociopolitical and rhetorical dimensions of texts.

Our experiences teaching John Singleton's *Higher Learning* in rural Oklahoma suggest similar strategies. Whether students are indeed "exhausted by the rigors of political correctness" (Bishop, 24) and able, once given the proper tools, to "get at sophisticated readings of the texts . . . for themselves" depends very much on the students' pedagogical and cultural environments. Our students, for example, by virtue of the culture they inhabit, are often more resistant to PC arguments than they are exhausted by them, because they often are unaware of, and isolated from, the social and historical conditions that legitimate these arguments.

Because we teach in an economically disadvantaged rural area, we are presented with particular challenges when we bring multicultural texts or issues into the classroom. Even though our learning environment is marked by a high percentage of ethnic students (more than 30 percent of the student population is Native American), many students identify with "white" mainstream American values and many, sadly, know very little or nothing about their ethnic heritage. The small towns our students come from are often the kind where "everybody knows everybody," and this focus on assimilation makes it difficult for some of our students to see explorations of difference in the classroom as anything other than a privileging of difference, bound to create trouble and conflict where none appeared to exist before. The students' general lack of cultural knowledge often leads them to reject all those perceived as "other."

Further, as the geographic and economic isolation of our students promotes monolithic "white" identities, it also renders print culture somewhat irrelevant to them: reading and writing have small relevance for many of our students, who—outside of school or local libraries—can only get whatever books are on offer at Wal-Mart. While many of our high school teachers do an excellent job, little reading or writing takes place outside of English class, with the result that one third of our students score below 19 on the ACT and must therefore take developmental reading and writing courses prior to entering freshman composition. Teaching strategies for active, critical reading and introducing students to rhetorical skills necessary for understanding and evaluating texts, including visual texts, therefore becomes a priority in our classrooms. Like Bishop, we see the need to enable students to develop their own arguments, and therefore we emphasize the need for a structuralist heuristic that includes close reading. Like Bishop too, however, we also see the need for a discussion of larger didactic and ideological frameworks that address our particular student population. It is in the context of our students' limited experience with reading and their resistance to cultural difference that we use film in our writing classes. Since cable TV and VCRs are readily available to most of our students, film provides a link to the world outside and a common popular literacy, one we have found helpful to build from on our way toward academic, critical literacies in the writing classroom.

A word about the use of film in the composition class: Film in some ways levels an uneven playing field for students, providing a literacy shared among teacher, student, and the world outside. Too often, however, this common ground is taken for granted, in ways that suggest film's rhetorical innocence. In many cases, films are used in classrooms merely to discuss the "messages" they contain. But questions of rhetoricity, interpretation, reader response, or rhetorical purpose apply to film just as they do to print text. Film has its own rhetoric, similar to but different from the rhetoric of the printed text, a rhetoric executed through such mechanisms as camera placement and distance, editing, and so forth. This rhetoric is read not only through codes specific to film, but also through codes specific to the viewer: whatever cultural knowledges the reader brings to bear upon the text as well as his or her understanding of that text's rhetorical situation.

If the visual text has its own rhetoric, albeit one highly dependent on the viewer's social constructedness, and if we want to sensitize students to the presence of rhetoric so they can use it themselves and fend off its bad uses, to use film merely as a handy visual aid seems to us to miss an important opportunity to show students how film shapes their world and experiences. Therefore we agree with James Berlin's (1996) imperative for writing instructors:

> Our business must be to instruct students in signifying practices broadly conceived—to see not only the rhetoric of the college essay, but also the rhetoric of the institution of schooling, of politics, and of the media, the hermeneutic not only of certain literary texts, but also the hermeneutic of film, TV, and popular music. (93)

In other words, by teaching students to read the rhetoric of film in the writing classroom, we are exploring two goals at once: we engage students in an analysis of the rhetorical and the cultural codes that operate to define subject positions—including redefining their own—and we seek to empower culturally underprivileged students by giving them access to a literacy that is both academic and critically self-reflexive.

In order to achieve these goals, we propose a threefold pedagogical strategy. In the first section of this chapter, we discuss how developing an empathetic understanding of "others" can help students move beyond simplistic cultural binaries and decrease defensive responses or outright hostility toward issues of diversity. John Singleton's film, we argue, can broaden students' cultural literacy by offering effective strategies for both identification and instruction. *Higher Learning* is also a perfect example of a film that renders explicit its own cinematic strategies and therefore encourages student analysis of its formal qualities. In the second section of this chapter, we therefore propose an inductive heuristic for learning to read the rhetoric of film and discuss our students' efforts at close reading and understanding cinematic codes. How rhetorical literacy is linked to cultural literacy is the subject of the third and final section, in which we argue that a formalist reading of "frames" and "shots" is best complemented by the introduction of a contextual and local hermeneutics that renders visible the students' participation in particular discourse communities. By analyzing the visual text as part of a rhetorical situation, students learn to contextualize Singleton's creative and polemic strategies and to (re)define their own positions as his intended audience.

## Creating Empathetic Identification: A Pedagogical View

Teaching a multicultural agenda in a fairly homogeneous classroom can unwittingly strengthen rather than weaken students' feelings of alienation and their ideas that their own identities are not being acknowledged. This problem is often compounded by college anthologies that present multiculturalism as a study of social and ethnic differences. Such differences are politicized into boundaries drawn around different groups and can serve as the basis for student prejudice or lack of interest. Multicultural anthologies, then, can reinforce rather than dismantle boundaries demarcating groups that students are already only all too willing to bracket off as irrelevant to their own needs or experiences. For instance, students have asked us: "Why do we have to study Indians in the writing class?" or "Why should we read Martin Luther King?"

By using John Singleton's *Higher Learning* in the multicultural writing classroom, educators can anticipate questions that register student hostility and annoyance toward the study of "others' lives." *Higher Learning* answers such questions indirectly by inviting students to examine contemporary social issues both empathetically and critically. By blending together the separate story lines of three characters, whose paths cross only at a few pivotal moments, Singleton highlights and problematizes the lack of connections among individuals from seemingly separate ethnic and social groups. The movie follows three "first-term freshmen who get a crash course in diversity, identity, and sexuality in writer/director John Singleton's bold look at contemporary college life" (back of video description). The three freshmen are Malik, a black male on an athletic scholarship for track; Remy, a white male from Idaho; and Kristen, a white female from California whose family is in financial trouble. By focusing on the academic and social struggles of the students, Singleton wanted to approach the film "on the level of a documentary" and to show

> what really happens on a university campus. . . . While Singleton acknowledges that he drew upon his own experiences while writing the screenplay, the film is also packed with issues burning on today's campuses: cultural diversity, date rape, homophobia, institutional and social racism, ever-rising tuition, and what some see as the exploitation of college athletes. (Bergman 1995)

When interviewed by college students, Singleton professed that his goal was to encourage discussion among students about these contemporary social problems.

Singleton's film successfully dispels hostility and self-pity by revealing the complexities and intersections of racial identity with class, economics, gender, location, and education. But *Higher Learning* does even more than complicate identity politics; it reveals the hidden privilege of "whiteness." Such a message is crucial in an institutional environment where many of our white students feel powerless, at the bottom of a class hierarchy, and lacking social recognition. Many have misconceptions about minority scholarships, welfare, and other social programs from which they feel unjustly excluded. In sum, because many of our students are economically underprivileged, they are willing to adopt narratives of representation that suggest that whites are victims of racial inequality. *Higher Learning* powerfully counters such popular narratives of white victimization—or, as our students often say, "reverse racism"—by offering instead a vision of identity grounded in personal agency and democratic responsibility. *Higher Learning* also teaches students that identity is never based monolithically on "race" but always also on those factors that interpellate the racial self with class, gender, education, location, nationality, sexuality, and so on. In that sense, *Higher Learning* offers our students intersections and possible connections between themselves and those they usually perceive as "others." Such new identifications, however, also involve painful recognitions about the students' own subject positions, including racial and sexual prejudices of which they are often unaware and that they prefer not to acknowledge.

In a lecture on education and psychoanalysis, Jacques Lacan argues that "teaching, like analysis, has to deal not so much with *lack* of knowledge as with *resistances* to knowledge" (qtd. in Penley 1990, 170). Constance Penley concludes from this that "this refusal [to know], then, is not so much a refusal of information as a refusal to acknowledge *one's own implication* in that information" (171). In order to facilitate the students' recognition of their "implications" in racism and homophobia (which students initially insist does not exist on our campus), Annette uses Singleton's film first to trigger empathy for and identification with subject positions different from her students'. For one of the first writing journal responses, Annette asks students to identify with a character and describe his/her problems. Students may initially feel that they do not have much in common with any of the characters because of gender or racial differences. But the movie offers multiple strategies of identification, among them economic and social positions. For instance, after careful consideration of the main characters, Darren, a white male, wrote: "If I had to choose one [a character] I guess it would be Malik. He has had problems with the scholarship that he thought he had gotten . . . " By realizing a common context of economic oppression, Darren, a white student from a rural background, was able to identify with Malik, a black student from a city. Amanda, a white female, chose

to identify with Kristen because of her positive attitude and political agency.
Amanda wrote: "She began participating in a women's help group, and she became more actively involved with the politics concerning her school. These actions helped her to overcome the anger and hurt inside of her so that she could
move on with her life." Thomas, a white male, chose to respond to what he saw
as the film's message:

> It sends a message that America is a divided country. . . . Coming from a smaller
> university, I do not witness that many acts of racism. Other than an occasional
> derogatory remark, I am not exposed to racial hate, therefore I can't relate to
> the film other than feeling pity for those that fall victim to the hate of others,
> and I think almost anyone can relate to that.

But that is exactly it: empathetic understanding means crossing a boundary to the "other" and relocating intersections of gender, race, and class. By
identifying with somebody else, somebody whom they are not, the students
are creating what multicultural educator Barry Kanpol (1995) calls an "intersubjective consciousness." An advocate of a "pedagogy of empathy," Kanpol
writes:

> Empathy, then, is reached through one's different subjective experiences of
> racism, alienation, and various other forms of domination, combined with an
> understanding of the dialectical meeting points of the similarities of these op-
> pressive experiences. (181)

But whereas Kanpol suggests that such empathy is produced through "personal
memories and histories" that can easily result in self-indulgent essays about
personal experiences with discrimination, Annette then shifts the locus of experience away from the student's Self as the center of consciousness. She uses
Singleton's film to create a potential for the empathetic representation of others
and a place for situating collective intersubjective identities. In Annette's classroom, Singleton's film acts initially as an invitation to identify with somebody
else, to create an "intertext" between Self and Other, the personal and the political. In a recent *College English* article, Lindsay Pentolfe Aegerter (1997)
supports this pedagogical strategy in the multicultural writing classroom. She
writes, "Identification, quite simply, decreases the possibility of oppositional
antagonism" (905).

## Academic Literacy and the Rhetoric
## of Film: Two Heuristics

Empathy, however, is only the beginning of our students' thinking and writing about their own identities in relation to the identities of "others." As they
attempt to come to terms with issues of difference, they must also learn to
speak to, and write about, these issues in a new and different literacy—the

language of academic discourse. As David Bartholomae (1985) says, our students must

> speak not only in another's voice but through another's code; and they not only
> have to do this, they have to speak in the voice and through the codes of those
> of us with power and wisdom; and they not only have to do this, they have to
> do it before they know what they are doing, before they have a project to par-
> ticipate in, and before, at least in terms of our disciplines, they have anything to
> say. (156)

In a recent *CCC* article, David Foster (1997) describes how students respond to texts that do not seem to include them in their audiences. Needing, and failing, to feel a reader-writer connection in some of the anthology pieces they read for his writing classes, Foster's students "cast about for alternative reader-constructions into which they could more readily project themselves" (525). Acknowledging the differences between themselves and the intended audiences they postulate for each piece, Foster's students, he claims, gain from their responses a heightened awareness of the complexity of reading but do not feel impelled to join any of the discourse communities these texts imply. Ignored by Foster, however, is the possibility that there might also be strategies for making oneself into the kind of audience a text requires, in order to then write one's way into its discourse community. This is one of the premises underlying the academic discourse movement in composition, a movement most frequently associated with David Bartholomae. Mariolina Salvatori (1996) asks, "What happens when students show little cultural, emotional, or intellectual predisposition for . . . reading? How can a teacher teach her students to perform a kind of reading that she herself has learned to perform mysteriously and magically?" (451).

Such questions occupy the nexus between the academic discourse movement and studies in developmental English, and are extremely appropriate in pedagogical environments like ours, where literacy is culturally undervalued. In order for students to gain academic literacy, they must be provided with a vocabulary and a heuristic or interpretive framework that enables them to read texts closely. In the case of film, this means learning to view film through such literary devices as plot, character, and symbol but also to consider more specifically filmic devices such as soundtrack, costume, setting, camera angle and distance, shot duration, and editing. Introducing the terminology of filmmaking into discussions of *Higher Learning* gives students the kind of critical vocabulary and interpretive framework that enables them to position themselves as experts.

*Higher Learning* is highly structured and overt in its rhetorical strategies, particularly in its self-referential commentary. To take the most obvious example, the film begins with a shot of the American flag. The homogeneous unity this flag presupposes is then undercut by the ensuing narrative, and by multiple flags displayed by different groups at Columbus College: the rebel flag, the flag of African national unity, and the swastika. The film ends with another shot of the American flag, this time with the words "unlearn" superimposed upon it. Hence the flag in the final frame comments ironically on the flag in the first frame.

The soundtrack comments on the screenplay as well. Singleton chose his own musical artists for the soundtrack and asked them to compose songs for specific scenes and characters—Ice Cube for Malik, for example; Rage Against the Machine for Remy; and Tori Amos for Kristen. In the closing credits, a song by Ice Cube (who also plays sixth-year senior Fudge) renarrates the whole movie from the perspective of Malik, offering a particular reading of the movie the viewer has just seen. Similarly, the soundtrack accompanying a scene of Malik running track contains the lyrics "You are young, gifted, and black, with your soul intact," and a scene of Kristen putting photos of her friends and family up in her room is accompanied by the lyrics "Just a photograph/Kinda makes me laugh."

Self-referential commentary also takes place at the level of editing. Transitions between scenes either repeat a visual or sound element, to show a commonality between scenes and characters (as when the same music and a book connect separate scenes of Malik and Remy studying), or to provide ironic commentary (as when a white fraternity boy proclaims, "Nobody parties like we do," and the scene then cuts to a black party in Fudge's dormitory, which is later broken up by campus security).

Because of the highly structured, self-referential qualities of *Higher Learning,* a formalist approach works well to foreground not just its style but also its political elements. In the case of writer-director John Singleton, it would be difficult to find any repeated element or pattern that did not in some way both register and convey his politics. Asking students to trace, for example, the occurrences of the flag in the film or to chart Remy's costume changes from Idaho loner to neo-Nazi skinhead inevitably draws students' attention to these highly rhetorical, political elements, making them available for class discussion. For example, John, asked to trace the contexts in which the word *class* got mentioned in *Higher Learning,* reported that characters used the word *class* in two ways—to mean socioeconomic class and the classroom—and that at times the two meanings intersected. The ability to "go to class," he noted, depended on how one was economically situated. John pointed out that at one moment in the film, Malik complains about the fact that he both has to study and run track in order to keep his scholarship. He says to Professor Phipps, "I don't see white folks worrying about nothing but going to class," and Phipps counters by suggesting that Malik's problem is therefore economic, not racial.

Johanna began her composition course with an interest in film and a curiosity to see how what her students possessed in the way of visual literacy might be exploited in the service of more academic literacies. Inspired by Salvatori (1996), Ann Berthoff (1984), and others, she believed that students could construct their own strategies for reading and thinking, and so she devised a two-part heuristic aimed at teaching students to teach themselves the rhetorical codes of film and then apply their understanding of filmic rhetoric to *Higher Learning.* By learning how to do close readings of film, Johanna's students would try on academic discourse in the context of "a project to participate in," to borrow Bartholomae's phrase.

Before giving them the heuristics, however, Johanna recognized the need to provide students with a certain vocabulary. Using a glossary from an introductory film textbook, she screened instances of shots and kinds of sound typically found in most movies. Each student was then given a type of shot, an aspect of sound, or a component of mise-en-scène (e.g., props, costumes, setting) to trace through *Higher Learning,* and to apply the first heuristic to it:

1.   How am I influenced by element X (the close-up, nondiegetic sound, etc.)? Or, what have I come to expect from X?

2.   Do I perceive any patterns in X (e.g., frequency of repetition, distribution, placement, surrounding context)?

3.   Do I perceive any changes in X? What can I attribute them to?

4.   Can I make any inferences about element X's nature or uses?

5.   Are any questions raised for me by my tracing of X?

The heuristic enabled students to learn the rhetoric of film inductively and to define for others how their particular filmic element functioned rhetorically—that is, when and for what purpose a director might use that element. For example, following the heuristic, Cristeena came to the conclusion that a close-up caused her to focus on a particular detail, often a facial expression or an object significant to the plot, that a close-up usually needs to be preceded by some sort of establishing shot showing the object in its context, and, based on her experience, that directors use it to draw the viewer's attention to something important. In an essay titled "The Common Closet," Katie noted that Singleton used repetition of visual objects to achieve transitions between scenes:

> The first easily noticeable transition through this method was the closet in the establishing scene of Malik and Kristen [moving into their dorm rooms]. Malik is seen picking up a stack of clothes on hangers and walking towards the closet. Just as he approaches the closet, a door opens and a light shines toward the viewer as Kristen hangs some clothes on the bar in the foreground of the frame.

One of the best writers in the class, Brad used the heuristic to trace background objects, and observed that in Singleton's movie backgrounds shift in and out of focus according to how important they are in illuminating the scene taking place. One scene in which the background was definitely in focus was the date rape scene in Billy's room at his fraternity house. Brad wrote:

> The "Conquerors" banner is used not only as the school logo but as a caption to express in written form what is occurring or will occur: the rape. Though the "Conquerors" banners are seen before the date rape scene, the repetitiveness helps to add to the ever-growing nature of the forceful scene to come. While the rape is taking place, other signs are in clear view [on the wall behind Billy's bed]: "No Exit," "No Stopping At Anytime." As if to express in both literal and symbolic form, the signs shout their messages. The red neon "No exit" signs reflect [Kristen's] mental image of no escape; the "No Stopping At Anytime" posts the reality that [Billy] is not going to stop.

After students understood some of the codes of film and how they function rhetorically, they were asked to isolate and describe any scene of twenty-five shots or less that drew their attention upon their first viewing, and to analyze their initial reaction in terms of Singleton's directorial decisions as well as their own prior feelings and experiences. The following heuristic helped them analyze their clip's internal relations and its relation to the larger narrative whole:

1.  How does your clip function in its surrounding context—both its immediate context and scenes similar to it throughout the movie? [Instructors might ask students to think of what would be lost if their clip had been edited out of the movie.]

2.  What kinds of shots does the film's director choose? Why are they effective or ineffective? [Instructors can prepare students to answer this question by having them mentally substitute other kinds of shots for the shots in question—close-ups for long shots, following shots for overhead shots, etc.]

3.  How does the audio portion of the film link up with the images? [Instructors might suggest that, after viewing their clip several times, students cover or turn down the screen to listen to the sound alone to make sure they can link changes in the soundtrack to specific images or events.]

Barrett, a student who went through the developmental courses at our university prior to entering freshman writing, used his newly acquired film terminology to describe how Singleton achieves his rhetorical effects. Having chosen to discuss a pivotal fight between Remy's skinhead friends and Malik's black friends, Barrett said:

> The eyeline match shots were used to see what the emotional responses between the groups were when they first met up in the lounge. The following shots, and close-up shots during the fight, help show that both groups are reacting in the same way even though they think each group is so different. And

the statement ["You worse than a fuckin' nigger"] is used to show the resentment the white supremacists have toward the black races.

Similarly, Jerry combined an analysis of *Higher Learning*'s narrative structure with his understanding of the rhetoric of shots and sound to explain the significance of Kristen and Malik's scene in the elevator. He noted that "Singleton had no verbal dialogue in this scene to show the separation of the races. This helped to set up the last scene with Kristen and Malik where there is actual dialogue." He continued:

> Singleton used careful judgment when using camera shots to shoot this scene. He starts with an establishing shot of Kristen. This is done for the viewers to get in their minds a set picture of Kristen [it's the first time we see her]. He uses a close-up of Malik's hand [thrusting through the elevator door] as a point-of-view shot. He does this to let us see how Kristen sees a big hand of a color that she is not used to and it defines her fears of people different races than her own. The two different close-up shots of Kristen and Malik's faces let us see how each one feels about being in the elevator. At this point both are acting as if they are in the elevator by themselves. Singleton uses this to show that each one would rather be in their own little world with their own people who they are comfortable with [than] to intertwine their different lives together with unfamiliar faces.

## Analyzing Discourse Communities: Toward Ideological Critique

A crucial step in decoding film for its ideological messages is to make students understand the relationship between texts and their intended audiences, and how that relationship produces specific forms of authority and power. Henry Giroux (1994) agrees that "by providing students with critical tools to decode dominating machineries of representation, their own locations and social formations can be understood in terms that allow them to introduce into their discourse 'a sense of the political which ultimately leads to a consideration of power'" (48). In her essay, Amanda correctly summmed up the importance of understanding cinematic codes and situating these codes in the structure of meaning of which they form a part: "If you aren't prepared to think about what each phrase or scene represents or symbolizes, you are at a disadvantage in understanding this movie." Careful textual decoding is particularly important for viewing *Higher Learning* because the movie urges its audience to probe complex questions of identity. In Amanda's words: "who am I? what is my place? who is at fault? and where do I find myself?" Amanda concluded that "finding the answers depends on the audience, the audience's understanding of the plot, and their perspective of the messages John Singleton is trying to relate." In other words, understanding and enjoying the film depends on learning how to be(come) the intended audience.

In order to facilitate this learning process, our students discuss ways of reading Singleton's film as a visual "text," as part of a rhetorical situation and therefore subject to the same tensions between reader (viewer), writer (director), and subject matter as any other text, such as the college essay, for example. The writing assignment—to write a movie critique and thereby join a professional and academic discourse community—invites the students to adopt the subject position of "an informed movie critic" aware of the conflicted discussions about Singleton's film. In the course of this exercise, the students were supposed to learn that any discourse is always a means of constituting and delineating an audience as well as a writer/director. As James Berlin (1996) reminds us, "for a postmodern rhetoric, the writer and reader or the speaker and listener must likewise be aware that the subject or producer of discourse is a construction, a fabrication, established through the devices of signifying practices" (82).

By discussing the relationship between director, subject matter, and audience, students realized that they could not write a successful movie review without taking into consideration Singleton's "identity" as well as his goals and intentions. Writing, like screen writing and directing, is always embedded in a social context that makes certain choices necessary, and students began to discuss Singleton's creative and polemic strategies in connection with his "messages" for the intended audience. For instance, most students found that "Singleton exaggerates the issues he explores." And Mark explains, "his reason for doing this is to bring the issues of discrimination on the basis of race, sex, and class to the attention of the American public . . . Singleton's objective is to shock and disturb you, to bring these issues to the forefront of [your] thoughts and discussions." Mark successfully constructed himself as part of the "American public" who "has long tried to overlook the effects of discrimination."

After taking into consideration the dynamics of the rhetorical situation, not all students thought that Singleton made successful choices as a writer/director. Millie wrote: "If Singleton intended for us white girls to relate to Kristen he should have written a brain into the script for her . . . Singleton did not succeed in creating a character that I feel most girls could identify with." By addressing the apparently failed effort at gender representation, Millie taped into an interesting conflict of the movie itself: while Singleton seeks to offer multiple strategies for identification—in fact, he planned on incorporating even more characters to make the film more "well rounded"—he establishes discourse barriers for some audience members. Singleton's rhetorical choices make it difficult for some of our students to feel properly addressed. For example, Kelli thinks that the "story contains outrageous amounts of adult language," which make the movie "vulgar" and "repulsive." For this reason, the film's "R rating is far too mild; NC 17 not even severe enough." Kelli's resistance to Singleton's ethos stems from her refusal to take into consideration the possibility that cinematic discourse is a calculated construction aimed at addressing a particular discourse community rather than a "natural" phenomenon. By referring to the language of Singleton's interview with Anne Bergman, which the students read, Kelli suggests precisely the "natural" basis for his language use in the movie: "[Singleton] uses that kind of language when he is simply chatting with students about *Higher Learning*. . . . For that reason, his language choice appears to be more than just a ploy at recreating a typical campus; it is *natural* to him, but not to a traditional audience" (emphasis ours). By "naturalizing" Singleton's signifying practices and simultaneously distancing herself from his intended audience, Kelli resorts to the safe binaries of natural/cultural; normal/abnormal; traditional/nontraditional. Thereby she fails to recognize the plurality of discursively constituted subject positions in Singleton's film. Whereas Kelli fails to consider and/or rejects the social constructedness of Singleton's ethos, she feels (self-righteously) empowered by what she understands as the norms and rules of public discourse. As Jeffrey Cinnamond (1995) explains, "discourse practices are specific and distinct for each community as it develops subtle, calculated mechanisms, including ritualized forms for disciplining itself and its members" (273). According to Kelli's understanding of public discourse practices, Singleton ignored rather than changed the ethical codes of communication and broke "the rules." Therefore, Singleton's discourse practices act as exclusionary boundaries for Kelli's construction of herself as a member of the intended audience. Cinnamond explains: "discourse practices not only constitute membership, they also regulate members both consciously and unconsciously. As such, discourse practices transmit, expose, anchor, and produce power" (237).

But whereas Kelli's (mis)understanding of Singleton's discourse practices, particularly his ethos, seems to exclude her from his intended audience, her (mis)reading also enables her own empowerment. In other words, Kelli's alienation is paradoxically grounded in her own empowerment as an academic student writer who feels that Singleton's (in)appropriate forms of address must be critiqued. By creating a discourse community that confers authority on our students *as* "students" who appear to be in a particularly privileged position to judge a movie *about* students, the writing assignment entitled students to their own voices and empowered them in their judgments. Thomas successfully joined the discourse community of reviewers when he wrote:

> In spite of being bashed by professional movie critics, this movie was a success. The film critics, probably quite a bit older than the average target audience member, completely overlooked the wonderful anti-racism, anti-violence message which this movie had to offer.

By establishing students as Singleton's intended audience, Thomas showed that age and professional background of the target audience, for instance, are important factors in determining the success of this film. For instance, Thomas argued that "feeling left out is a major issue for most college students" and "while the movie is busy pushing these points of importance across to a young audience, the same points may not seem as important to an older viewing group." By joining a professional discourse community and analyzing Singleton's rhetorical strategies, the students were eventually able to investigate their subject positions as Singleton's intended audience. And in articulating the relationship between Singleton's intentions and their own identities, many were able to acknowledge their readings and movie critiques not as universal responses but rather as indications of their own cultural location and experiences. In other words, many students recognized that spelling out the challenges of Singleton's rhetoric challenged them in turn to recognize and articulate their own ideological positions.

Asking students to enter the field of rhetorical and ideological critique is an exercise, we think, that seems rather appropriate for a film that is about the power of competing ideologies. Self-consciously aware of its own ideological position, Singleton's film urges the students to broaden their cultural knowledge and to develop their political ideologies for the sake of their own democratic empowerment. Darcy articulated this insight best when she wrote: "Either way, these leaders [Professor Phipps, Fudge, and skinhead Scott] know that knowledge is power. Singleton delivered the message that education is essential to survive."

Teaching students to "survive" means teaching them to identify, challenge, and rewrite changing cultural and political representations. In "From Outside, In," Barbara Mellix (1996) describes both the pain and success attached to acquiring new literacies. "To seek knowledge, freedom, and autonomy," she writes, "means always to be in the concentrated process of becoming—always to be venturing into new territory, feeling one's way at first, then getting one's balance, negotiating, accommodating, *discovering oneself in ways that previously defined others*" (83, emphasis ours). Because learning to read and write requires adopting new subject positions and discourses, multicultural educators must find ways to admit students into the lives of others as well as into the larger discourse communities that contain them.

Film can help forward these objectives because its codes consist in a widely shared literacy, providing links to worlds and subject positions outside the viewer's immediate experiences. At the same time, however, by virtue of its commonly shared codes, film is also in part responsible for constructing hegemonic subject positions. A multicultural pedagogy must therefore also address itself to film's rhetoric. By combining strategies for empathy, close reading, and rhetorical analysis, educators can help students investigate their own subject positions in the process of investigating others'. Such a critical investigation enables students to write their way into various discourse communities as they move toward critical literacy and democratic emancipation.

## Works Cited

Aegerter, Lindsay Pentolfe. 1997. "Michelle Cliff and the Paradox of Privilege." *College English* 59: 898–915.

Bartholomae, David. 1985. "Inventing the University." In *When a Writer Can't Write: Studies in Writer's Block and Other Composing Problems,* edited by Mike Rose, 134–65. New York: Guilford.

Bergman, Anne. 1995. "Laying It on the Line." *Los Angeles Times,* 15 January, B8.

Berlin, James. 1996. *Rhetorics, Poetics, and Cultures: Refiguring College English Studies.* Urbana, IL: NCTE.

Berthoff, Ann. 1984. "Is Teaching Still Possible? Writing, Meaning, and Higher Order Reasoning." *College English* 46: 743–55.

Bishop, Ellen. 1997. "Film Frames: Literacy and Satiric Violence in Contemporary Movies." *Postscript* 16 (2): 18–34.

Cinnamond, Jeffrey. 1995. "Safeguarding Empowerment." In *Critical Multiculturalism,* edited by Barry Kanpol and Peter McLaren, 235–55. Westport, CT: Bergin and Garvey.

Foster, David. 1997. "Reading(s) in the Writing Classroom." *College Composition and Communication* 48: 518–39.

Giroux, Henry. 1994. "Living Dangerously: Identity Politics and the New Cultural Racism." In *Between Borders,* edited by Henry Giroux and Peter McLaren, 29–55. New York: Routledge.

hooks, bell. 1994. *Teaching to Transgress: Education as the Practice of Freedom.* New York: Routledge.

Kanpol, Barry. 1995. "Multiculturalism and Empathy: A Border Pedagogy of Solidarity." In *Critical Multiculturalism,* edited by Barry Kanpol and Peter McLaren, 177– 95. Westport, CT: Bergin and Garvey.

Mellix, Barbara. 1996. "From Outside, In." In *Writing Lives: Exploring Literacy and Community,* edited by Sara Garnes, David Humphries, Vic Mortimer, Jennifer Phegley, and Kathleen R. Wallace, 75–85. New York: St. Martin's Press.

Penley, Constance. 1990. *The Future of an Illusion.* Minneapolis: University of Minnesota Press.

Salvatori, Mariolina. 1996. "Conversations with Texts: Reading in the Teaching of Composition." *College English* 58: 440–54.

Singleton, John, dir. 1996. *Higher Learning.* Columbia Pictures.

# 8

# Mapping the Use of Feature Films in Composition Classes

Dulce Cruz

As the only Latina in my department, I've been forced to pay close attention to my ethnic identity and how it affects my pedagogical stance, especially because I teach composition to an array of multicultural students. My own struggle for self-actualization and acceptance in the academy has sharpened my awareness of the various perceptions about writing that "world majority" students bring to my classroom. I have learned to acknowledge that my students' differences in cultures may also mean particular differences in what they privilege about writing, and in what they understand when we discuss "organization," "development," or "voice," for instance. Making that acknowledgment places me in a tenuous position: I want to validate each of their own culturally rooted versions of college writing, yet I am charged with teaching them "academic" writing. The situation is intricate, as Helen Fox (1994) affirms:

> It is not enough, anymore, to see the difficulties our students may have in the university as "language problems" or inadequate academic preparedness that can be alleviated with remedial work in English or basic skills. Nor is it enough to think of students who come from other cultures as having distinctive, culturally based writing styles which we can either encourage or ask them to change. (xx)

It is perhaps even more complex to teach college composition as a culturally constructed process that consequently entails coding and decoding as a context-specific experience. But that difficulty is diminished, I have found, if the polemics of that stance are integrated into the discourse of the class, and if I consistently emphasize to all my students that their cultural uniquenesses are welcome, that their ways of making meanings are as valid as our nebulous "United States mainstream" ways, and that they're certainly as worthy of being

100

incorporated. For me that stance requires that I also continuously reconceptualize why and how I teach composition. And that recursive examination of my teaching is productive in that it nourishes my enactment of, as bell hooks (1994) terms it, an "engaged pedagogy."

Like hooks and Paulo Freire (1970), I believe that classrooms—particularly composition classrooms—ought to be decentered, democratic places that provide occasions for raising consciousness and mobilizing social action: places where students can be practitioners, not receptacles; where they can feel safe and encouraged to challenge and question critically; and where teaching can be a genuine learning experience for the teacher as well. Above all else, I hold that classrooms ought to be places where all of us can be driven to grow as whole human beings, where we can self-actualize, and, as hooks affirms, where teachers can fully practice "our work." And "our work" entails going beyond merely sharing information and helping to shape "the intellectual and spiritual growth of our students" (13).

I deliberately choose approaches that help me cultivate that "work" in my college composition courses; one of the most productive is using feature-length international films. Movies are an inextricable part of our expandingly multimedia-centered lives, and students spend a lot of time watching them. Hence, it is a medium that is accessible and stimulating—so much so, it is my experience, that incorporating movies provides an invigorating common ground and therefore a way to quicken the creation of a learning community where the majority can be fully engaged and invested. In such a generative environment, it is easier to prompt my students to be critical thinkers and active agents (not just consumers) who make significant and authoritative meaning in everyday life as well as in reading and writing. Movies allow students to see the process of composing; they facilitate the inclusion and affirmation of myriad cultural backgrounds, diverse levels of skills, and multiple ways of thinking about college reading, writing, and communicating. Films provide opportunities for students to create bridges that link them with disparate places and ideas. Overwhelmingly, students are pleased to see films in the composition class; one explained in her journal:

> I'm so glad we'll get to see movies! When I was a senior in high school, my teacher was introducing the *Canterbury Tales* by explaining Chaucer's unique method. She explained how their occupation, clothing, and method of travel contributed to the character. She asked if anyone could think of an example that duplicated Chaucer's concept; the class was silent. Then I said *The Breakfast Club*. One smart alec chuckled, and my teacher just looked at me with a look that said get serious. During the rest of the day my thoughts would wander to this incident. John Hughes did accomplish the same effect as Chaucer: Hughes used the student's clothing, their lunch, their parents, their parents' vehicles, how students said "goodbye," and how they reacted to one

another in Saturday detention to build characters. Thinking about the film made the *Canterbury Tales* interesting for me and it gave me a lot of ideas that helped me write the paper.

Using movies in the composition class helps me to teach students (in introductory to advanced courses) aspects of the composing process that, I believe, are transcultural and important if they are to live in more engaged ways. Those aspects include:

- viewing films, other cultural texts, reading, and writing as tools that they can use to understand themselves and their relationship to the world

- thinking critically (from multiple perspectives and beyond the surface)

- identifying and exploring socially relevant themes and issues (for personal growth and/or for writing in my and other courses)

- formulating informed answers to these questions:
  What statement do I want to make?
  To whom?
  Why?
  What kind of evidence will I use?
  How will I determine what evidence to include and exclude?
  How will I organize that evidence and why?
  How will I conclude?
  How do mechanics and presentation hinder or facilitate access to my
    prose and statement?
  What difference do my choices make?

- understanding that if the process of composing is approached in the ways suggested above they will also be nurturing the process of self-actualization, intellectual, and spiritual growth.

## Preliminaries

My composition classes focus on reading and writing—the composing process; they're not film courses—but films are not ancillary. I use films as an integral part of teaching students to compose written documents, partly because films tell stories in the language of light, color, movement, and sound; they provide ready-made images, and so they capture the senses and emotions promptly, thus potentially exerting great influence. In order to get my students to start seeing beyond the familiar, I prefer to use internationally made films that address issues relating to race, politics, ethnicity, gender, class, and economics. I choose one or two generative themes and relevant films for the semester (e.g., portrayals of the body across cultures; nationalism and colonialism across cultures). Most recently, I've begun to poll students as soon as they register; that way, I can make the course more democratic and inclusive of their interests and needs.

Invariably, my aim is to set up occasions for the students to engage in these intertextual and recursive (not hierarchical) yet increasingly sophisticated tasks for working with written sources: exploring, summarizing, comparing, evaluating, and synthesizing. I select foundational readings (students are encouraged to share their own materials) and activities to challenge them to see, read, write, discuss, and think in progressively critical ways. I meet with each of them often during conferences, but most sessions are workshops in which they work as an entire class or in small groups; they consistently critique all texts, especially their own drafts.

To set the tone for the class as a place where students enact writing as a process, where they take charge of their own learning, and where they follow the inquiry model (that is, emphasizing the use of reading and writing as tools for reflection and investigation), at the beginning of the semester I ask that they read Adrienne Rich's "When We Dead Awaken: Writing as Re-Vision" (1979); Paulo Freire's "The 'Banking' Concept of Education" (1970); Jean Franco's "High-Tech Primitivism: The Representation of Tribal Societies in Feature Films" (1993); and "The Language of Film: Signs and Syntax," a chapter in James Monaco's book titled *How to Read a Film* (1981). Other readings include movie reviews, essays, and creative nonfiction pieces that are challenging in content and that serve as models of effective writing. As the semester progresses, they find further information by conducting their own traditional library and ethnographic research.

Depending on the length of the class sessions, I show films in their entirety, or I ask that students form small groups and screen the films in the library or some other place. In either case, I always show clips because they help to illustrate and clarify the task for the day. Since I aim for students to enact revision in every respect, I request that they see the films at least twice, preferably with different people with whom they can discuss and share notes. Sometimes I provide a handout with key questions and observations for them to consider during and after screening. Throughout the semester they complete different assignments (reviews, memos, personal narratives, analyses, descriptions, etc.), which function as parts of their term research paper, but all of their writing is rooted in the double-entry journal they maintain, and which they circulate among at least two other peers. That journal provides yet another forum for exchanging and reseeing ideas. Those entries are revised into position papers, recomposed into various kinds of writing of their choice, and turned into drafts of their formal pieces. At times, I direct their journal entries by asking that they answer or ponder specific questions and issues.

On a typical day, the session is divided in two: during one half I show clips (chosen by me or the students) that illustrate our target task (e.g., composing conclusions, identifying types of supporting evidence, composing effective transitions); during the other half students workshop their drafts in small groups or as a whole class. In both cases, they begin by reading or distributing portions of their journal entries. They discuss what surprises them, what they do not understand, and anything else that strikes them about the content and process of composing (in the film or in writing). Then they share information gathered from the Internet and other sources. That way, they learn from their peers' reactions, comments, and questions, and simply from voicing their own ideas. They do a five-minute freewrite before, after, or during the conversation (or a combination of these). In these exchanges, especially at the beginning of the semester when they are exploring and seeking topics, students identify themes and issues, and they become more metacognitive of the ways they construct meaning. As the semester progresses, they add findings from traditional library and ethnographic research. Consequently, they engage in an increasingly sophisticated recursive process of reseeing ideas as filtered through new information and experiences. Sometimes I make that process more obvious by asking that they scrutinize the composing process through other senses, such as hearing (listening to music) or tasting (eating a meal).

## Tool(s) for Understanding the Self and the World

Making those incrementally critical moves in shaping ideas and composing them in writing, particularly when it means examining potentially controversial revelations, is easier for students if the catalyst is a film, a medium that is intimate to them yet allows distance and time while they make significant meaning, reflect on it, and then return to consider their own ways of seeing the world. The process, therefore, is always a reflexive act of probing texts and themselves—particularly as writers. As a result, my students have shown, they gain a more acute understanding of what really happens when they compose, and therefore greater control over their actions generally and over their decisions specifically when determining diction, voice, and other aspects of writing (and by extension, when making any decisions).

For example, comparing is a task that students do constantly in their lives, but when asked to produce a written comparison, they have trouble. "Do you want me to list one version first, then the other; is that a comparison?" they ask. Often students don't realize that comparing can be a complex task that extends beyond summarizing two views, or that it is at the core of enacting more involved tasks (like synthesizing). Therefore, I have them scrutinize at lease three versions of a topic, preferably with subtly clashing stances so that they have to sift through similarities and differences. Then they write a short paper that places the views either in relation to one another or in the context of a broader issue. One of the most effective brief exercises requires that students examine samples of prose written by feminists and nonfeminists. First, I ask that they compare the differences and similarities, if there are any, in the ways they are composed; then I give them the following excerpt, a characterization of feminist writing composed by Rae Rosenthal, so that students can compare, contrast, and add to their own analyses. Rosenthal claims that written pieces by feminists are

> Less combative, definitive, and formulaic and more anecdotal and question-ing than is academic discourse generally. And in the intertextuality and self-referencing of many of these essays, there is a spirit of cooperation, a sense of building upon one another rather than in place of one another. Noticeably absent is the oftentimes embarrassing tone of aggression, which frequently characterizes academic writing. (145)

That brief exercise does more than get students to compare differences and similarities; it helps to clarify that in my classroom traditional "academic" prose is not the only privileged kind of writing, and it helps to clarify that comparing is not synonymous with cataloguing. Movies are central in the way that I elaborate that issue. For instance, I might have them compare the ways various movies based on Jane Austen's *Pride and Prejudice* depict Elizabeth's body, which means they screen all the films made in the United States. If I want to extend the exercise through a longer set of tasks, or if the students choose, we broaden the category to include all films made in England too, and so on. If I want the exercise to be brief, they can compare, for instance, how Elizabeth's body is depicted in a 1950s British and a 1990s Hollywood version. They examine the differences and similarities, and then (to be more critical) they discuss how re-presentation is determined by cultural context, and how the historical moment in which each film is made (by whom, and for what audience) influences the way Elizabeth's body is depicted. That initial probing might be extended with additional research on the ethos of each time and place. The last step is perhaps more important, since it asks that students be reflexive: they scrutinize how their own historical moment determines the ways they understand those depictions. And thus, I explain to students, comparing critically means enacting versions of other skills (e.g., summarizing, evaluating, and synthesizing).

Summarizing is equally challenging for students. In its simplest form, summary assignments ask students to "read" a single film or article and to report, in their own words, what is said. That may seem easy, but it can be a formidable task when it is presented as an activity requiring that they characterize what deems certain information as evidence, or that they identify key points, what constitutes logical development, cause and effect, and effective transitions.

Films like *Barcelona, Red Sorghum,* and *Mindwalk* (a screen version of Fritjof Capra's *The Turning Point*) are excellent models of methodically developed and cohesive arguments, and thus productive tools for illustrating what is involved in a summary. The first two of these films have little action and much dialogue; in order to understand them, students have to pay close attention to all details. The third of these films, Zhang Yimou's *Red Sorghum,* is truly a challenge because it involves a series of flashbacks and flash-forwards. I really like using it, though, for that very reason, and because it is infused with literary devices such as metaphors, epiphanies, allegories, and satire. Since it is a Mandarin Chinese visual and audio interpretation of Mo Yan's novel (with English subtitles), students can see that a summary requires translation and interpretation. And since it presents versions of a history that is not widely known in the United States (Japan's invasion of China), students can also see that constructing a summary is as context-dependent as "making" history.

Aside from that, I like using *Red Sorghum* simply because it is forthright and bold. One critic notes that "detractors in China dismiss the film as mindless sensationalism, a libidinal impulse for the ugly, a regressive effort at 'the uncivilized and savage,' and a stylistic horror indulging in moral and visual 'crudities'" (Berry 1991, 86). I think it provides a visually gut-wrenching examination of colonialism and nationalism in intense colors and magnificently vivid photography. The violence and brutality may be too graphic for some, and so I usually warn students, chiefly freshmen about it; I explain, notably to Chinese students, that the film goes against Confucian cultural praxis, favoring decorum, concealment, restraint, delicacy, and refinement. Many cringe when I describe the scene in which Japanese soldiers flay a Chinese male character; others are captivated by the "blood, guts, and Hollywood action" they immediately envision. *Red Sorghum* is very useful in illustrating how to be aware of your audience (how to appeal—to emotions in this case), and in examining how parts (e.g., camera angles, colors, lighting, and such) contribute to building the entire text. Certainly, it is a source for generating many socially relevant themes that students can pursue, and so I also use it to get students to explore.

At the beginning of the semester, particularly, students need to learn how to orient themselves to the topic they are going to investigate in depth. Part of this orientation and exploration involves finding a connection to the topic, a reason to be interested in the issues and ideas under consideration. I want them to ask, Why do people think the topic is important? Why should I care about it? What do I know and feel about the topic already? In addition to using films, reading, and journaling, I prompt students to explore a topic by asking them to attend lectures, theater performances, and art exhibits, and to pay critical attention to everyday life events. The aim is always to get students to sift through complexities, to seek out a range of views, to investigate options, and to have them resist the urge either to take a stance on the basis of prior commitments or to settle an issue before examining arguments.

*Red Sorghum* is productive for getting students to explore and wrestle with profound issues. It certainly motivated one of my African American students: she was struck with the representation of Chinese women's condition in the 1930s, since to her it was parallel with that of black women in the southern United States at the same time. For her term project she wanted to analyze those similarities; her ultimate aim was to reflect on her own condition as a 1990s black woman wanting to teach English in China. She focused on that issue all semester, conducting traditional research and then a brief ethnographic study that included interviewing elderly members of her family. When she finished researching, she stepped back to consider how all of that information helped to explain her situation as a black woman. She compared representations of women's oppression in Zhang Yimou and Mo Yan's *Red Sorghum,* and two other works she was reading (and screening) for pleasure (Alex Haley's *Roots* and Terry McMillan's *Waiting to Exhale*), and her own family's stories. As she began to explore her own condition, she posed provocative questions about the legacy of slavery in the United States and our continued reluctance to discuss it: "we see slavery as if it is over and done, as if there are no lingering effects," she wrote. Her final product was a lucid historical and autobiographical essay that unpacked newfound realizations. She explained that watching *Red Sorghum,* the film, allowed her to see similarities in the ways women have been oppressed, and that in doing so she began to understand the degree to which she had unconsciously "internalized negative images" of black women. More important, she wrote, she consequently saw the need to recompose her self-image.

Similarly, another student seized the occasion of screening *Red Sorghum* and turned it into an opportunity to examine, as he said, his "inadvertent" notions about the process of interpreting and making meaning. He too chose to read Mo Yan's novel and wrote a comparative essay on how Zhang Yimou interpreted depictions of women and how he in turn interpreted both texts. He concluded with astute positing on his realization that no image or idea is "ever truly objective or static." All meanings are "mediated translations," he wrote. That realization, he explained, meant that he had to examine his own belief system seriously, whether or not he changed his views. That was a significant revelation and thus a step in cognitive growth for him. For this student, as for most in the class, films functioned as the generative catalyst for exploring and probing ideas and the crafting of written pieces. Engaging in that process then prompted self-analysis and thus self-empowerment.

Tarzan films can be equally provocative. I use them to focus on evaluating, that pivotal skill students find so difficult. In evaluative tasks, students review various positions critically, making judgments about the adequacy of claims and evidence about the efficacy of their recommendations and proposals. Students don't often feel the "authority" to evaluate, but it is easier to have them understand and enact evaluation when they see that they exercise that skill all of the time when they talk about movies. I show that evaluation is a complex and multilayered process like the other skills. Evaluating effectively requires that they think about subtext, inferences, connotation (versus denotation), and subliminal messages; it means paying close attention to details and understanding that, for instance, no representation is ever "transparent."

To illustrate all of that I show multiple versions of a film in the chronological order in which they were made. Tarzan films are very useful, since so many of our students grow up viewing them, usually uncritically. One way

students begin to hone their critical skills is by doing close readings—by notic-
ing and unpacking re-presentations they deem problematic. Usually I wait for
students to identify such scenes; sometimes I ask that they pay attention to a
particular part, like the scene in the 1932 version of *Tarzan, the Ape Man* (the
first "talkie" based on Edgar Rice Burroughs' novels) in which Jane and her
father's entourage are walking a steep mountain ledge. Africans carry heavy
loads of equipment; one of them falls screaming to his death, and no one reacts,
except Mr. Porter, Jane's father, who simply asks, "what was in that package?"
In contrast, a little later, when Jane almost slips, there is massive commotion
and a successful attempt to rescue her.

Another scene depicts a tribe of pygmies, who, students discover on closer
inspection, are really white midget actors painted black. For the 1981 version
of that same Tarzan film I ask students to pay close attention to Jane, played by
Bo Derek, who, unlike in the 1932 version, is the central focus. She awakens
Tarzan's sexual appetite. When he first sees her pale white skin and blond hair,
he becomes disoriented, as if he had never seen a female, even though he grew
up among many Africans. But black women are not sexually appealing to him,
or even human. Similar issues on race and gender can be identified in the scene
with the pygmies. The 1981 version is slightly different than the 1932 version:
the leader of the tribe, a muscular blue-black demon-looking man, threatens
Jane with rape. Of course, Tarzan rescues her and brutally kills several of the
Africans.

Most students do not notice such things right away, or the repercussions.
Often it is difficult for them when they finally see the subtext, when they begin
to unpack the messages being conveyed about black people, or women. It's
"stealing" their innocence, they say, or it is "indoctrinating" paranoia and hy-
persensitivity. That is one instance when my ethnicity takes center stage: when
students say (implicitly or explicitly), "It's *just* a movie; you see all that because
you're Latina." It is also an instance I turn into opportunities for discussing sub-
jectivities and positionality (where and why we stand) and how they shape our
worldviews.

More often than not, students are stunned when they begin to unpack and
evaluate subtexts. That, in turn, opens them up to seeing the process of composing with renewed eyes. Many of them, consequently, begin to seek deeper
awareness of everything around them. Some are so "changed" that they begin
to question and challenge ideas and ways of making meaning and understanding the world. At the end of one semester a student sent me this e-mail:

> Just wanted to let you know how much I "hated" [your class]. Yes, HATED—
> because it made me think and re-evaluate. Who wants to go through that?
> Who wants to look inwardly and assess her ingrained values and ideas? I sure
> didn't. And you forced me to do just that through the [readings] that you
> forced down my throat (with no spoonful of sugar to make it easier), and that
> $#@%^&! journal in which I had to reflect on what the readings were say-

ing—you didn't even let me dismiss them out of hand—no you made me not just "think" about them, but then "write" about what I was thinking! Sort of makes your thoughts official when they're down on paper . . . So, I just wanted to let you know how much I hated your class—and how privileged I feel to have been [part of it].

## Synthesis

Teaching synthesis can be even more challenging, since it is a skill that encompasses exploring, comparing, summarizing, and evaluating, but also builds on them. Students find it difficult to understand how those skills are imbricated, or how they are subtly different. To help them grasp and enact synthesis, I have them discuss and write about several (often conflicting) versions of an issue (a sort of summary). Then they investigate the relevant ongoing "conversation" (a sort of exploration), identify points of connections and contention (a sort of comparison), place their findings in a larger framework (a sort of evaluation), and then decide where and why they stand in relation to that issue. Each of those skills, and all of them together as a synthesis, requires recursive and incremental reflection and reflexivity.

When we address synthesis, usually toward the end of the semester, I also explicitly enact my own reflexivity. Consequently, that is when I am most self-conscious about my pedagogical stance, personal geography, internal landscape, and the external spaces I inhabit, and when I methodically and rigorously include work by or about Latina/os. Recently, I refocused an advanced three-hundred-level required composition course so that we could spend the entire semester writing about and wrestling with issues and scholarship on Latina/os. I chose "The Arts and Culture of Cubans and Cuban Americans" as the generative theme; I left it as general as that so that students could refocus according to their individual interests.

One of my aims was to have us examine what we knew about this particular segment of the Latino/a population, how we arrived at that knowledge, and how we could recompose it, partly because I wanted to problematize and help shatter stereotypes. My aim was certainly not to inculcate my worldview, nor to convert; but it was to have us examine the processes by which we make meaning, especially with politically charged issues. I did not want my students to think that I was just indoctrinating ideology, or that they would be penalized if they expressed views different from mine. Teaching and learning is always political, I explained, but success in my class would be measured not by the "adequacy" of positions, but by the evidence that proved an engaged process of researching, being critical, being reflexive, and reseeing their written texts until their positions were coherent, cohesive, and accessible to the target audience. They could and should resist; I wanted them to see and understand what it means to be free active agents.

Thus, I thought it important to acknowledge my personal and professional investment in Latina/o culture and scholarship; that was one way I could "expose," as Henry Giroux (1983) suggests we should, my agenda, and thereby, in the tradition of feminist pedagogy, share (not negate) my power in the classroom. I wanted all of us to be aware of how our practices both prescribe and describe meaning making in our culture, and to understand, as Raymond Williams (1981) writes, that culture is a "signifying system through which necessarily (though among other means) a social order is communicated, reproduced, experienced and explored" (13).

I wanted us to cognizantly engage the process of synthesizing. I also wanted students to enact intertextuality—to research scholarship, popular publications, scripts, the writers, the actors, films, and the literary and/or social commentary that they and critics composed about films we had screened. My plan was to create a "behind the scenes" opportunity for reflecting, and to have students become meta-conscious of how their increasing awareness of the process of composing written texts paralleled their own recomposing of information on Latino/as.

To help meet those aims, I had graduate students in my other course, a proseminar on composition theory and practice, read and screen the same material, I asked for volunteers who would interact with the undergraduates as readers of their work, sometimes as tutors, and who'd participate in a semester-long e-mail discussion and exchange of ideas. Films were a significant part in both classes, and students welcomed them, even if they grumbled at occasionally having to read subtitles. Watching films facilitated the way they made connections, the way they began to resee/revise ideas: to synthesize.

For example, Tomas Gutierrez Alea's film version of Zenel Paz's play *Strawberry and Chocolate* helped me show synthesis from at least two perspectives: what's in the film; what's written about it. Students can see synthesis in the content: the film presents a powerful critique of Castro's regime, especially in the conclusion, which movie critic Frederick Kaufman (1995) calls "paradoxical" because it presupposes "that the truest patriot of all must always act, in equal measures, as both dissident and a revolutionary" (71). That critique attests that in living, as in writing, we can and should examine the very ideals we hold dear, and that that process necessitates that we synthesize— that is, that we investigate, discuss, and discern points of connections and contention; that we review, summarize, and evaluate; and then, in an informed manner, that we decide why and where we stand. The film shows that process most obviously in the evolving relationship between the two main characters, David and Diego. One student, a computer science major, noted:

> Diego really educates David, a young university student, and a peasant's son; he shows him how to see differently, how to step outside his tightly built worldview, by showing him the architecture in disrepair, music other than what is approved by the government, like the voice of Maria Callas, and art, and censored literature such as Ibsen's *A Doll's House*. I saw the limitations

of David's world (maybe my world too?) when he doesn't recognize a famous Walt Whitman poem, and when he thinks Diego is a traitor just because he's drinking whisky. I saw how David fights with all that, how he has to weigh ideas, and compare them, and make decisions about what he believed, how he got to believe that, and how to come up with a new belief. That was real hard for him; I think he must've felt like he was being skinned.

Students also see the process of synthesizing by comparing the film with what is written about it and Alea. For instance, though the movie is very critical of the Cuban government, in researching students find that Alea was decidedly not a dissident. He was an integral part of Cuba's officially sanctioned cultural affairs and a founding member of the Cuban Institute of Cinematographic Art and Industry, which was established in 1958.

After screening *Strawberry and Chocolate,* one undergraduate student, a professional woman in her late forties, wrote candidly in her journal: "It became evident that my background knowledge [on Cubans and Cuban Americans] was woefully inadequate." The film piqued her interest—so much that she proceeded to, as she told me, "drag" her partner to various Cuban restaurants, "subject him" to reading all her work and to watching any film she found that had anything to do with Cubans, among them, the Hollywood version of Cuban American Oscar Hijuelos' novel *The Mambo Kings Play Songs of Love.* Over and over she commented on how the combination of films and writing "pushed" her to search herself for (up to then) unrecognized and unexamined disparate and long-held beliefs. She explained in a journal entry:

> Here I am in the first English comp course I've taken in thirty years. Somehow I assumed that grammar and punctuation would have been the focus . . . instead I'm "synthesizing" and learning about Cuban and Cuban Americans, their arts and culture. That means that I have to "re-compose," like Dr. Cruz says, my notions about that. What did I learn so far from Alea's films? More importantly, does any of this knowledge change my life? My perception of the world? I learned that all is not well in Castro's Cuba, but is it because the Marxist ideal is not being followed, or is it because capitalism, in the form of black markets, is corrupting what could be a paradise? And what did I learn about composing: music in the film is the transitional device, the refrain provides cohesion. And so what? Cuban culture is becoming more accessible to me; I'm re-seeing my beliefs—for one thing.

This student wrote substantially more than I required, partly, she maintained, because the films exposed her to ideas and images she had not encountered, and therefore she was continuously surprised by new insights about her worldview. In another journal entry she commented:

> Watching *The Mambo Kings* made me see the difference between Hollywood and Cuban visions of Cubans. I liked the scene at the Club Babalu when they meet Desi Arnaz (portrayed by Desi Arnaz, Jr.—he managed to sound just

like his father). There is some very clever splicing of the film with old footage of *I Love Lucy*—(talk about blurring realities!). It may be because of our assignment to watch *I Love Lucy* reruns that I was more attuned, or because I actually remember the original *I Love Lucy*. For many in this class, these reruns are pieces of history first aired before they were born. For me, it is my life. And while I remember watching Lucy growing up, I don't remember being aware of the stereotypes portrayed. It's disconcerting to see how blatant they were and to reflect on how these images might have influenced who I was to become.

Alea's last film, *Guantanamera,* is equally effective for illustrating the skill of synthesizing. As critic Paula Nechak (1997) notes, this movie "comments upon the political scene in Cuba while managing to be a bittersweet story about lost love and the follies that prevail when social change is in the air for both an entire country and an intimate group of traveling passengers"; it is "an anarchic movie" that requires piecing of various stories, images, sounds, and allusions (1). The plot, for one, entails the transporting of a corpse, which, students realize, is a metaphor for the slow demise of Cuba's economy, and a device that allows Alea to "pan" the geographical and psychological landscape of Cuba and its people. Students also see synthesis while researching—when they find that the plot is based on an actual event, a newspaper story Alea clipped in the late 1980s, "when Cuba's shortage of gasoline was becoming acute," says Mirtha Ibarra, Alea's widow and the main female actor in both films (Rohter 1997, 3). Movie critic Larry Rohter writes:

> Indeed, anyone who has traveled the length of Cuba in recent years will quickly recognize scenes from daily life in *Guantanamera* Alea reproduces almost intact: the eerie absence of traffic on the highways; the families that wait for hours and hours for buses that never come, then crowd into the back of the rare passing truck; the flourishing illegal roadside commerce in meat and vegetables, which are bought and sold in American dollars, not Cuban pesos. *Guantanamera,* in short, is a road movie that shows a society dispirited and in decay. (3)

But no matter how interesting and creative the exercises, not all students were as receptive, engaged, and willing to unpack "synthesis" or to be nearly as enthusiastic and invested in the project as I am. In fact, some could or would not commit to methodically sifting, sorting, being introspective and reflexive about Cubans and Cuban Americans for an entire semester. One, a white male in his mid-twenties, resisted to the end of the semester primarily because of my choice of topic. Why, he questioned, did I "force" the subject on them; why was I "pushing" him to rethink and synthesize any of his positions? As this journal entry illustrates, he was honest, though:

> Part of me hoped that Guantanamera was Spanish for the empire strikes back. I had never seen pictures of Cuba. I guess I understand why some Cuban immigrants are bothered by having to be there or in this country. If I had to flee

my home I'd miss it too. But it made me mad when I read [in doing research] about how some Cubans try to turn parts of Miami into Havana. They flee their homes, the U.S. accepts them with open arms and sets up government programs to help them out; they are free to come and go; they have the opportunity to make a better life—like they don't have in Cuba. And yet they don't like being here. They want to shelter themselves in their own little fantasy world. Instead of just being an American they want to be called Cuban American. That's how they repay America? That is what bothers me.

## Temporary Closure

Films are not the complete answer to all our needs in the composition classroom, but they can be the catalysts that help students understand the process of composing. Following are samples of successful activities that have been instrumental for teaching each of the critical skills I discussed in detail. Hopefully, with any or a combination of these exercises, students will gain a deeper understanding of what John Berger (1972) has so articulately stated: "We only see what we look at. To look is an act of choice" (8).

*Summarizing.* Stop the film in the middle and ask students to describe where their allegiances lie, with what character or situation; have them enumerate the evidence that sways them. Repeat the exercise at the end of the film, but this time have students also determine how and why the new evidence shapes the final outcome. This initial exercise can be further developed into a piece that analyzes types of evidence and their impact on positionality, voice, or point of view.

*Comparing.* Ask students to identify the stereotypes they have about a topic (e.g., Latino/as); show the film, and then ask them to compare similarities and differences with what they find in the film. This initial exercise can be developed a day or so later, once they have had time to think, by asking students to write about how and why they learned those stereotypes, and where they are embedded.

*Exploring.* Have students play the roles of movie critics. The oral arguments they formulate and substantiate can be further developed into position papers.

*Evaluating.* Have students attend a screening of a silent film that is accompanied by a live musical performance (for instance, Charley Chaplin's *City Lights*). Have them journal about the relationship between sight and sound, how the music (violins, cellos, brass) "talks" for the characters. Those entries can be further developed into essays that unpack the symbolism of certain cultural artifacts, or that discuss transitions and cohesion.

*Synthesizing.* Have students read a Vietnamese and an American version of some event during the Vietnam War—a few editorials, and perhaps some oral histories. Then have them read Joseph Conrad's *Heart of Darkness,* and screen Francis Ford Coppola's film version, *Apocalypse Now* (and even supplement the assignment by asking that they also screen a Vietnamese film, like *The Scent of Green Papaya*). Finally, have them sift through all those texts and write a substantiated essay detailing how and why they arrived at the belief they hold about that event.

Alan Kennedy (1995) notes that we ought to "regard writing as similar to map making when one is setting out on a journey as an explorer"; and that in teaching writing we ought to "ask our students to consult existing maps, or representations, of the territory they intend to explore," and then to "lead them into the practice of making their own maps, or written contributions" (35). Using films in the composition class allows me to elucidate that map-making process, those socially anchored meaning-making events, because they make it easier for students to see the invisible practices of composing, and to be reflexive about the ways we understand and represent (how we map) our own discourses and conditions. Films can facilitate reflection and analysis, and that in turn allows students to be more aware and therefore more skilled in manipulating conventions. Consequently, students tend to feel a greater sense of control, and therefore a sense of power that allows them to compose more authoritatively and articulately. For many students that self-awareness also means that they take greater responsibility for what they say, and in some cases that they are prompted to seek positive change actively for themselves and some aspect of our society. And if my students reach a measure of self-actualization, then my "work" as the professor is partly done.

# Works Cited

*Apocalypse Now.* 1979. Directed by Francis Ford Coppola. Paramount Home Video (United Artists).

*Barcelona.* 1994. Directed by Whit Stillman. Westerly Film.

Berger, John. 1972. *Ways of Seeing.* New York: Penguin.

Berry, Chris, ed. 1991. *Chinese Cinema.* London: British Film Institute.

Burroughs, Edgar Rice. [1914] 1990. *Tarzan of the Apes.* New York: Penguin.

Capra, Fritjof. 1982. *The Turning Point: Science, Society, and the Rising Culture.* New York: Simon & Schuster.

*City Lights.* 1931. Directed by Charlie Chaplin. United Artists.

Conrad, Joseph. 1996. *Heart of Darkness.* 2d ed. Boston: Bedford Books.

Fox, Helen. 1994. *Listening to the World: Cultural Issues in Academic Writing.* Urbana, IL: NCTE.

Franco, Jean. 1993. "High-Tech Primitivism: The Representation of Tribal Societies in Feature Films." In *Mediating Two Worlds: Cinematic Encounters in the Americas,* edited by John King, Ana M. Lopez, Manuel Alvarado, et al., 81–94. London: British Film Institute.

Freire, Paulo. 1970. "The 'Banking' Concept of Education." In *Pedagogy of the Oppressed*. New York: Continuum Publishing Corporation.

Giroux, Henry A. 1983. *Theory and Resistance in Education: A Pedagogy for the Opposition*. New York: Bergin.

*Guantanamera*. 1997. Directed by Tomas Gutierrez Alea. ICAIC.

Haley, Alex. 1976. *Roots*. Garden City, NJ: Doubleday.

———. [1977] 1992. *Roots*. Warner Bros. Home Video.

Hijuelos, Oscar. 1989. *The Mambo Kings Play Songs of Love*. New York: Farrar, Straus & Giroux.

hooks, bell. 1994. *Teaching to Transgress: Education as the Practice of Freedom*. New York: Routledge.

Kaufman, Frederick. 1995. "Polemical Pillow Talk: Strange Bedfellows in *Strawberry and Chocolate*." *Aperture* (Fall).

Kennedy, Alan. 1995. "Politics, Writing, Writing Instruction, Public Space and English." In *Left Margins: Cultural Studies and Composition Pedagogy*, edited by Karen Fitts and Alan W. France, 17–36. Albany: State University of New York Press.

*Mambo Kings*. 1992. Directed by Arne Glimcher. Warner Brothers.

McMillan, Terry. 1992. *Waiting to Exhale*. New York: Viking.

*Mindwalk*. 1993. Directed by Bernt Capra. Paramount Pictures.

Mo, Yan. 1993. *Red Sorghum: A Novel of China*. New York: Viking.

Monaco, James. 1981. *How to Read a Film: The Art, Technology, Language, History, and Theory of Film and Media*. New York: Oxford University Press.

Nechak, Paula. 1997. "*Guantanamera* Fuels the Human Spirit." *Seattle Post-Intelligencer* on LatinoLink Web Site.

*Red Sorghum*. 1987, 1991. Directed by Zhang Yimou. New Yorker Video.

Rich, Adrienne. 1979. "When We Dead Awaken: Writing as Re-Vision." In *On Lies, Secrets, and Silence, Selected Prose 1966–1978*. New York: W. W. Norton.

Rohter, Larry. 1997. "A Final Journey into the Heart of Cuba." *New York Times* News Service on LatinoLink Web Site.

Rosenthal, Rae. 1995. "Feminists in Action: How to Practice What We Teach." In *Left Margins: Cultural Studies and Composition Pedagogy*, edited by Karen Fitts and Alan W. France, 139–55. Albany: State University of New York Press.

*The Scent of Green Papaya*. 1993. Directed by Anh Hung Tran. Cine Company, UK.

*Strawberry and Chocolate*. 1993. Directed by Tomas Gutierrez Alea. ICAIC.

*Tarzan the Ape Man*. 1932. Directed by W. S. Van Dyke. MGM-UA.

*Tarzan the Ape Man*. 1981. Directed by John Derek. MGM-UA.

*Waiting to Exale*. 1995. Directed by Forest Whitaker. 20th Century Fox Film.

Williams, Raymond. 1981. *The Sociology of Culture*. New York: Schocken.

# 9

## Inherit the Text

### *An Interdisciplinary
Perspective on Argumentation*

### Loretta F. Kasper and Robert Singer

Developing proficiency in writing presents a major challenge to many students in college developmental writing programs, especially for students of English as a Second Language (ESL). Nevertheless, ESL students must become proficient writers if they are to achieve their academic goals. In order to become full participants in the mainstream, students must meet increasingly stringent institutional standards for writing. College writing assessment examinations often require students to develop an effective argument on an issue of interest. Proficiency in argumentative writing is a skill that unfortunately eludes many students.

ESL students' analytical writing skills can be improved through discipline-based instructional programs (Kasper 1996, 25–33), which use material drawn from one or more mainstream academic disciplines (e.g., psychology or biology) as the medium of English language instruction. Discipline-based courses are designed both to increase language proficiency and to facilitate academic performance. Research has shown that ESL students' overall linguistic skill acquisition is enhanced when instructional activities involve as many of the senses as possible (Collie 1987, 8). The students' increased sensory involvement improves both motivation and performance in the classroom.

The rationale for discipline-based instruction is founded on the principle that intellectual and linguistic growth are interdependent and that successful development of linguistic skill occurs when ESL learners are presented with material in a meaningful, contextualized form in which the primary focus is on the acquisition of information (Brinton 1989, 3). This suggests that classroom

116

learning contexts, where ESL students learn both language and multidisciplinary content through an abundance of language-mediated activities and projects, promote enhanced English language literacy (MacGowan-Gilhooly 1996, 52). This literacy is achieved as students learn to use the English language in an increasingly complex and broader range of activities which reflects how knowledge is constructed in the mainstream of academic discourse.

In particular, the incorporation of film into the discipline-based ESL course helps to make difficult subject matter more accessible to ESL students. Film studies facilitates the acquisition of expository writing skills by providing a stimulus which activates the students' imaginations. Film visualizes ideas and information for its audience, in this case, students, and presents it as "knowledge"; in reality, these narratives are encoded ideological briefings, cultural constructs. As film offers a graphic presentation of what is often abstract, dry subject matter, for example, legal concepts and issues, film makes the classroom discussion more concrete. This leads to a lively and wide-ranging level of discourse, thereby encouraging levels of awareness and comprehension (Keyser 1985, 8).

In this paper, we will describe how to integrate the film, *Inherit the Wind* (1960), directed by Stanley Kramer, and the adaptation of a 1955 play written by Jerome Lawrence and Robert E. Lee, into a discipline-based unit incorporating science, history, and anthropology, while utilizing a postmodern critical perspective, and how to use this film to teach students to develop effective written arguments. *Inherit the Wind* presents a "factual" account of the historical and legal reactions in American society to Darwin's theory of human evolution as it dramatizes and recalls the infamous Scopes trial—another "trial of the century." As a result of contemporary media-saturation from various commercial films, the Simpson trial, cable television's "Court TV," "The Peoples' Court," and other sources, students have had even greater exposure to and experience with the jury/trial format and the ideological narratives of justice as an almost pop-culture gesture/phenomena, in which everybody participates and has an opinion. For most students, film, or television, is the medium of choice, which unites entertainment with information—a complex source of personalized truth and knowledge. Films such as *The Accused* and *Dead Man Walking,* that depict provocative social issues, challenge students "to probe, investigate, and draw conclusions that are problematic—often unresolvable—and will give rise to questions, especially as they involve a clash of competing values" (Knoblauch qtd. in Trillin 1985, 15). In fact, the historical Scopes trial placed two historically conflicting ideological forces against each other—religion and science—as well as two major figures from early twentieth-century American culture: William Jennings Bryan and Clarence Darrow.

The Scopes Trial took place in Dayton, Tennessee in 1925. John Scopes, a science teacher, was accused and convicted of violating the Tennessee statute known as the Butler Act, which prohibited teachers in any state-supported schools from teaching the theory that man descended from the apes; thus, the state utilized legal mechanisms to control the dissemination of ideas deemed subversive ideologies. Scopes was found guilty and fined $100 for his offense. Clarence Darrow, the attorney for the defense, knew that his client was guilty of violating the law, but he wanted to have the law reviewed and thrown out by the Supreme Court. Darrow maintained that the Butler Act violated the First Amendment of the Constitution, which prohibits the mixing of church and state. Darrow's argument appealed to scientific knowledge and logic—the idea of progress—a mainstay of modernism.

The attorney for the prosecution was William Jennings Bryan. Bryan maintained a creationist point of view, arguing that the Bible contained the entire history of man. The argument advanced by William Jennings Bryan appealed to dominant fundamentalist Protestant views and emotions and reinforced the traditional narratives of religion and class prerogative. Since "ideology refers to the representing of reality which goes on in specific historical settings for each culture" (Andrew 1984, 112), the film, *Inherit the Wind,* read as a cultural artifact/product, can only interpret and reconstruct this historical event. This film represents the trend in post-World War II American cinema to encode messages of humanist tolerance concerning race, religion, and other ideologically troublesome areas. Films such as *Compulsion, Twelve Angry Men,* and *To Kill a Mockingbird* appeal to a broadly defined audience and its individual/collective sense of humanity, which is, in reality, an ambiguous concept. Students should be made aware of and discuss how the various media, especially film, interprets historical events and people and the distinctions between documentary and fiction.

In his essay, "Visual Composition," Les Keyser reports on the successful use of the animated film, *Clay, or the Origin of the Species,* which generates discussions of evolution. Keyser states that the intense in-class discussions generated by this film encouraged students to share ideas on this provocative subject and further stimulated students to explore individual attitudes through written exposition and argumentation. Keyser believes that the film helped students to "find an authentic voice and then redefine it, progressing from self-discovery to argument and exposition" (7). *Inherit the Wind* is also a strong stimulus in the classroom because it is highly dramatic and based on real-life events, providing "a creative interpretation of actuality" (Grierson qtd. in Barsam 1985, 20). The film is a polemic recreated, which enables the contemporary viewer to discover personal insights and cultural perspectives on history and society. Even in the contemporary classroom, Darwin's theory of human evolution still provides a potential wealth of material for students to explore: first, through discussion, and later through written expository or argumentative essays. For example, a recent newspaper article stated that in Tennessee "the State Legislature is considering permitting school boards to dismiss teachers who present evolution as a fact rather than a theory of human origin" (Applebome 1996, 1) which involves issues of academic freedom and curriculum control.

## The Film as Text

Prior to a close, in-class reading of *Inherit the Wind,* students conduct preliminary library research and collect material on Darwin, the theory of evolution, the Scopes Monkey Trial, and turn-of-the century American culture in order to provide a summary of the major figures and events. This summary is followed by an introduction to the film *Inherit the Wind;* the instructor might wish to discuss the major stars of the film, the subgenre of the "trial film," or any topic of relevance. It is recommended that the whole film be viewed by the class to develop a sense of continuity; key dramatic sequences might be rescreened for additional analysis.

The opening shot of *Inherit the Wind* is the exterior of a courthouse in Hillsboro, Tennessee; this is complemented by the singing of the hymn "Old Time Religion." The developing narrative sequence connotes a sense of historical importance, a time of tension and destiny, as a man, then some men, cross through this "anytown" in America and into a schoolroom. Power and urgency dominate the frame, as an over-the-shoulder shot—from the Reverend Brown's point of view of the approaching men—establishes images of traditional male authority. This is the self-appointed morality squad, who represent the fundamentalist precepts common to the era and apparently, today. By the time this group reaches the back of the schoolroom, and the ill-fated teacher, Bert Cates, pulls down a large chart with the figure of a huge ape to illustrate his discussion of evolution, the sides have been drawn and the outcome is inevitable. The lesson is stopped and the teacher is arrested. What follows is the fall and rise of one man.

A discussion of the fictional characters in *Inherit the Wind* facilitates the awareness of how argumentation is creatively represented in the film text and perceived by the audience; each character reflects both a particular dramatic function and philosophical predisposition towards the greater narratives of religion/science most clearly espoused by the attorneys, Henry Drummond (portrayed by Spencer Tracy) and Matthew Brady (portrayed by Fredric March). For example, the Reverend, and the majority of townspeople, clearly support the status-quo and traditional patriarchal views of religion, natural law, and God. When Brady, via legal maneuverings and biblical invocations, ridicules Darwin's theories, the citizens largely agree. *Inherit the Wind* represents the majority of these people as intolerant and somewhat primitive, if not slow-witted, when it comes to technology and scientific "progress," but these people are also quite cunning when it comes to the commercial benefits the town will likely experience. In addition, women in the film are represented as either ferocious furies, wholly supportive of "their man," or confused by the issues;

gender representations should be evaluated in the classroom for the manner in which they affect perceptions of an argument.

As the national, "big-city" newspapers learn about this incident, they ridicule the arrest and inevitable trial of Bert Cates, who is not represented as heroic and is often unsure of himself and uncertain of the issues. Cates—along with his students—represents the more tolerant and socially progressive modern views of science and knowledge rather than the provincial views of traditional morality and religion. A reporter, E. K. Hornbeck (portrayed by Gene Kelly), will appear as an important figure in Hillsboro. He is the Mephistophelean voice of iconoclasm and ironically states that "the future is obsolete"—a rather prescient postmodern perspective. Hornbeck argues without genuine passion and is very condescending. However, Hornbeck is not a dramatic foil to Brady; that is Drummond's role.

The main characters in this film who represent the basic antithetical points of view are the attorneys Matthew Brady and Henry Drummond. Matthew Brady argues for the creationist viewpoint and rails against "the gods of science." He is the last gasp of the nineteenth century. Brady's legal argument, aside from the obvious point that Cates broke the law, is based primarily on the interpretation of biblical/religious dogma. He states that scientists cannot explain the most basic of God's creations, e.g., the watermelon, and believes that science cannot be reconciled with creationism (religion). Brady argues that since God made everything on earth, he can change everything, even Natural Law. He says that we should only believe in the things that are in the Bible. Brady quotes Bishop Usher, an "authority," as to the time of creation—"in the fall of the year, 4004 B.C., at 9:00 A.M." Therefore, Brady's argument is wholly based on biblical precepts and not the kind of evidence students would be accustomed to seeing in a modern courtroom; it is his opinion passing as facts. Yet the authority of the man, the Bible, the cause, and the traditions of shared religious values are sufficient to persuade the citizenry of that era.

Brady's heightened emotionalism is often difficult for our students, especially nonnatives, to understand or accept about twentieth-century American culture; however, this film segment illustrates why it is imperative to provide a thorough in-class cultural context of the historical (and contemporary) legal and moral conflicts generated by Darwin's theories, especially when it involves teaching those theories in the classroom.

Henry Drummond's legal arguments are different, but not completely. Drummond represents the evolutionist viewpoint held by Clarence Darrow. Drummond argues that the fundamental right to think is on trial. He states that "truth has meaning" and that, as lawyers, "we're here to serve truth," thus alluding to his belief in abstract notions of progress and a liberating (prenuclear) science triumphing over a restrictive, dominant religion. He counters Brady's argument, that we should only believe in the things that are in the Bible, by asking whether a tractor or a telephone is sinful because neither is in the Bible. He calls several scientists as expert witnesses on Darwin's theory of evolution.

When the judge disallows the testimony of these experts, Drummond calls Brady as an expert witness on the Bible. The idea is to subvert Brady's position and argument by revealing its inherent fallacies, to deconstruct his legal discourse in order to make visible its foundation in a strictly literal faith, and to represent scientific progress as the freedom of one man—all men—to think. This will be the dramatic highpoint of the film; it is also consistent with the nonconfrontational, postwar liberal ideology of the early 1960s which did not directly pit Hollywood against God and country.

The trial film, as a product of the commercial film industry, consistently paces its narrative so that it leads to the "moment of truth" as a dramatic, affective staple. The main arguments and viewpoints are presented and either accepted or ridiculed, depending on the producer's awareness of audience expectations. In *Inherit the Wind,* the Bible will not be mocked, but Brady, as a larger-than-life figure whose time has passed, can be deflated; therefore, his creationist argument deflates with him.

This courtroom sequence, in which Drummond calls upon Brady to testify as an expert on interpreting the Bible, visualizes the conflict between the two opposing forces in a mix of medium and close-up shots. For almost every shot in this extended sequence, Brady is placed to the right of the frame, Drummond to the left, and the judge is in the middle, slightly above the others. It is a triangular and politicized positioning. As Drummond questions Brady's expertise and interpretation of several biblical passages, Drummond effectively deconstructs the fundamentalist argument informing Brady's legal reasoning. Drummond exposes the inconsistencies behind some biblical narrative, especially when he asks if everything in the Bible should be taken literally. The Bible states that the sun stood still and that it moves around the Earth. According to Copernicus' theory of natural law, if the sun stood still, the Earth would be destroyed. Brady replies that God can control even natural law because God created natural law.

Drummond then shows Brady the ten million-year-old fossil remains of a prehistoric marine creature; he asks Brady if it is possible that, at the time of creation, a day were longer than twenty-four hours. Eventually Brady admits that he does not know how long a day was at the time of creation. After this admission, Brady, and his legal argument, begin to unravel.

Drummond states that "progress has never been a bargain"; for every loss, there is a gain. The gain to be won in this courtroom, according to Drummond's argument, is the unencumbered freedom to think. "The man [Cates] wishes to think," he says, thereby equating personal, individual liberty, thinking with knowledge and progress. Drummond then attacks Brady in a series of questions which he cannot answer: does a sponge think? What do you think a sponge thinks? Do you think a man should have the same privileges as a sponge? The argument is devastating to Brady, whose position of legal/moral authority is reductio ad absurdum. Brady might historically win the courtroom case, but he has lost the real argument. He and his position collapse by the end of the film, largely because he is tripped up by his own rhetoric. Perhaps the same could have been done to Drummond and his beliefs in the humanist abstractions of freedom and progress. In the final sequence of *Inherit the Wind,* Drummond marches out of the courtroom—towards the camera and audience—and in his hand he clutches both the Bible and a law book. This sweetens the ending by attempting to reconcile both narratives and their discourse/arguments, to the soundtrack cries of "glory, glory, hallelujah."

## In the Classroom

The in-class viewing of any film should be followed by a lengthy discussion of character, plot, and issues. Perhaps the most important way for students to read *Inherit the Wind* is to consider the entire film text as a trial of ideological (narrative) imperatives: custom versus progress, religion versus science, intolerance versus tolerance, old versus new (young), and other antithetical positions, generally only resolvable in the spirit of postwar/early 1960s reformist films.

With *Inherit the Wind,* the method and effectiveness of the legal arguments are the fundamental pedagogical concerns. The instructor might wish to begin the discussion with the statement that a student need not agree with a particular character's point of view, as long as that point of view can be evaluated and eventually written about. In fact, the instructor might wish to discuss how various arguments, in this commercially produced fiction film, represent a form of discourse subject to its own interpretation/sensibility—the 1960s reading the 1920s—and how the arguments are never quite neutral, or should not pass as "truth." Each position is an interpretation of reality, not reality. Another way to illustrate this concept could involve taping and editing sequences from contemporary trials covered on television, whether from a high or low profile case, and have the students analyze how legal positions are constructed. There have been several "trials of the century," as well as daily broadcasts of "Court Room" television, which could provide adequate instructional examples.

For *Inherit the Wind,* the students might be asked to divide a sheet of paper into two columns and instructed to use this sheet to list the important points made by Drummond and Brady as each presented a courtroom argument for or against Darwin's theory of evolution. Students then engage in a discussion of the effectiveness of each legal position as they identify and evaluate the statements they found most persuasive; they also search for additional sources or contemporary references in the library which could have been added to either sides' argument. Students then write a one-paragraph summary of the arguments and explain why they think each was effective. The statement might read like this: "Both Henry Drummond and Matthew Brady present strong arguments to support their position on the issue of evolution versus creation. Write a summary of the arguments on each side of the question. Which of these arguments do you find more convincing? Explain why." The students might enumerate the arguments for and against Darwin's theory by writing several of their responses on the chalkboard.

Since *Inherit the Wind* appeals to the social consciousness of the viewer, via the creative representation of moral, educational, legal, and social issues, the film does provide an effective means of stimulating critical thinking and for teaching ESL students how to construct a convincing argument. *Inherit the Wind* also provides a stimulus for writing samples of varying length and forms, and at the same time, it suggests a model for the writing process. In the film, the characters (like our students in the classroom) are struggling to discover meaning, truth, in their attempts to make sense of the world as they debate profound ideological questions. By watching and analyzing the opposing arguments presented by the attorneys, students learn how to develop an effective argument, from the emotional to the intellectual. In addition, they have been exposed to and might continue to research and explore recent legal issues, such as contemporary trials, the power of the media, and other timely classroom topics.

After students have thoroughly analyzed the arguments presented by the characters in the film, they are given an at-home writing assignment which asks them to choose an issue about which they have a strong opinion and to write a persuasive essay in which they argue their position on this issue. The student must be sure to include a rebuttal of the opposing viewpoint in the essay. Multiple drafts and revisions of these essays will facilitate genuine growth for these students as writers. As another assignment possibility, students can analyze various other courtroom dramas ranging from the O. J. Simpson trial footage to the popular TV show, "The Peoples' Court," in the terms they have just used with *Inherit the Wind.*

The lesson, as suggested here, requires a total of four to six hours of preparation time and three to four hours of class time. The preparation time consists of class time used to provide students with relevant background information. The class time consists of two hours to show the videotape of the film, and one to two hours to complete and discuss the in-class writing activities.

If the contemporary classroom's utilization of the medium of film is to be an effective stimulus for critical thought, it should help students to organize and shape their ideas toward an issue as well as give them a forum for the experience of "generating chaos" (Berthoff qtd. in Trillin 1985, 16), of being confused, and finally, of discovering form as a way out of that chaos (Trillin 1985). *Inherit the Wind* meets each of these criteria. By the end of the successful classroom analysis of the film, students will see patterns of discourse and critical connections which provide a focus for the piece they will write. As students listen to and discuss the conflicting emotional and legal views presented in *Inherit the Wind,* with the purpose of defining the most convincing argument and writing about it, they are encouraged to suspend their own preconceptions on a variety of issues (in this case, evolution), and to develop an open mind. In this way, students assume not only the role of the writer, but also that of the informed reader. Thus, film can illustrate for students that writing is not so much a matter of mastering technical skills, but of engaging in an active process of inquiry and communication in which "ideas are generated and not just transcribed" (Susser 1994, 35). Using *Inherit the Wind* as a rhetorical teaching device helps to focus students' attention on the process of writing, not the product of writing. This is especially important for ESL students, many of whom are preoccupied with producing accurate grammar and mechanics at the expense of developing and expressing powerful ideas (Kasper 1998, 1–17).

Because it is planned as part of an interdisciplinary, humanities-based course in developmental writing, *Inherit the Wind* helps to develop the skills necessary for the ESL student's success in college. The interdisciplinary activities detailed in this paper develop critical thinking skills as students become aware of the elements of a good argument and its theoretical foundation; these activities provide an additional forum for classroom discussion and debates to generate authentic and complex use of the English language in an academically challenging situation.

# Works Cited


Andrew, Dudley. 1984. *Concepts in Film Theory.* New York: Oxford University Press.

Applebome, Peter. 1996. "70 Years After Scopes Trial, Creation Debate Lives." *New York Times,* 10 March, A1.

Aronowitz, Stanley, and Henry A. Giroux. 1991. *Postmodern Education.* Minneapolis: University of Minneapolis Press.

Barsam, Richard. 1985. "Nonfiction Film and/as Composition." In *Images and Words: Using Film to Teach Writing,* edited by Jeffrey Spielberger, 19–26. New York: City University of New York.

Brinton, Donna, Marguerite Ann Snow, and Marjorie Bingham Wesche. 1989. *Content-Based Second Language Instruction.* New York: Newbury House.

Collie, Joanne, and Stephen Slater. 1987. *Literature in the Language Classroom.* Cambridge, England: Cambridge University Press.

Kasper, Loretta Frances. 1996. "Writing to Read: Enhancing ESL Students' Reading Proficiency Through Written Response to Text." *Teaching English in the Two-Year College* 23: 25–33.

———. 1998. "ESL Writing and the Principle of Nonjudgmental Awareness: Rationale and Implementation." *Teaching English in the Two-Year College* 25: 60–68.

Keyser, Les. 1985. "Visual Communication." In *Images and Words: Using Film to Teach Writing,* edited by Jeffrey Spielberger, 7–12. New York: City University of New York.

Kramer, Stanley, dir. 1960. *Inherit the Wind.* MGM/UA.

MacGowan-Gilhooly, Adele. 1996. "Fluency First: Reversing the Traditional ESL Sequence." *Writing in a Second Language: Insights from First and Second Language Teaching and Research,* edited by Bruce Leeds, 48–58. Chicago: Addison-Wesley.

Susser, Bernard. 1994. "Process Approaches in ESL/EFL Writing Instruction." *Journal of Second Language Writing* 3: 31–47.

Trillin, Alice. 1985. "Film and the Teaching of Writing." In *Images and Words: Using Film to Teach Writing,* edited by Jeffrey Spielberger, 13–18. New York: City University of New York.

# 10

## Using Film to Teach Coherence in Writing

Kate Chanock

## Introduction

This paper is about my experience with using a documentary video to raise my students' awareness of various aspects of academic argument. I wanted to look at elements such as structure, point of view, voice, use of evidence, attribution, and coherence in the film and to talk with students about how these were similar to, and different from, their equivalents in academic writing. In the event, coherence was the area in which we found the most interesting differences, which will be presented in this paper as they became apparent to us in the workshop. I have taught this workshop for three years now, and each time produces further insights: this paper is a composite narrative of this process of discovery. It will discuss the aims of the workshop; the activities; and the benefits of using a video as a text. I will also touch on some problems to consider when choosing a video for this purpose.

## Aims of the Workshop

As an adviser in academic writing in a Faculty of Humanities, I have found that one of the more puzzling ideas for first-year students is that of argument. They are confused by the overlap between the academic and the general meanings of "argument." Many students, when they write their early essays, think of argument in its familiar usage as a quarrel. When asked to find the argument of some piece of reading, therefore, they are puzzled if it does not appear to contain a debate, and do not know how to proceed. Conversely, many assignments do not mention argument, but the essays come back with comments like "I cannot follow your argument here" or "What does this section have to do with your argument?" Students tell me "I didn't know I was having an argument" or "There was nothing to argue about." Because of this confusion, I wanted to go into the nature and the characteristics of academic argument in depth, and I offered a series of workshops, an hour a week for four weeks, to any interested students. Each year between ten and thirty students have attended.

I began by unpacking the confusion over the term, and suggested that they think of an argument as a demonstration that some idea is the case; it may or may not be controversial. It is true, however, that many academic arguments are presented in a context of debate, for this is the process by which an idea becomes (or fails to become) knowledge. When a scholar puts forward an idea, colleagues will scrutinize the formulation of the question, the adequacy, relevance, and use of sources, the scope of discussion, and the validity of interpretation, in terms of its logic and coherence. Students are expected to recognize this critical process, to participate in it, and to be open to similar criticism of their own discussions. For this reason, I wanted the workshop to look at an argument presented in a context of debate: first to recognize how the argument was constructed, and then to consider the problems with it—including both the problems pointed out by dissenting scholars, and also those which the students themselves might notice.

I chose, for this purpose, a ninety-minute television documentary called *The Riddle of the Dead Sea Scrolls*. This program outlines Dr. Barbara Thiering's controversial interpretation of the documents of the Essene Community at Qumran, in Israel, before and perhaps during the time of Jesus. Dr. Thiering focuses on similarities between the scrolls and the Christian gospels, and casts doubt on the widely accepted dating of the scrolls to the first century B.C., a date which would rule out any suggestion that they refer to Jesus. In her view, Jesus appears in the scrolls as an enemy of the Essenes, expelled because he tried to reform their practices and open the ministry to all, rejecting the strict religious hierarchy and insistence upon ritual purity of the Essene community. Her interpretation rests upon a method of reading scripture—common at the time the scrolls were written—which extracts two levels of meaning from religious texts. At one level, the scriptures are read as lessons about supernatural intervention in human lives, for those who "need miracles." At another level, the same stories encode, in metaphors many of which have become obscure over time, a record of actual events. Dr. Thiering suggests that, if first-century scholars read scripture this way, they probably also wrote it this way; we should, therefore, reread the gospels by the same method and we will find there a message of reform. The stories about Jesus' ministry are, in this view, stories about freeing spiritual practice from the grip of priests and opening it up to lay people.

The program discusses the finding and processing of the Dead Sea Scrolls; the problem of dating them; and Dr. Thiering's interpretation. She explains the special method of reading scripture and its implications for the meaning of stories such as the Virgin Birth, the miracles of Jesus' ministry, the Crucifixion, and the Resurrection. Along the way, other Qumran scholars are consulted, and several of them disagree with points of—or all of—Dr. Thiering's interpretation, giving reasons for their disagreement. Thus, the program presents an unresolved debate, on a matter of general interest, among established scholars, with a discussion of methodology and a scaffolding of evidence. I chose it because it seemed to do well what I wanted to show being done; moreover, I hoped that a video might hold the interest of an audience accustomed to taking in information from television, and would also provide a focus I could manipulate to make sure we were all doing the same thing with the same piece of text at the same time.

In the event, the choice of a video turned out to be useful chiefly because it was not a written text; the differences between the two media provoked discussion which brought out the nature of academic argument more fully, and more precisely, than I had thought possible. In talking about what the video did, we talked about what academic writing does not do—and then we were looking at what it does instead.

## Activities

After discussing the confusion over what is meant by argument, I explained that the purpose of the workshops would be to help students to understand the term; to learn to recognize the arguments they read and hear in lectures; and to become conscious of effective ways of expressing arguments in their own writing. I described the materials we would use, and sketched my reasons for choosing the video (making it clear that I did not endorse anything in it but intended to look at it from a scholarly rather than a religious perspective). I then explained the ingredients and the structure common to arguments in our academic tradition, in accordance with the following handout:

**WHAT ACADEMICS MEAN BY THESIS, ARGUMENT,
AND EVIDENCE, & HOW TO FIND THE ARGUMENT
IN WHAT YOU READ**

An ARGUMENT is a DEMONSTRATION that some idea is true. It has
Two elements:
1.   A statement that something is the case: a THESIS
2.   A demonstration consisting of POINTS, each with EVIDENCE

THESIS: What the writer thinks
POINTS (why s/he thinks so) + EVIDENCE (how s/he knows)

|   |          |
|---|----------|
| 1 | facts    |
| 2 | facts    |
| 3 | facts    |

In one kind of argument, the points build up in a logical sequence to prove the thesis. Order and linkage are important, and the argument should be outlined in the introduction so the reader can anticipate the relationship between the parts.

In another kind, several sources or kinds of evidence are examined. Each one suggests that the thesis is right, and together they make it very likely. Here it may not matter in what order the sources are discussed; but the different kinds of evidence should be outlined in the introduction.

After the introduction, the point made in each section is often stated in the first ("topic") sentence. The link to the next section is often in the last sentence of the section. Thus you can often see the argument by reading the first and last page and the first and last sentence of each paragraph (Clanchy and Ballard 1968, 23–36).

In any academic argument, all the material presented should be relevant to the thesis; its relevance should be spelt out; and the progress of the argument should be signposted (signposting is telling the reader where you're going, where you've got to, and where you're going next).

This brief presentation introduced the students to the language academics use to talk about argument, and to the invaluable technique of skimming for argument which is demonstrated in Ballard and Clanchy's book.

## Raising Awareness of Language

We were now equipped for a critical examination of the *Riddle of the Dead Sea Scrolls*. Before plunging in, I suggested that they be on the lookout, too, for academic language, nonacademic language, language of persuasion, language of bias, and changes in the role of the narrator. Some of what we were about to hear would be considered sound academic practice, while some of it would not; and I thought it would be useful to talk about the difference. The group turned out to have a good ear for the relevant expressions, pointing out the language by which academics cover their rear ("It is likely that"; "If we accept x, then y would go like this"; "would be" rather than "is"; "there is very strong reason to believe"; etc.). They heard, also, expressions of bias when the narrator described some academics as "clinging to" accepted theories, while others were "more open-minded." And, connected with this, they noted the points where the narrator's "voice" merged with that of Dr. Thiering; that is, instead of presenting the debate objectively, he put her side of it in such a way as to sound like established fact. These were useful observations because students often have difficulty, in essays, with sustaining their own voice as distinct from that of a source they are closely examining.

## Watching the Video

We began viewing the video, treating it as a draft. That is, we were going to identify the sections of the argument, consider whether they needed reordering and/or more explicit signposting or linking, and evaluate the use of evidence. Because this process would be new to the participants, and because the video was quite long and the material complex, I had prepared an outline of the argument to help us to follow and to talk about it. This outline owes a great deal to two different models: the analysis of a text in Ballard and Clanchy (1984, 54–58) and the "Descriptive Outline" in Elbow and Belanoff (1989, 37–39). Both of these are concerned with drawing students' attention to two different, but concurrent, ways of analyzing a text. Elbow and Belanoff focus students on what the text "says" and what it "does." The concern in Ballard and Clanchy is similarly rhetorical, but, as they are addressing foreign students, they highlight the language involved. In a column to the left of the text, they ask, "What is happening in the text?" while a column to the right asks "Which key words help us to understand what is happening in the text?" My outline of the video, similarly, was presented in two columns, with "content" on the left and "structure" on the right.

The outline follows this paper as an appendix. Each student had a copy to annotate as we went along; I stopped the video whenever someone wanted to comment, or when I wanted to consider a "chunk" of the argument.

## Observations

Points 1 through 5, we could see, made up an introduction to the program. At that point we expected a discussion of the dating of the Dead Sea Scrolls, but we did not get it. Instead, we were offered evidence that the Essene community was a monastic one (Point 6). We were not told the relevance of this, perhaps because we were able to guess that it suggested a connection between the Essene way of life and the later development of Christian religious institutions. The filmmaker, then, was relying on the audience to supply the "so what" for this part of the argument; here was an opportunity to talk about how much needs to be made explicit when building one's own case.

The relevance of Point 7 was not explained either, but we pressed on and by 15 we could see that this section, overall, was about reasons for thinking that the Scrolls did refer to Jesus and reasons for thinking they did not. We thought this should have been signposted before Point 6, and the material reordered thereafter to put the case for, and the case against, in two visible clusters—the sort of operation it is useful to do to one's own draft. Here I showed the students how one can label each paragraph of a draft in the margin, to show in a few words what point it is making, as a basis for reordering where necessary.

From 18 to 21 we found ourselves in a patch of unconnected points which could not be repaired by identifying the links between them and making these explicit. There were no links between them (as I've indicated in the appended outline with question marks). This was as useful for the purposes of the workshop as a well-built section would have been; perhaps more useful, since instead of being shown a good model, the students were able to see that professionals also have problems stitching their material together in places. As they became involved in the question of organizing the material coherently, a closer examination revealed that two themes had been mixed up in this sequence, and that Point 20 belonged between 16 and 17. The suggestion was being made that the publication of the Scrolls had been delayed because scholars were reluctant to make the new material available, on account of the challenge to Christianity which it might present. Having placed 20, we could then see that 18 and 21 went together, while 19 remained anomalous. Much later, when we reached 32, we realized that 19 belonged there!

While it became an interesting challenge to treat the video as if it were a draft in need of revision, someone pointed out, and the rest agreed, that, had they been watching in couch potato mode, the lack of connections would not have bothered them. They had pictures to look at, and a narrator acting as guide, and in any case, if you stopped to worry about what you had just seen you would miss the next bit.

## Comparing Watching with Reading

This brought up a whole set of questions about the difference between printed and video texts. In one sense, we found, reading is more active, because you can always pause and reconsider as you read. The mental "hey, wait a minute" is not possible when you are watching something that will not stop and wait for you.

On the other hand, the video required the reader to provide links between different kinds of information. Some points were being made verbally, while others were presented by pictures. Moreover, while some of these images were straightforward—for example, after we were told that the Essene community had been monastic, we were shown film of the physical remains on the site, with their communal layout—others communicated by suggestion points which were never made explicitly. For example, at 22, the spoken text claimed that the Jesus of the Gospels had behaved like the "Wicked Priest" of the Dead Sea Scrolls, rejecting ritual purity and asceticism, criticizing the financial practices of the priests, and opening the priesthood to all. This was followed by film of a modern ceremonial procession in a church, the clerics in elaborate regalia which marked them as separate from and superior to the congregation. The implication, that Jesus' attempts to erase the distinction between priest and laity were subsequently overturned by the Catholic Church, was not lost on us. It was not articulated in the program, but contributed powerfully to the undercurrent of criticism of the Church for having, in Thiering's view, lost sight of the original meaning of Jesus' ministry.

We were fascinated by messages like this, for we realized that we were quite prepared to accept them without putting into words what it was that we accepted. The students found that their critical faculties were suspended, at least with regard to the visual aspects of the film. A picture was accepted as being worth a thousand words, and you did not ask yourself what those words might have been.

Another thing on which they were prepared to suspend judgment was the form of what they were watching. If it did not seem to fit together, that was not a problem. Many films, and also novels, work this way: different situations, different characters, different times and places are juxtaposed in quick succession and you have to trust that they will come together in the end. Indeed, this is a form—it is the form of the whodunit, and, by extension, of much psychological drama. The characters are confused, and if the audience is to participate, it must also be confused, if slightly less so. However, it is not the form of academic argument. Thus, the students were helped to realize what is characteristic of academic argument by contrasting it with another form, and one about which they had interesting comments to make. They gained some confidence by looking at argument as a form, rather than the form.

It is, therefore, probably worth reflecting on the fact that many students get much of their factual information, and a good deal of interpretation surrounding it, via forms and techniques which belong to the visual media. They may not distinguish between news documentary and academic texts as sources, but these are in fact very different ways of presenting material. It is probably more useful to explore the kinds of differences with students rather than simply to categorize one form as better than the other.

One further difference which they noted was that the video "had no footnotes." It was not always possible to tell who thought what, or where one could go to sort it out. The position of the narrator increasingly merged with that of Thiering, while opposing views were sometimes attributed to individuals, but sometimes to "critics." Of course there was no point in criticizing the program for omissions which the medium virtually entailed; but the students wanted to! Their frustration with this showed them the value of exact referencing, careful attribution of views, and language which made clear the status, as well as the provenance, of the material they were meeting. Was it a claim, a suggestion, a question, a fact? Was it a guess? They were not prepared, for example, to let Thiering get away with the formulation that Jesus' walking on water was "probably an old anti-priestly joke." Probably? Why?

## Implications for Writing: Cohesive Devices

In all these ways, our analysis of the video brought out important characteristics of academic argument, either because they appeared in the video or because they were conspicuous by their absence. Of these, the most important may be the absence of what Mina Shaughnessy calls "words and phrases that point up connections" (1977, 206). These, she says, are used by "advanced" writers at tertiary level, agreeing with the findings of a study by Cooper et al. (1984). The researchers collected compositions from a freshman class in an American university, and analyzed the writing in order to discover what distinguished the best writing from the worst. They found, to their surprise, that it was not spelling, grammar, or vocabulary generally which made the difference, for the compositions were much the same in these respects. What distinguished the good writing was the elaboration of points in the argument and the use of cohesive words and devices, chiefly connectives. If cohesion is achieved largely by nonverbal means in film, it may be that some students who take in a good deal of information this way will not recognize a need to articulate the relations between the things they write. My students were not bothered by the absence of verbalized connections in the video we watched; on the other hand, they were able to verbalize what was missing, and they enjoyed doing so. We took some time to pool the cohesive expressions we knew, sort them into various categories (contrast, result, building up an idea, changing direction, moving from general to particular, etc.) and put them into a handout for other students' use.

## Structural Revisions

Between points 34 and 35, again, there was a disjunction; otherwise, we were able to see how the argument fitted together. Nonetheless, it was apparent that a written version would be a good deal more satisfactory if it had a tighter structure, with all the historical context together in one cluster and all the textual interpretation together in another. The result would probably be too dense for a video presentation, but suitable for a written text. This brought up the whole issue of "tight" and "loose" organization in academic writing, which is characteristically denser than students are used to. It was interesting to consider the density of lectures, which should be closer to that of film than to that of writing. When a lecture has been written to be read, it is often too dense to be heard, as some of the students were able to confirm!

## Summarizing

For about three sessions we watched the video and fiddled with the outline, considering revisions, additions, and reordering which would be useful if it were a draft of an essay. In summing up this activity, I drew a diagram to show what we meant when we asked ourselves "How well is this argued?" In answering this question, we had looked at both content and form, as shown below:

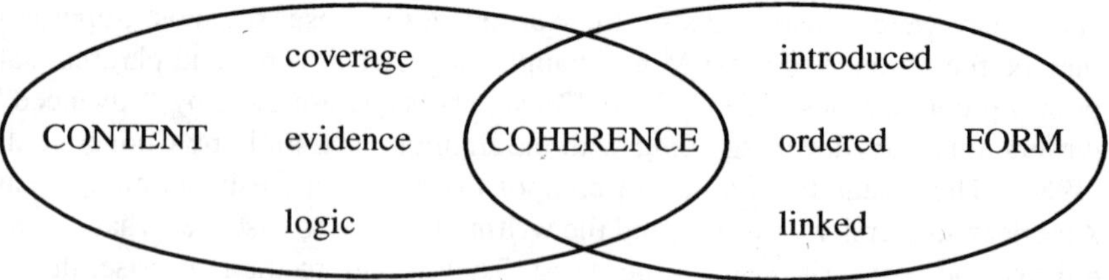

Students should, I urged, ask the same question of their own drafts, and consider the same areas of form and content. Finally, to see how transferable the lessons of the video activity would be, I asked the group to think about revising a sample essay from another useful writing guide, by Jones and Grant (1981). I chose a history essay (67–72); there are others in this collection, but this one proved to be a useful choice, for the students saw at once that there were problems of relevance, organization, and signposting, and, more fundamentally, that the essay lacked a thesis. On the other hand, attention to all these things would produce a viable essay, as the material was there, and the writer's intention was discernible, though not yet realized in the essay. By the time they had decided what could be done to solve these problems, I felt quite confident about their readiness to construct and revise arguments of their own.

## Considerations

For anyone thinking of using a similar approach, various considerations will, I think, arise. First, the video, while popular with students, is a long one, and this raises questions both of time tabling and of use. It is difficult to assemble students for a noncredit-bearing activity of more than an hour a week, so I run these workshops during lunch time, once a week, for four weeks. This means that students drop and join, and in any case it is difficult to remember the details of the video from one week to the next, so we begin each time by recalling where we were. If it were possible to find a whole morning—perhaps as part of an orientation course—it might be more efficient to do the whole thing in one piece. On the other hand, it might be possible to shorten the activity by finding a much shorter video.

In terms of the use that could be made of it, too, there may be some advantage in finding a shorter film. One could then try eliciting the outline from the students (which is really out of the question with the *Dead Sea Scrolls* as it took me several days to outline, and this would be still more difficult for students coming to it cold). My students, in responding to questionnaires evaluating the workshop, tend to think that they need the outline as a model, and that the opportunity to do it themselves, with the sample essay, is as much as they could handle when the ideas are new. Nonetheless, I would like to try working one up together.

It is not easy, of course, to find suitable videos for this purpose. Probably the best ones are in the area of popular science, where a new idea is being introduced or an old one contested. These are often very clear in the presentation of background, the putting of a thesis, the production and ordering of evidence, and the consideration of alternative explanations. In using them, however, we would have to bear in mind that they are not dealing with "humanities" material. For our purposes, programs on psychology, language, history, or social institutions such as the legal system are likely to be useful. Archaeology is particularly fruitful for a mixed group, because it tends to draw on more than one discipline for method and context; the *Dead Sea Scrolls* program is a good example. Moreover, the material is rarely completely unfamiliar to an undergraduate audience, though some students will be more knowledgeable than others. Whatever the material, it will provide a useful opportunity to discuss the problems students encounter in every essay: what audience should they imagine, and how much background, fact, and explanation should they provide? We were surprised by how much knowledge our program took for granted.

## Conclusion

This series of workshops has shown that students can make good use of an approach which asks them to look at academic argument in terms of both content and rhetorical structure. In addition, it has raised some points of comparison between written and visual texts which may have implications for the way we talk to students about creating coherence in their work.

## Works Cited

Ballard, B., and J. Clanchy. 1984. *Study Abroad. A Manual for Asian Students.* Kuala Lumpur: Longman Malaysia.

Clanchy, J., and B. Ballard. 1986. *Essay Writing for Students. A Practical Guide.* Melbourne: Longman Cheshire.

Cooper, C., et al. 1984. "Studying the Writing Capabilities of a University Freshman Class: Strategies from a Case Study." In *New Directions in Composition Research,* edited by R. Beach and L. Bridwell. New York: Guilford Press.

Elbow, P., and P. Belanoff. 1989. *Sharing and Responding.* New York: Random House.

Jones, J., and B. Grant. 1981. *Writing, Setting, and Marking Essays.* Aukland: Higher Education Research Office, University of Aukland.

Shaughnessy, M. 1977. *Errors and Expectations.* New York: Oxford University Press.

*The Riddle of the Dead Sea Scrolls.* 1990. Surrey Hills, NSW: Ariba Pty. Ltd. 1 videocassette (VHS PAL) (81 min): sd., col., ½ in. Based on the book *The Qumran Origins of the Christian Church* by Barbara Thiering. Produced for Beyond International Group. Distributed in Australia by Roadshow Home Video. Credits: producer, J. R. Mitchell; writer/narrator, Rowan Ayers.

# Appendix

## *The Riddle of the Dead Sea Scrolls*

| *Content (What it says)* | *Structure (What it does)* |
|---|---|
| 1. New evidence may throw new light on origins of Christianity: DSS found in Qumran 1947, are documents of ascetic Jewish monks, "Essenes" | Theme<br><br>Background |
| 2. DSS challenge Christian tradition:<br> Maybe: Jesus was an Essene<br>    there is a 2nd layer of<br>     meaning in Gospels<br>    Rational explanation for<br>     Virgin Birth,<br>    resurrection,<br>    Miracles | Thesis: newly discovered documents lead to reinterpretation of major existing source |
| 3. This new interpretation can demystify modern Christian rituals; Therefore opposed by Church and scholars | Implications, if true, must encounter resistance by others in the field: controversy |
| Signposting: What is the new interpretation and how credible is it? | |
| 4. New interpretation rests on crucial error in previous scholarship | Methodological error in previous scholarship suggested |
| 5. If consensus dating of DSS to 140 BC wrong, DSS may refer to Jesus | Implications of correcting error: new document refers to same events as existing one |
| Signposting: Rest of program stems from this interpretation | |
| 6. Essenes were a monastic community<br> A. Nature of site<br> B. Themes of Manual of Discipline: penances, exclusions, celibacy, physical and moral purity | |

| | |
|---|---|
| 7. DSS tell of conflict of 2 leaders and parties | |
| 8. Consensus: struggle occurred before Jesus | Incompatible consensus interpretation of same material |
| 9. One leader was a fiery preacher, threatened punishment, baptized | Evidence of a connection |
| 10. If consensus date was wrong, the leaders were probably John Baptist and Jesus | Connection between new and existing documents |
| 11. Previous interpretation based on consensus date: leaders probably rival candidates for high priest | Counterargument |
| 12. Not enough information for high priest theory | Evidence for counter-argument insufficient |
| 13. DSS contain parallels with Christianity: groups doing same things, using same terms, as in Gospels | Evidence for connection between documents |
| 14. Big differences from Christianity: strict observance of law, priestly community | Acknowledgment of problematic evidence |
| 15. But similarities must be faced | Insistence upon connection |
| 16. Previous scholars refuse to face these because new theory may threaten "sacred ground" | Explanation for resistance to new theory |
| 17. New theory not destructive: instead, removal of myth leads to truer idea of what Christianity was about | Claim that resistance is based on misunderstanding |
| 18. Dating method which rules out connection is not applicable to DSS | Rejection of methodological rejection |
| 19. Thiering's on-site research matches DSS details to site of Qumran | New theory does not rely on one method alone |
| 20. Publication of DSS has been very slow | Reasons for delay in publishing sources |
| 21. To accept Thiering's case we must reject consensus dating | Conditions for accepting new theory |

22. John the Baptist was Teacher of Righteousness and Jesus was Wicked Priest of DSS — *Characters in new documents identified with characters in existing ones*
    A. Essenes and other Jews were expecting Messiahs
    B. Jesus of Gospels behaved like Wicked Priest of DSS: rejected ritual purity, asceticism, financial practices of priests, and he opened priesthood to all
        [Cinematic implication here that Jesus' opening of priesthood was overturned by Catholic Church]

23. Virgin Birth crucial to world view of Western civilization, showing divine intervention — *One element of existing source identified as crucial to previous interpretation*

24. Virgin Birth intended as metaphorical rather than supernatural in terms of DSS — *This element has been misunderstood*
    A. Essene "virgins" could be fiances of monks
    B. Gospels are inconsistent on Jesus' ancestry: line of David or Holy Spirit? — *Evidence*
    C. Essene monks called "Holy Spirits" so impregnation of virgin by Holy Spirit could describe Mary's pregnancy by Joseph — *Evidence*

25. Fr. Murphy: Virgin Birth not a Judaic idea, but unique to Christianity — *Likelihood of new interpretation challenged by other scholars*

26. Others: Virgin Birth is probably a metaphor, but stands for divine significance rather than ordinary event — *Relevance of new interpretation challenged by other scholars*

27. Dependence on symbolism of supernatural unnecessary to moral code of Christianity: DSS gives more realistic basis

*New interpretation destroys previous one, but replaces it with one more satisfactory*

28. Metaphors that seem miraculous to us were used in DSS to describe ordinary events:
   A. Heaven = sky
   B. Camel & eye of needle = grades of monks

*Reason for proposing different methodology*

29. Qumranis believed scripture had 2 levels of meaning and encoded history discoverable by pesher reading method. So, it's likely that Apostles encoded history into the Gospels accordingly.
   A. Qumranis read Old Testament for historical prophecy
   B. Gospel writers similarly read prophecy in Old Testament
   C. Qumranis may have written New Testament according to their ideas about the Old Testament, as implied by Jesus' use of Parables

*Reason for proposing different methodology*

30. Pesher method makes historical sense of miracle stories and cleans up anomalies in Jesus' behaviour
   A. Water into wine
   B. Raising dead
   C. Loaves and fishes

   Jesus assumed priestly power and extended membership to excluded groups

*Problems which new method can explain*

31. Pesher reading reveals true meaning of early Christianity: Kept best aspects of Judaism but reformed exclusionary attitudes and financial practices so attracted abuse in DSS

*Summary*

32. DSS provide history of the Church before Jesus
    A. Qumran modeled on Jerusalem
    B. Center for exiled and scattered Jews
    C. Association with Zealots (anti-Roman)

*Interpretation of new document meshed with historical sources*

33. Jesus and Judas (Zealot) were allied, then split because Jesus preached peace
    A. They shared opposition to priestliness
    B. They fell out over opposition to Rome
    C. Temptation by Satan = debate between Jesus and Judas

*Resulting extension of new interpretation*

*Evidence*

*Evidence*

*Evidence*

34. Raising from dead wasn't a miracle
    A. Membership at Qumran = life
    B. Excommunication = death
    C. Lazarus excommunicated
    D. Jesus received him as ally

*Further interpretation of existing source by new method*

35. Pesher technique may offer ordinary explanation of Crucifixion and Resurrection
    A. Jesus fainted, didn't die
    B. Friends revived and rescued him
    C. He used sanctuary to stay at large

*Further interpretation of existing source by new method*

36. This history not invented; read from existing documents by reliable method

*Argument recapitulated*

37. Religion has obscured true message of Jesus but we can rediscover it

*Benefits of acceptance recapitulated*

38. Not all evidence is in

*Scholar's doubts reiterated*

39. Are these readings destructive and irrelevant, or do they lead to better understanding?

*Questions left open*

# 11

## Educating *with* Rita

### Victoria Salmon

For several years I searched for an appropriate introductory writing assignment for my community college composition students. I sympathized with their anxiety over entering the academy, their concerns with public versus private discourse, and their need to learn the skills to find jobs in the American economic system. In addition to these issues, diversity in my classroom meant more than multiculturalism; it also encompassed the issues of gender, age, and educability. While taking a graduate course at George Mason University, the professor assigned the movie *Educating Rita,* and as I reviewed this movie, I recognized that the thematic elements of the story can be connected to the academic experiences of my students. In particular, the movie speaks to the margins; students who are on the borders of American higher education. It addresses the issues of inclusion/exclusion in the academy; it articulates the obstacles that nontraditional college students endure. Therefore, for the past four semesters I have used this movie as a medium for the introductory composition assignment. Each semester's students revealed exciting and intriguing responses to Rita's entry into the academy.

## Rita and the Community College Student

In *Educating Rita,* Michael Caine plays an alcoholic, disorganized literature professor; Julie Walters plays Rita, a hairdresser who craves an education. From the outset of the movie, Rita teaches Frank even before Frank has the chance to teach Rita. Demonstrating a practical knowledge of the world, Rita explains to Frank how to repair his door. This initial scene establishes Rita's knowledge and talents as worthwhile. An exchange of knowledge continues throughout the movie, and both characters grow as individuals because they share in the learning process.

Rita often wonders if she is able to learn, yet the viewer realizes that she continually learns throughout the film. Her strong desire to pursue her formal education emanates from a willingness to learn from life's experiences. However, she candidly states, "All I know is that I know nothing." Community college students often feel this same sentiment. Their marginalized status in society and in the academy emphasizes this statement. They are the nontraditional college students who may be older, or younger, or a minority, or perhaps students who have not succeeded in high school or a prior college. As with the character Rita, they have "not been similarly shaped by an academic and literary culture, and so from the perspective of that culture . . . [they are] sure to look deficient" (McGrath and Spear, 94).

Yet, the number of community college students in the United States is impressive: 35.8 percent of all college students, and 44.3 percent of all college freshman attend American community colleges (Dougherty, 3). These numbers certainly demonstrate the two-year schools' value by extending higher education to a broad citizenry. In addition, the "open door" policy—a policy many four-year public institutions have adopted—allows for a much more diverse population not often viewed in the university setting. Some community college students return to school after dropping out of four-year colleges. Some of these students are in their sixties and seventies and attend school for personal fulfillment. Some of these students are graduates of four-year colleges who return to school to learn a business skill. Some of these students are studying to earn associates degrees in nursing, technology, and child development. Moreover, the classrooms are filled with students who "zigzag" through their college and professional careers (Griffith and Connor, 2).

Furthermore, these two-year college students on the borders of higher education are often depicted as "losers" in the media. Television in particular offers "demeaning and discouraging portrayals of the two-year schools" (Griffith, 271). Yet, the "people who define [the community college and its students] are not the people who know" them (Griffith, 270). Community colleges gladly offer a place in the classroom to the "unglamorous" members of our society. They come into the classroom to retrain for positions in business and industry. They come from welfare lines to learn the skills necessary for their first job. They transfer to many of the best colleges and universities in the United States. These schools allow students who are normally shunned placement in the academic conversation.

## Inclusion/Exclusion Within the Academy

Rita's initiation into the academy was a writing assignment on Forrester's *Howard's End.* Her paper compares the book to one of Harold Robbins' popular novels, which astounds the professor and provides a great comic scene for the audience. Comparing one of the classics to a pulp novel is "just not done" in the academy. Frank's outburst at this travesty deserves to be reviewed. When an educator chooses to teach in an "open university" forum, he needs to consider the students' academic backgrounds and histories before assigning texts. Many community college educators agree that a gradual introduction into the world of classical literature is best. Total emersion often creates frustration, and often, apathy in a student, "If I don't understand this, I can't understand anything." Among the goals of many community college educators is the desire to keep students in the classroom, offer encouragement, and guide them toward further learning.

Rita's enthusiasm for her first encounter with *Macbeth* demonstrates how the adult learner suddenly "gets it." She runs to the university, interrupts Frank's class, and blurts out her fervor over the play. This heartening scene reminds me of some of my own students who have experienced similar joy. Skeptical about Rita's response to the play, Frank responds that he is "honored" that she chose to share her enthusiasm with him and invites her to share it with his class. She does, and she does this well. She then begins to devour literature; she develops confidence as a learner, and is willing to move forward with her education.

As in any good educational environment, the teacher learns from the student. Mutual growth permeates this movie. Frank teaches Rita to channel her enthusiasm into her writings, and then he teaches her how to transform her honest feelings into scholarly prose. He reminds her that what she is and has as a person is valuable, but she must also adapt to the university forum. He reminds her too, however, to ask questions, criticize, read carefully; she should not simply memorize the material. He tries to enlighten Rita to live a life of fullness and harmony *with* the world; he warns her about an academic life separate from the outside world. Rita offers her own encouragements and warnings. After a few drunken and embarrassing moments, Frank is forced to take a leave of absence. He does not leave though without a final lesson from Rita. She encourages him to stop drinking, take advantage of a new life in Australia, and grow as an individual. As an experienced hairdresser, she offers what she can to Frank—a "new look." Therefore, as he leaves her at the airport, the audience may assume that Frank is also transformed.

Rita's educational process recalls a term often used in community college education, "the lifelong learner." Her experiences as a student are similar to those we encounter in the community college classroom: adult learners sharing space, time, and energy with younger students. These schools attempt to attract the adult learner, and the institutions adjust their methods of instruction, administration, and scheduling to meet their needs. Like Rita, the average age of a community college student is about twenty-nine, is employed, is female, and possibly is a parent. All of these demands provide for a diverse undergraduate student body for the school and for the educator who must take into consideration differences on the basis of race, class, gender, educational background, age, and ethnic origin.

At the outset of the semester, I ask my students to formulate their goals. We discuss these goals, and then I develop and organize a curriculum reflecting their needs. Diagnosing their knowledge with written assignments and skill objectives allows me to change or adapt the program as the semester progresses. A gradual introduction into the worlds of composition and literature allows students to gain confidence as they perform. Moreover, I participate as coach rather than lecturer; connected learning, rather than arbitrary requirements, are the instructional goals. I employ portfolio assessment to define the development of the students; this allows the students as well as the instructor to see educational process.

The students in my classroom are similar to Rita. They wish to be "transformed." Two-year college students know the meaning of transformation; they live it. They are participants in higher education on one level and are marginalized in society on other levels. For them, a college composition course represents the potential to transform themselves into student-writers, to comprehend the academic language they encounter on campus, and to decode the nuances of language in the business world.

Entry into the academic and business worlds demands that students must learn "to speak our language, to speak as we do, to try on the peculiar ways of knowing, selecting, evaluating, reporting, concluding and arguing that define the discourse of our community" (Bartholomae, 134). Rita and the marginalized community college student recognize that a hierarchy within the academy exists and demands that a writer must "imagine and write from a position of privilege" (Bartholomae, 139). As a community college educator, I try to demonstrate respect for both the individual's private language community and the demands of the academic language community. Accepting the value of the student's private literacy affords a more flexible attitude toward the composition process. Harold Robbins' work may be more familiar to my students than Forrester's, yet with effort academic literacy can be "more accessible" to community college students (Courage, 485). I try to "explore . . . literacy practices outside of the context of the college classroom" (Courage, 493). Therefore, I bring in a medium students are familiar with, films.

## The Assignment

The critical goals of the *Educating Rita* composition assignment include debating the value of standard English as public language in an "educated" society, examining the conflicts that students experience when entering (or reentering) college, and defining the meaning of "a college education." While we review these issues, students are asked to determine the significance of Rita's husband's attitude toward her education and his attempt to burn her books. Students argue about Rita's family's desire for her to quit school and have a baby. Moreover, students express interest in the interaction between Rita and Frank.

They examine this relationship as an example of professor/student relationships they desire.

This assignment flows into a unit from Jack Selzer's reader, *Conversations*. We read the section titled, "What's College For?" and discuss essays by Alice Walker, bell hooks, Adrienne Rich, and review a Garry Trudeau cartoon. Each of these works question the value of higher education. As in the film, these writers ask if college does more harm than good. They examine the integrity of private language vs. public language. They challenge the values inherent in higher education. They warn students about the "dangers" of a college education. After this unit is completed, students realize that education is not a neutral tool.

Students receive a handout which explains the assignment. I keep two copies of *Educating Rita* on reserve in our library; students are asked to watch the movie within a two-week period. Then they are asked to write a two- to three-page paper on one of the following issues:

> "What's College For?" Sometimes the student experiences conflicts: between home and college cultures, the role of college in the creation of the educated person, teacher/student relationships, should college be primarily vocational or purely educational in nature. What does it mean to have "a college education"?
>
> Choose one of the topics above and think about it in relation to Rita's educational experience. Does Rita's academic experience reflect any of the conflicts? Write a clear, concise thesis statement which analyzes Rita's encounter with the academic world. While reviewing the story, think about the conflicts you have experienced while adjusting to college life. You may want to discuss any similar conflicts/relationships in connection with your analysis of the film. You may also integrate your opinion about the movie with your analysis.

## Student Responses

Several themes are embraced in the students' essays. Most of these students sincerely believe in the myth/dream that higher education is the passport to economic and personal success. If they, too, achieve academic success, they will be able to participate in the "American Dream." Even though they have experienced discouragement, anxiety, and frustration in their academic careers, their essays reflect optimism about their potentiality.

Farah, a sixteen-year-old college freshman, wants to attend medical school. Her essay demonstrates how optimistic many of my students are. She states that:

> College has an important role in the creation of an educated person. Classes provide knowledge and skills practiced in a person's chosen profession. It

also provides an environment which allows the person to think, explore, experiment, and express himself . . . College will expand a person's network of personal and professional acquaintances for many chances at a successful career.

She continues her essay with:

College is like a ticket to a different life. It might be an expensive ticket, but in the end it will be worth it . . . Having completed college, sends one on the road to a new life and to a more independent and responsible future.

Lucia, a young woman beginning her college career, reflects upon similar issues:

A college education and experience contributes much to the creation of the educated person. Rita's success in self-discovery is largely due to [her] college education. More importantly, it enables one to recognize opportunities and choices to decide what is best for his life. Ultimately, a college education helps one establish the lifestyle that allows for fulfillment of one's own interests and priorities.

Jenny, who is also beginning her academic journey, struggles with her opinions about the movie. She finds the movie uplifting and a journey for self-discovery, and she expresses her belief that "Education is very important in this world. To be an educated women [sic] is to be someone important, who people look up to with respect." The movie proves to her that obstacles stand in the way of Rita's—and many college students'—attempts at an education. Jenny celebrates Rita as "a winner" because "she pulled through no matter how difficult it was and succeeded in becoming an educated woman." Although Jenny recognizes the struggles that Rita experience, this student felt ambivalent about her own attempts at attaining a college education.

Carina expressed ambivalence also. She thoughtfully expresses concern about why students attend college, "motivations for becoming a college student have changed drastically over the past century." She states, "The principal [sic] intention of . . . college students is to acquire a trade status in society. College is currently a necessary implement for achieving success in society."

After discussing Rita's desire for a new life and relief from an oppressive family, Carina continues her thoughtful reflection about a college education in the twentieth century.

Growth in technology and growth in population has [sic] rapidly increased in the past century causing a shift in society's perspective on life and success. This expansion has also created an increase in career options that require extensive knowledge and training which, in turn, has affected people's reasons and decisions for going to college. People, in general, no longer attend college purely for learning how to think. The rare individual who has traditional

> views on education and wants to learn for the sake of learning is looked down
> upon as an under-achiever who isn't fulfilling his duties in life . . . Time has
> altered what college is about to the point that one is required to go, whether
> he has an interest to learn or not, in order to survive.

These students reflect noted community college critic Dale Parnell's attitude about how community colleges can help students from various backgrounds and cultures seek potential (10). He acknowledges that there "are many kinds of talents and many kinds of excellence" and the most significant aspect of education should encourage progress (8). This progress can be achieved through community, technical, or junior colleges which offer to the "ordinary" student postsecondary education and training. He asserts that a worker—the ordinary middle-level person—deserves a broad education. Yet, his view corresponds more with Lucia, Jenny, and Farah rather than Carina. Parnell and other proponents of community college education stress the schools' contributions to the economic and social welfare of a society. They rarely ask the questions Carina's essay acknowledges. Today, four-year institutions also insist upon their abilities to help create an individual's participation in the business aspects of society. Although this trend in American higher education may be distressing to college educators, it is a reality which deserves more attention.

However, in this movie Rita already has a job as a hairdresser; her pursuit of an education reaches beyond employment potential. This pursuit causes much anxiety and anger within her family and close friends. Often community college students experience these same conflicts. Endalkachew, a young man from Africa, wrote about Denny's efforts to burn Rita's books:

> By burning books, he attempts to destroy her basis of knowledge. As Adolph
> Hitler burnt books to keep knowledge away from people, Denny tries to pre-
> vent her consciousness. Like Hitler, Denny does not want Rita to have control
> or power.

His comments about Rita's husband and this scene reflects the struggles and conflicts that Endalkachew experienced in his native country, Somalia. He, along with other students from Africa, constantly discussed the suppression of knowledge in their war-torn countries. Not only does the ruling government cause suppression, often family members verbally and physically abuse young men and women who want to earn an education.

Bisrat's essay reveals his struggle to attend schools both in his native country and here in the United States. Throughout the semester his writing centered on the challenges he faced throughout his educational career. His alcoholic father "used to force [him] to work in the garage instead of going to school. [The father] gave examples about his relatives, who were auto mechanic [sic], and how they became successful." This constant desire to have his son join him in the auto repair business caused Bisrat to feel confused and anxious. He states, "My mind was split in different ways; I couldn't concentrate on my education. I wasn't comfortable to speak in front of my father because he switched my words, and punished me verbally and physically."

This student compares his suffering and abuse to Rita's. He notes that her father wants her to settle down and become pregnant, as other women in her culture do. Her husband's desire to have children was thwarted by Rita's taking birth control pills. This conflict causes verbal and physical abuse which reminds Bisrat of his father's controlling abusive behavior.

Another issue students wrote about was Rita's attempt to become a member of the academic community. Several students felt that the scenes in the movie which depict this struggle resonated with their own efforts and discomforts. Ismail speaks quite honestly about this matter:

> When Rita comes to school, she is afraid of speaking to the students. She told her teacher that if she spoke to the students, they will notice that she is an uneducated person, and will make fun of her. I remember the first time I started school, I was afraid to speak to students because I didn't know if I was saying the right words or not . . . Even if I wanted to say something important about the discussion, I would keep my comments with me.

Ismail rarely participated in class discussions, and when we began our semester's collaborative research and presentation project, he dropped the class. His composition skills improved, yet his apprehension about participating in verbal projects was a roadblock he refused to overcome. I spoke with him about this problem, and failed to convince him to complete the semester.

Senait left her native country in Africa to attend college in India. She feels that her academic experiences taught her how to accept people from different cultures. She felt that she grew into a more responsible and independent woman, and compares her situation to Rita's abilities to grow as "a person with a better understanding of life, a new view of life . . . college offers more than just an academic development. A college education helps us become mature and wiser. We learn to interact with each other and develop our minds through the challenges of the various assignments we face."

Another woman who attended my class, Inez, was fascinated with the conflicting behavior between those considered part of the academic community and those who are not. She questions Rita's motives, and Inez wonders if Rita chooses appropriate role models. "Her academic life is flowing with false skimpy models, and people full of knowledge and hypocrisy whose behavior impress deeply Rita [sic]." Yet Inez also notes Rita's difficult lifestyle, "She fights her way out of an unfulfilled life style where cultural differences between spouses and among family members, become unbearable." For Inez, Rita's search for knowledge is more than an academic education, "through difficult steps Rita grows culturally . . . [she] captures Frank's message on the importance, and especially, on the strength of character a person has to hold, to be able to keep the *self*." Inez, perhaps reflecting her own desire to gain knowledge, applauds Rita's personal and cultural development.

Dania also applauds this development, yet she demonstrates an idealistic attitude when she discusses Rita's growth:

> In college a student learns how to act and react to different everyday situations, he/she feels strong and confident, like having a weapon to carry around, the weapon of knowledge and education. The person learns how to say no and stand up for his/her own rights, and defend his/her own opinions and sayings.

My response to Dania's comments was, "A person without a formal education cannot do these things?" I wanted her to realize that an academic education does not guarantee these abilities. Her optimism remained even in the rewritten version of her paper where she continually referred to Rita's strength and confidence. This student felt that Rita was brave to leave her husband and family, and she "is now educated and has a weapon in her hand. She can make her own decisions." Dania declares that she too has grown like Rita, and she too can "stick to [her] own opinion." Perhaps Dania's reaction is due to her own cultural heritage; she is a Muslim woman who came to the United States to earn an education. She insisted that her own growth and development is a result of her college education.

Finally, the remainder of the students discussed the teacher/student relationship in the movie. Frank's initial reaction to Rita's behavior and enthusiasm impressed them, and his ability to learn from her also influenced them. Most important, these students were heartened by Frank's patience and compassion.

Jennifer wrote several pages focusing on this teacher/student relationship. Because Frank willingly leads Rita through the academic writing process, Jennifer believed that he demonstrated qualities that make a strong educator, "faith, trust, and understanding." For Jennifer, faith is the initial quality a professor must have to create a relationship with a student, "when a teacher shows the student he/she has faith in what the student is doing, the student will trust the teacher." She uses Frank's faith in Rita's abilities as an example, "Rita . . . feels out of place because she doesn't understand what is happening in the world around her . . . Bryant never criticizes her . . . he never interrupts her . . . Bryant never abandons her because he has faith in her."

Faith in a student's ability builds self-confidence, according to Jennifer. This quality encourages the student to trust the professor and develop a willingness "to return to the teacher for help." Jennifer's essay reflects her current actions as a student, she is trying to cultivate relationships with her own teachers:

> At first I thought it would be too difficult since there are so many students in each of my classes . . . A little encouragement from any teacher helps me move a step closer to figuring out whether or not I trust them and feel that they understand me.

She continues by stating that a teacher/student relationship can influence a student well past the completion of an academic degree. "What the student learns from the teacher will continue to enforce and support the decisions the student must face throughout his/her life." As her composition professor, I hope that this is true; most of us in education live by this ideal. Yet, the responsibility is enormous.

Jennifer's close friend, Katharine, also took my composition class. They sat together every period, shared texts, and worked collaboratively during peer review sessions. The themes of their essays often mirrored each other's opinions, and this assignment reflected their mutual convictions about the student/teacher connection. Katharine was interested in the Frank/Rita relationship as an example of a teacher's interest in a student's development. Yet for Katharine, communication between professor and student was the most significant issue in the movie. In the communication process, the "student must trust that the professor will not mock or look down upon her work. When a student is able to ask questions and receive help, she is building skills that can be used for the rest of her life. [Rita] can ask questions without being afraid that Dr. Bryant's answers will be said in a ridiculing way." Katharine insists that teachers must be open to a student's "serious intentions of learning and receiving help."

In addition to verbal communication, Katharine views her composition assignments as written communications with her professors. Actually, she views written communication as the precursor to verbal communication. How an instructor writes comments or grades a paper determines if a student feels confident enough to communicate verbally with her professor. "When trust has been achieved through written communication, verbal communication starts," she states. In addition, these forms of communication aid the student with "ways to deal with everyday difficulties in communication between other people: friends, family, spouse, coworkers, neighbors, relatives, and acquaintances."

These comments put teachers in a tenuous and powerful position. If a student is discouraged by a professor's comments, perhaps she will become disheartened with the course work. According to Katharine's reactions, the student may actually become cautious about relationships outside of the classroom. These remarks reflect many studies about community college students' real or perceived marginalized status in the academy and in society. Most educators in this field of higher education realize these perceptions and make serious effort to communicate in a positive manner with their students.

Yvette, a woman who is using her military benefits to attend college while serving in the Navy, recognizes the issue of power in the Rita/Frank relationship.

> Initially, Frank possessed all of the power. He had the wisdom Rita so desperately desired. He worked with her week after week, molding her into a college-level student, instructing her which books to read, and the proper from of writing an essay. As Rita progressed, she eventually needed more than Frank could teach her. This is when we again see the threat that education manifests. Frank had been at the helm of Rita's education the entire time, now loosing control, he began to feel obsolete.

Yvette acknowledges the shift in power evident in this movie. Rita must move beyond Frank's academic support; Frank must investigate his personal life and correct serious flaws. College professors often have difficulty confronting their own powerlessness. However, each of my students consistently reminded me in their essays that education is about empowering *them;* I serve as their guide. The movie *Educating Rita* helps them discover and explore their position in the academic community.

Peter Elbow encourages his student to use texts, to manipulate them, to approach them as tools rather than icons (74). He promotes the notion of writing on a continuous basis, as a form of knowing, as a way of perfecting the "techniques and approaches toward getting words on paper" (74). This practice provides the writer with an opportunity to discover an authoritative voice and ownership of knowledge. My students see Frank Bryant attempt this same goal with Rita, and they know that this is my goal in my own classroom. Through composition assignments and class discussions, my effort is to include my community college students in the academic conversation often occupied by the traditional college student.

These two-year college students are like Rita. They confront many pressures not felt in the four-year college classroom: managing a job, a home, a family, financial struggles from job loss or blended families, and loss of self-esteem because of past academic failures. The respect for diversity evident in today's composition theory is encouraging to community college educators whose goal is to empower their students with the knowledge necessary for academic and economic success. The students outlined in this chapter mirror the students who populate the composition classrooms of most American community colleges. They are *different,* not in the hierarchical sense of "deficient, deformed, or secondary," but in the straightforward sense of heterogeneous, consequential, and determined (Brunette and Wills, 7).

## Works Cited

Bartholomae, David. 1985. "Inventing the University." In *When a Writer Can't Write,* edited by Mike Rose. New York: Guilford Press.

Brunette, Peter, and David Wills. 1989. *Screen/Play: Derrida and Film Theory.* Princeton, NJ: Princeton University Press.

Courage, Richard. 1993. "The Interaction of Public and Private Literacies." *College Composition and Communication* 44 (4): 484–96.

Dougherty, Kevin J. 1994. *The Contradictory College: The Conflicting Origins, Impacts, and Futures of the Community College.* Albany: State University of New York Press.

Elbow, Peter. 1995. "Being a Writer vs. Being an Academic: A Conflict in Goals." *College Composition and Communication* 46 (1): 72–83.

Griffith, Marlene, and Ann Connor. 1994. *Democracy's Open Door: The Community College in America's Future.* Portsmouth, NH: Boynton/Cook.

Griffith, Marlene. 1996. "Getting Our Story Out." *Teaching English in the Two-Year College* 23 (4): 269–73.

McGrath, Denis, and Martin B. Spear. 1991. *The Academic Crisis of the Community College.* Albany: State University of New York Press.

Parnell, Dale. 1985. *The Neglected Majority.* Washington, D.C.: American Association of Community and Junior Colleges.

# 12

## Challenging Antiwriting Biases
## in the Teaching of Film

John Heyda

In "So What's Wrong with Current-Traditional Rhetoric, Anyway?," a chapter from *The Methodical Memory,* Sharon Crowley considers the development of "full frontal teaching," the pedagogy instrumental to current-traditional rhetoric's gaining control of so many first-year writing classrooms and programs. "Full frontal" pedagogy made it possible to teach writing "by the book," gearing the classroom to lectures on textbook prescriptions and drills on their requirements; under its sway, textbooks came to dominate the classroom. Teachers organized class time around textbook study of guidelines for writing featured in lectures, analyzing "textbook exercises that drilled" their charges "in current-traditional prescriptions about grammar, diction, and style." To maintain so imposing a classroom style, the full frontal approach came, then, to depend on current-traditional textbooks, "popular originally because they gave untrained teachers something to teach." When "current-traditional thought prospered, that 'something' became the core of the composition course. It dictated the organization of syllabi and of whole composition programs. . . . Its prescriptions were identified as the ones that governed the writing done for English classes and for other courses as well" (147).

Full frontal teaching's reliance on textbooks to teach writing has proved highly marketable to many courses besides composition that require writing of students, most notably introduction to literature courses and courses in film, theater, and other arts. Such courses often draw large enrollments, too large, it is thought, to make room for much more than cursory attention to student writing, let alone the discussion and workshopping time necessary for sustained engagement of student texts. Even when teachers of such courses are not beleaguered by large, lecture-sized classes, a lack of training or experience in teaching composition can inhibit any recasting of course work in more writing-centered ways. Texts with titles like *Writing About Literature* and *A Short*

152

*Guide to Writing About Film* find a ready market, then, among teachers who need "something to teach" students about writing assigned papers, but who lack the class time or training to teach writing in their subject areas. Not surprisingly, the "something" such textbooks teach puts instructors in the same "full frontal" position as composition teachers bound to current-traditional textbooks; writing on film or literature becomes all too similar to the "antiwriting" promoted by such texts, "a series of exercises wherein students demonstrate their mastery of textbook trivia" (Crowley, 148–49). In Crowley's view, the prose "antiwriting" encourages "establishes no voice, selects no audience, takes no stand, makes no commitment. It can be produced by anyone, anywhere, at any time, on demand." The pedagogy for such prose, as Jasper Neel sees it, sends this message: "'I am not writing. I hold no position. I have nothing at all to do with discovery, communication, or persuasion. I care nothing about the truth. What I am is an essay.'"

## Eliminating the Antiwriting Bias

In this essay I argue that, at the outset of any conversation about "ways of thinking about film and composition pedagogically," film and writing teachers need to address the legacies of "full frontal teaching" and "antiwriting" pedagogies in shaping (re)presentations of writing in film texts and curricula. If film and writing teachers are to start such a conversation, they would do well to look first at the writing typically required of students in film courses. Were they to do so, they would find "full frontal teaching" as much, if not more of an issue in teaching film as it has been in teaching composition.

I begin by examining a number of prominent film texts for what they reveal of "antiwriting" biases. Next, I consider antidotes to antiwriting biases in the teaching of film, drawing on my experience in redesigning an introductory film studies course so that my course plan now bears considerable resemblance to syllabi for my composition courses. Finally, I will detail writing assignments I have developed to challenge the antiwriting biases current-traditional textbooks and pedagogy impose and that students bring with them from previous encounters with writing in school.

## Film as Art

Biases against writing show up in textbooks for introductory film studies in a number of ways. The most obvious bias appears in the stance such texts take against student writing. Designed for large, lecture-sized courses, film texts discourage sustained attention to writing. They assume that teachers will be too busy with other classroom responsibilities to devote much time to the teaching of writing. Consequently, student writing on film rarely appears in such texts. If it appears at all, it shows up only in the form of model student essays included in appendices on writing about film. (Most film texts do not even include the most perfunctory, end-of-chapter writing assignments.) In other words, student writing appears, in good current-traditional style, as product rather than as process. This antiwriting stance is by no means limited to student writing, however; the contributions of professional writers on film receive scant attention as well. In truth, film studies textbooks play up to full frontal teaching and antiwriting pedagogies by consistently erasing, marginalizing, and masking the many roles writing has played in the history and criticism of film.

This severing of ties between writing and film study is achieved, in large part, through textbooks' reliance on what Richard Maltby refers to as "a critical tradition that makes significant claims for Hollywood cinema as an art practice comparable to the practice of literature or painting." Maltby acknowledges that, while "this tradition has many strengths," it has a "weakness . . . in its tendency to take movies out of the context of their production and consumption as objects of an industrial and commercial process" (2). In this way, the cultural work produced by a wide range of writers, by consumers, critics, publicists, and screenwriters is quite strictly subordinated to the work of "artists," whose performances cover virtually every phase of film as art—acting, directing, photography, costume and set design, and so on. One very popular text acknowledges this hierarchy in its preface, noting that "our main concern has been with film as art, but when appropriate, we also discuss film as industry, and as a reflection of popular audience values, social ideologies, and historical epochs" (Giannetti, xi). Another leading textbook wants "to introduce the reader to the aesthetics of film"; its "aim is to survey the fundamental aspects of cinema as an art form," seeking "to isolate those basic features of film which can constitute it as an art." This text claims to direct "itself at the person interested in how the film medium may give us experiences akin to those offered by painting, sculpture, music, literature, theater, architecture, or dance" (Bordwell and Thompson, xiii).

Maltby notes that "most introductions to film studies argue that the common technological and aesthetic properties of film mean that the various forms of cinema can be treated as a single subject for study." This narrowing of perspective to "how movies work in terms of their formal or aesthetic properties" eliminates from view other possible perspectives, among them movies' "function as consumable goods in a capitalist economy." In this regard, Maltby cites Pauline Kael's dissatisfaction with the teaching of so narrow a perspective. For Kael, there was something quite wrong "about classes in which students who interpreted a movie's plot as a mechanism for producing audience response were corrected by teachers who explained it in terms of a creative artist working out a theme." It was "'as if the conditions under which the movie is made and the market for which it is designed were irrelevant, as if the latest product from Warners or Universal should be analyzed like a lyric poem'" (2–3).

Textbooks' narrow focus on "how movies work in terms of their formal or aesthetic properties" works hand in glove, then, with the limited view of writing such texts offer. Both work to strip film study of context, save the context offered by the "art practice" tradition to which Maltby refers. Radically decontextualized, students' response has nowhere to go, then, but to the novitiate's position already inscribed for them in film texts. As novitiate, the student is left to express herself in the terms texts prescribe, terms that focus attention on appreciation for the artistry to be found in movies.

Crowley has cited the tendency of current-traditional composition texts "to portray student writers as having been extracted from any community they might have inhabited prior to entering the classroom." In this regard, she notes Ohmann's observation that "the student writer acts not only outside of time and history, but alone—framing ideas, discovering and expressing himself, trying to persuade others, but never working with others to make a theme that advances a common purpose" (151). Film texts' film-as-art treatment often achieves much the same isolating effect with regard to students as moviegoers, extracting them from the moviegoing communities in which they participate. So positioned, students asked to write about film have little recourse but to write in accordance with current-traditional dictates.

Texts could be organized differently, of course. They could open up spaces for writing by introducing students to more than just cinema's formal and aesthetic properties. They could focus on a range of issues and problems that have figured prominently in the work of screenwriters, publicists, film historians, and critics. They could devote space to writing for the screen, examining excerpts from screenplays with an eye to William Goldman's claims that "today you must give the star everything," and that "there is no single more important commercial element in screenplay writing than the star part" (62). Texts might feature sections on writing's roles in manipulating the imagery of celebrity, glamour, and stardom. Here students could investigate publicity's powerful effects in the autobiographies and biographies of stars, articles from fan magazines, and advertising and promotional initiatives. Textbooks might examine the discourses of practicing critics of film, from the work of newspaper review writers to the prose of more occasional or academic critics. A range of more reflective writings on film might merit space in texts as well. Both amateur and professional moviegoers' encounters with specific movies and venues, and with recent trends in the ever-changing experience of "going to the movies" could serve well here. To date, however, textbook publishers have kept the multivocal realities of so broad a range of writings at bay, substituting in their place the single voice of the textbook author.

Over time, three textbook types have come to dominate the market for film studies. A first type follows a chronological plan, organizing the study of film historically, via major figures and film movements. Prominent texts of this sort include Cook's *A History of Narrative Film,* Giannetti's *Flashback: A Brief History of Film,* and Sklar's *Film: An International History of the Medium.* A second type engages a topical plan, ordering film study in a survey of basic features, from editing and mise en scène, photography to sound. Major texts of this kind include Boggs' *The Art of Watching Films,* Bordwell and Thompson's

*Film Art: An Introduction,* Giannetti's *Understanding Movies,* and Prince's *Movies and Meaning: An Introduction to Film.* A third type, meant to supplement either of the first two, serves the quite specialized function of counseling students on how to write papers for film courses. This advice giving, not surprisingly, closely resembles the current-traditional rhetoric of writing themes about literature guides. It is an unhappy circumstance that, as the following paragraphs will argue, textbook adoption decisions involving either of these two text types can easily set a teacher on a pedagogical course decidedly anti-writing in character.

None of the above-mentioned texts propose anything like a significant role for writing in their programs for film study; some, notably the chronology-based texts, offer no pedagogical apparatus whatever. Cook, Sklar, and Giannetti's *Flashback* provide no questions for discussion or study, let alone any writing-related apparatus, even of the most conventional sort of topics for writing, guidelines for student writers, sample papers. If chronological texts erase writing, texts following a topic-based plan do only a bit better, pushing writing to the margins of film study. Boggs' *The Art of Watching Films* puts a section on writing in an appendix, "Writing a Film Analysis," with ten of its twelve pages taken up by two sample student essays, a long critical analysis and a shorter analysis of "selected film elements." Besides these samples, the book offers only end-of-chapter study questions and video exercises "designed to engender either class discussion or written response" (xiii). Prince's *Movies and Meaning* includes no writing-related apparatus at all; only a two-page subsection of a chapter on "Film Criticism and Interpretation," "Writing Film Criticism," instructs students in criticism as an activity that might involve them as writers. Bordwell and Thompson's *Film Art* contains no apparatus either, except for a brief, four-page "Appendix: Writing a Critical Analysis of a Film," appearing at the end of a chapter on film criticism. Giannetti's *Understanding Movies* offers no writing-related materials at all, though its last chapter, "Synthesis: *Citizen Kane,*" described as a "recapitulation of the main ideas of the previous chapters, applied to a single movie," can be made to serve, as the preface suggests, "as a rough model for a term paper" (ix).

To make up for the displacement of writing in such texts, a third sort of text has found a niche, the guidebook, a representative example of which is Corrigan's *A Short Guide to Writing About Film,* now in a third edition. Designed to serve as a supplementary text, Corrigan's *Guide* assumes a film course with little or no time to spare for writing instruction, its professed aim "to fill the gap between writing handbooks and film studies texts by distilling writing lessons as they apply specifically to film criticism" (x). How little impact emergent composition pedagogies have had on the teaching of film is only too evident in writing lessons this guide "distills." Corrigan's *Guide* assumes a writing program for film courses tied securely to current-traditional practice, one that reinforces full frontal pedagogy at every turn, but especially at its first turn, that of invention. The guide's two key chapters, "Preparing to Watch and

Preparing to Write" and "Film Terms and Topics," treat invention extensively, and in the controlling and prescriptive manner of current-traditional rhetorics. From the outset, students learn that they cannot be very inventive in how they write about film. While, as Corrigan puts it, "our primary experience of a movie is the singular and perhaps private one of watching it for the first time—involved and enjoying it, one hopes, but possibly annoyed yet still somewhat involved," this unique involvement cannot serve as a proper source for invention. For "either as preparation before the screening or shortly afterwards, . . . a writer needs to sort out that personal and primary experience along manageable lines, and this sorting out should become the groundwork for your analysis of the movie." Managing, sorting out, analysis—constraints such as these define invention for the student. "Should you talk about the characters? Technological innovations? The film's effect on an audience? Where, in brief, should you start to direct your attention and your analysis, so that you do not give yourself the impossible task of 'writing about the whole movie'?" (16). Lost in such admonitions is any concern that the student writer define for herself the possible and impossible in her inventional repertoire.

Crowley observes of the current-traditional model of invention that it involves "the construction of a mental forecast of what was to appear on paper," composed of "a retrospective review of the writer's thought processes . . . assumed to be natural to all normal persons." Provided the student is "normal," then, "she should be able to get her writing right on the first go-round." Consequently, "she needed no assistance with invention proper; indeed very little could be given her. What teachers could do was lecture about how a finished discourse should look, if it were to accurately reflect the uniform, 'natural,' composing process put forward in current-traditional theory" (147–48). Lecturing on "how a finished discourse should look," intervenes, then, in any process of invention a student might construct on her own, taking over any authority she might have over her own discourse. If, in classical rhetoric, "a writer's appropriation of discursive authority was necessarily tied to invention," so that "to establish an authoritative voice, a writer must be able to choose the rhetorical situations she will address," at liberty "to select a voice, a stance, her material, and her arguments," current-traditional rhetoric "denies all of these choices to student writers" (148).

Not only do textbooks for film courses strip students of their inventiveness, they deprive teachers of their own powers of invention as well. In this regard, what film texts do when they give teachers "something to teach students about writing," only mimics and reinforces the controls texts have imposed on composition classrooms and programs. Crowley notes that by the end of the last century, "teacherly authority began to be displaced by the authoritative voice of the current-traditional textbook." For writing teachers

> the upshot of this situation was that teacherly authority was replaced by the
> institutional authority represented in composition programs and in textbooks

> selected by a faculty committee . . . . The institution further usurped teachers'
> authority by imposing on them the standardized expectations about the for-
> mal features of discourse derived from current-traditional rhetoric. (153)

Unless film texts are used judiciously, such books can impose the same sorts of standardizing expectations on teachers and their students.

## How to Reclaim Writing and Film

What steps might teachers of film and composition take, then, to reclaim for themselves something of the pedagogical inventiveness and discursive author-ity full frontal teaching can so easily strip from them? How can they free them-selves from film textbooks' vicelike grip? I would propose four measures teachers might take to counteract antiwriting biases and their effects. As a first step, teachers need to take a hard look at the institutional constraints course scheduling imposes, and that full frontal teaching and its textbooks take for granted. If, for instance, class time is divided up into a couple of fifty-minute meetings a week, with an additional, longer session set aside each week for screenings of entire films, countering antiwriting biases becomes all but im-possible. If class size is set much above twenty-five students per teacher, mak-ing much of writing becomes next to impossible as well. Workable scheduling alternatives such as two 100-minute classes per week, combined with smaller classes or team-teaching assignments, can offer the flexibility needed to make room for writing.

A second step teachers might take to create a classroom environment more supportive of writing is to set aside class time for group presentations, for which students select and screen excerpts, and for which they write at least one detailed handout. Handouts can serve as "liner notes" to presentations, as study guides for classmates working on related individual projects, or as useful refer-ence points to ongoing class discussion or reading assignments.

A third measure teachers might take involves the process by which films are selected for in-class screenings. This step may not bear as directly on stu-dent writing as other moves teachers might make, but it can pay dividends in ways that support student writing. Crowley notes that "in current-traditional pedagogy, students don't perform: teachers do" (147). This is especially evi-dent in the way films are selected for full-length screenings, where teachers typically make the decisions and students learn to live with them. I work from what I consider a better plan, which is to present students with lists of up to ten films for each full-length in-class screening, asking them to vote on the films they want to watch. Compiling and revising such lists adds work for teachers, but the extra effort is repaid in heightened student investment in what they see and write.

Redesigning course calendars, making class time for class presentations, and letting students vote on the films they see—all can help in challenging antiwriting biases in the teaching of film. None of these moves can make much of a difference, however, without a writing program that can offer students something more than what textbooks provide. A fourth move teachers need to make, then, is to replace the narrow regimen for writing dictated by film texts with a wider ranging and more inventive program of writing project options. Film texts provide remarkably little variety in this regard; in text after text students are force-fed a steady diet of assignments in analytical and analytical-critical writing. A broader range of options, including assignments in argumentative, critical, investigative, and narrative writing could give students needed opportunities to explore powers of invention long denied them.

In the paragraphs that follow, I offer additional information on these four steps, along with suggestions as to how a teacher might build them into a more writing-centered film studies course.

## Course Calendars

If textbooks for film courses devote little or no space to student writing, course scheduling often reinforces such antiwriting biases, and in ways that can undermine any attempts to change course emphases. Consider, for instance, the aforementioned course schedule calling for two hour-long meetings and one two-hour session a week, and designating the two-hour slot for full-length screenings. With close to 50 percent of total class time set aside for weekly screenings, this arrangement can send the message that a movie every week represents the centerpiece of the course. Showcasing full-length screenings might tie in well with the textbook goal of providing students maximum exposure to major films and industry figures, but it can make more passive students' relations to the films they see. If students are to learn to watch movies in more active ways, more class time must be devoted to such learning, and to the kinds of activities that can sustain it—writing workshops, group presentations, discussion of readings, and so on. To make room for such activities, I limit the amount of time I set aside for full-length screenings to about 35 percent of total class time. For a fifteen-week semester comprised of twenty-nine 105-minute class meetings, this means that ten or eleven meetings are devoted to screenings, the rest to other activities.

Clearing additional time for activities supportive of student writing allows me to take on another difficulty textbooks can pose for course planning. If current-traditional rhetorics give full frontal pedagogy ways to teach writing by the book and "on schedule," with their table of contents clearly suggesting a week or so to focus on prewriting and invention, another week or so to do arrangement, then revision, and so on, film texts organized chronologically and topically are set up to work in much of the same fashion, by the book and by the calendar. With considerable ease the full frontal teacher can abstract week-by-week lesson plans from both text types' chapter-by-chapter organizational schemes. Teaching film chronologically might prescribe a week on Griffith and early American cinema and a screening of *Broken Blossoms* or *Intolerance,* a week on German expressionism with a viewing of *The Cabinet of Dr. Caligari, The Joyless Street,* or *M,* another on Italian neorealism and a showcasing of *Open City* or *The Bicycle Thief,* and so on. Teaching topically might proscribe weeks on acting, editing, mise-en-scène, and photography, along with the appropriate full-length screenings. In either case, an invariant, text-based organizational scheme dictates course planning, rather than a teacher's evolving practice.

In my own teaching, I have moved away from basing my course calendar on a textbook's table of contents. The calendar I have devised begins by dividing the work of the course into three five-week units, each characterizing a relationship students have with cinema—moviegoer as consumer, as fan, and as critic. I use Maltby's *Hollywood Cinema* to provide readings for each unit, using these texts as sources for discussion topics, "viewing strategies," and writing assignments. Maltby's text is a difficult one for my students to read well; his prose style, they report, can be abstruse and off-putting. But *Hollywood Cinema* stands apart from rival introductory texts in its commitment to reviewing major issues and problems in the critical literature of film studies, rather than just surveying basic elements of film as art.

The first unit, "moviegoer as consumer," focuses on how the motion picture industry positions us to watch movies in ways that support industry aims. It features packets of readings on moviegoing experiences I have compiled for an initial section entitled "Encounters," and readings from Maltby's "Entertainment" and "Industry" chapters. This unit invites students to reflect on their own expectations of "going to the movies," to tell stories of especially memorable moviegoing experiences, even to respond to the claims of critics that the era of blockbuster movie making drastically limits our expectations as consumers of movies. The second unit, "moviegoer as fan," looks at how moviegoers identify with and at times resist industry aims. This unit draws on Maltby's "Genre," "Technology," and "Performance" chapters, as well as on outside readings on such topics as the star system, action heroes, and gender inequities in the casting of movie roles. Here we study, especially, the impact on moviegoers of cinema's dependence on the star system, on action and spectacle, and on ever more elaborate costume and set designs. The third unit, "moviegoer as critic," addresses issues of more scholarly and critical interest, in particular the "look" of a film, its mise-en-scène, its direction, its editing. Maltby's chapters on "Space," "Time," "Narrative," "Politics," and "Criticism" provide most of the readings for this unit.

## Group Presentations

I tell my students on the first day that the class will not be a lecture course, but rather a course built on their active participation in conversations, discussions, and group work. To assure that everyone in class has the chance, at least once, to lead a class discussion, I schedule a number of group presentations during the term. Early in the semester I hand out a sign-up sheet listing possible topics for presentations, among them the star system, the "empire of genres," the spectacle of movement, star performance, the three "looks" of cinema, film time/movie time, clarity and ambiguity, and Hollywood versus Washington. I ask students to list their first, second, and third choices, then work out a schedule for presentations based on their preferences. Topics are based on readings from Maltby and additional readings from outside sources.

A part of students' group presentation assignment is to lead discussion for a portion of a class, another part to select excerpts to be screened that day, and another part to prepare a detailed, two- to three-page handout for class members. I serve as a "limited partner" in all class presentations, playing the role of coproducer. I offer suggestions and make recommendations, sharing ideas as well as any relevant materials I've already collected. I advise that presentations not be elaborate or formal ones, but more like conversations or discussions about concerns or issues presenters would like to raise about the day's readings and/or the excerpts they bring to class. I counsel presenters to gear discussion to some part of the work assigned for the day—readings from the textbook or from handouts, short writing assignments, even discussion of films selected for full-length screenings. On selecting excerpts, I note that most of the clips I bring to class cover the period between the mid 30s and the early 90s, but that if presenters are more inclined to bring in excerpts from more recent, or even current films, this is OK, that I welcome clips different from those I rely on. I ask that excerpts be in "reasonably good taste," and that they take up no more than five to ten minutes. I offer guidelines, as well, on handouts to accompany presentations.

## Selecting Full-Length Screenings

When pundits and scholars inveigh against the decline in literacy among the young, it is students' lack of exposure to literature that concerns them most. In "Reflections on the Freshman English Course," for instance, Richard Marius points to his students' lack of familiarity with the Bible, with Shakespeare, even the Gettysburg Address, lamenting that "this generation does not read." For Marius, "they are strangers . . . to those points of reference that might help them navigate the literary sea. . . . They cannot write because they have not read and they cannot hear" (178). In "Why Do We Read?" Katha Pollitt cites her students' not knowing any poems over a decade old, observing that "Robert Lowell was as far outside their frame of reference as Alexander Pope" (328). Were film teachers to weigh in with their own observations regarding student familiarity with culturally or historically significant films, they might make similar claims about young people's cineliteracy. One key difference they would do well to acknowledge, however, is that, while students may not read much literature, they do watch movies, and plenty of them. My own experience has been that my students know relatively little about major films and figures of the past, but they have had a lot of exposure to today's more successful films, follow the ups and downs of many contemporary stars, and recognize a number of the major directors of the day. When it comes to cinema, illiteracy is not so much the problem as it is students' having grown into a different kind of cineliteracy than previous generations. If their reading skills suffer due to a debilitating lack of exposure to literature, their motion picture viewing skills may suffer from overexposure to movies made in what Susan Sontag has called "the era of hyper industrial films," a time when "the sheer ubiquity of moving images has steadily undermined the standards people once had both for cinema as art and for cinema as popular entertainment" (16).

Like the prevailing pedagogy for introduction to literature courses, which aims at exposing students to texts they should but have not read, the pedagogy built into film textbooks positions teachers to take on students' lack of exposure to landmarks of cinematic art. The assumption is, of course, that teachers will make the decisions as to which landmarks students will see. The thinking is that if teachers show students the right films—*Modern Times, Citizen Kane, The Third Man*—they will have succeeded, at least, in exposing students to great cinematic achievements they might not otherwise see. The problem is that, while teachers taking charge of text selection can work relatively well in literature survey courses, since students have had little exposure to or investment in such texts, it can meet with resistance and resentment in film courses due to students' considerable investment in their own moviegoing experiences, not to mention their overexposure to the "hyper industrial films" to which Sontag refers. Plus, so prescriptive an approach to the selection of films for screening ties in only too well with guidebook models for writing about film, which assume that teachers, in good current-traditional fashion, will determine the limits of students discursive authority.

To restore to students some measure of authority over which films they see and write about, I give them the chance to choose the movies they see and write about. To do this, I present them with lists of ten movies for each scheduled screening date and ask them to vote for the three they would be most interested in seeing. After I tally each of these votes, I conduct a second, runoff vote among the top three vote getters, with these winners emerging as the films the class sees in their entirety. Screening dates are tied to textbook chapters, so that, for instance, for a chapter on industry I prepare a list of ten films relevant to issues the chapter raises, for the chapter on cinematic space a list of films significant for their contributions to study of mise-en-scène, and so on. To provide students with information about each film listed, I compile synopses from guides such as Leonard Maltin's *Movie and Video Guide* and Videohound's *Golden Movie Retriever.* One limitation I face is that, since class meetings run only 105 minutes, I can only screen films of roughly that duration. The listings in the appendix cover all films that students had a chance to vote on the last time I taught the course. Headings appearing at the beginning of each list represent my own occasional, but slight modifications to chapter titles from Maltby's textbook. I experience both delight and chagrin over the votes my students have cast. I am delighted that they so often vote for films I think of as the right ones for an introductory course in film studies; *Bonnie and Clyde, Diner, The Graduate,* and *Psycho* have won with regularity. But black-and-white, foreign, and pre-60s films rarely, if ever win. Great films like *The Bicycle Thief, The 400 Blows,* and *M* never come close to winning. (This last semester's lists included no foreign titles, in keeping with my use of Maltby's *Hollywood Cinema,* though a better plan might be to compile a single list comprised entirely of major foreign titles. In this way, students would be assured of seeing at least one foreign film during the course of a semester.) Documentaries, musicals, and westerns do quite poorly as well. Still, by the end of most semesters, when I consider the films students have voted to see, I find them quite comparable to lists I might compile on my own. Plus, I learn a good deal about my students as moviegoers, something I would lose were I to choose the films we see.

## Options for Writing

I assign a good deal of writing in my film studies classes—eight or nine short, 250- to 350-word journal responses tied to readings and full-length screenings, and three longer projects, each one linked to a major unit of the course—moviegoer as consumer, as fan, and as critic. Journal assignments give students the chance to write in response to full-length screenings, assigned readings, and shorter versions of longer project options. They help, too, in focusing class discussions; students are always better prepared and have more to say on assigned topics when they have had the chance to formulate written responses ahead of time.

For each longer unit project, I offer students four or five options. The aim of all three options packages is to counteract perhaps the most distressing aspect of conventional, writing-about-film assignments—their hostility to individual voice. In place of individual voice, current-traditional pedagogy requires, as Crowley puts it, "a standard authorial voice for student-written discourses—a voice that could be put on for any occasion." In this regard, Crowley recalls Ohmann's critique of composition textbooks. In *English in America,* Ohmann cites textbooks' typically representing the "student writer as a person who lacked location in either space or time, who was newborn, unformed, without social origins and without needs. . . . He has no history. Hence the writing he does and the skills he acquires are detached from those parts of himself not encompassed by this new identity as a student" (151).

My assignments try to restore to students those parts of their moviegoing selves film textbooks routinely fail to address. Textbooks address students, narrowly, as beginners without experience of cinema as art, and new to the academic study of film; it is to this still nascent academic self alone that textbooks direct student writers' attention. Project options I have developed counter this textbook approach by acknowledging students' considerable experience of movies and moviegoing and by inviting them to draw on these experiences in their writing.

A first set of project options solicits response to assignments that represent the student writer as a consumer of moviegoing experiences not just of the movies themselves, but the rituals associated with theatergoing, renting movies, even frequenting drive-ins. These rituals construct moviegoers' receptivity to cinema in ways that students need to recognize and rethink as a part of their introduction to the study of film. The project option that follows asks students to reflect on and to critique their own expectations of "going to the movies," and in a way that allows them to give voice to their own experiences of cinema as art *and* as industry.

In "The Decay of Cinema," Susan Sontag argues that the cinema, which "began in wonder," and was "once heralded as the art of the 20th century, seems now, as the century closes, to be a decadent art." She sees "the onset in the last decade of an ignominious, irreversible decline" that's left us with "a disincarnated, lightweight cinema that doesn't demand anyone's full attention." Sontag's main concern is not with the deteriorating quality of movies themselves, however; she is more alarmed that, with the movies' decline, "the love of cinema has waned." She contends that while "people still like going to the movies, and some people still care about and expect something special, necessary from a film," It's hard to "find anymore, at least among the young, the distinctive cinephilic love of movies that is not simply love of but a certain taste in films (grounded in a vast appetite for seeing and reseeing as much as possible of cinema's glorious past)." We've reached the point where "you can't look forward anymore to new films that you can admire," unless, that is, they are "exceptions," "actual violations of the norms and practices that now govern movie making everywhere."

If you choose this option, I'd like you to consider and reflect on your own expectations of "going to the movies." How have your own experiences with moviegoing affected what you now expect of your visits to the theater? Would you say that you "expect something special," something "necessary from a film," or are your expectations better described in some other way? Sontag speaks of a conflict in the making of films between "cinema as routine and cinema as experiment." It might be useful to think of our own moviegoing experiences in much the same way. Do you follow a routine in what you allow yourself to experience of movies and moviegoing, or is your approach more experimental? What impact has your approach had on what you've come to expect of movies and moviegoing?

Once you've addressed what you've come to expect of "going to the movies," I'd like you to develop a critique of your own expectations of moviegoing. What might you do differently in how you approach going to the movies? What positive changes can you envision yourself making? In what ways is your position in the marketplace for movies such that changing your approach could prove difficult or impossible? In speaking to such questions, address yourself to Sontag's reading of the current state of moviegoing.

Do you regard the desire to lose yourself in other people's lives and faces a virtual impossibility nowadays, as Sontag suggests? Can you know the experience of surrender to, of "being transported by," what is on the screen? What of wanting "to be kidnapped by the movie," to be "overwhelmed by the physical presence of the image"? How valuable are such experiences to you? Or are there other moviegoing experiences Sontag fails to mention that you find as valuable or more valuable?

A second set of project options invites student writers to reflect on their own experiences with movies' fan-making powers. I ask students to consider the power movies have to construct them as fans of stars, spectacular action, and special effects. I ask them, for instance, to interrogate what and how much they require of stars, whether there are star qualities they identify with more strongly than others, and how much action or spectacle they require of the movies they see. The option that follows asks students to develop a reading of the manufacturing of stardom in the star treatment created to bring about audience identification with a particular actor or actress.

In Alfred Hitchcock's view, "casting is characterization." This can mean, as Louis Giannetti has noted, that "once a role has been cast, especially with a personality star, the essence of the role of the fictional character is already established. In a sense, stars are more 'real' than other characters, which is why many people refer to a character by the actor's name, rather than by the name of the person in the story." In "Everything You Always Wanted to Know About Stars" (see handout), William Goldman argues that "today you must give the star everything." For Goldman "there is no single more important commercial element in screenplay writing than the star part. . . . Studios crave stars, and, more likely than not, what will make stars commit [to appear in a film] is not necessarily the quality of the project as a whole but the part they're going to play."

Choose a scene from a feature-length film with which you are familiar and show how the role for which an actor has been cast gets the "star treatment." What is built into the role in this scene so that you are encouraged to identify with the star qualities this actor is made to possess? In what ways, for instance, is the star actor's role made more "real" than roles assigned other actors in the scene? How is the star actor "protected," to use Goldman's term, so that the star "gets everything"? (As Goldman puts it, "Stars will not play weak and they will not play blemished, and you better know that now.") You might show how the scene is "shifted to suit" the star, how the star part works so that other people in the scene "do the expository talking." You might consider how the star part is drawn so that the glamour of the star actor figures in how his or her role is played out in the scene. If, for instance, you are more inclined to refer to the "character by the actor's name, rather than by the name of the person in the story," how is this tendency encouraged by the scene?

> Once you've established how the role gets the "star treatment," offer a critique of how well this treatment works for you as you watch the scene. What satisfactions, if any, do you find in this treatment? What frustrations do you encounter? Does the "star treatment" help or hurt the scene? Does it enhance your experience of this part of the film, or does it throw up obstacles to your enjoyment or involvement with the scene?

A third package of options posits the student writer as critical of moviegoing by calling on them to identify and think through moments of difficulty, frustration, or resistance they experience while watching movies. In the option that follows, I ask students to address issues involved with the "social problem" movie:

> In "Controversy with Class: The Social Problem Movie," a section from his "Politics" chapter, Maltby contends that "there are contradictory impulses behind the social problem movie, involving both the recognition and disavowal of Hollywood's power." He makes the point that "by indicating its ability to deal responsibly with issues of political import to American audiences, Hollywood has sought to acknowledge the political influence attributed to its movies by social scientists and lobby groups, but also to show that such power is indeed safe in its own hands." Moviemakers figured that "if handled appropriately, overtly concerned cinema could lend prestige to its producers, by demonstrating a serious-minded concern for a wide range of social problems" (383). Maltby goes on to claim that "Hollywood still routinely insists that committed movies such as *Mississippi Burning* are about characters caught up in political events rather than politicized statements in their own right. What political charge they may possess is thus an expression of the audience's political convictions, rather than those of the producers" (389).
>
> Select a social problem movie, possibly *Falling Down, Mississippi Burning,* or another such film you know well, and develop a critique of Hollywood's handling of "issues of political import" in a single, "powerful" scene from the film. What "contradictory impulses" do you find at work in the way the scene is put together? Does the "Hollywood treatment" of these impulses suggest that the scene is dealing responsibly with the impulses it arouses, with the issues it raises? Is its power "safe," or is there something dangerous or risky in the emotions the scene stirs in you as you watch it? If the scene conveys a "political charge," how do you read and respond to this charge? Is it "safe" to let this political charge have its way with you, or does it make you feel "unsafe"? What might be said about the power of its political "charge"? How safe do you feel with the thought that this power might express your own, or the audience's political convictions? Or, how safe do you feel with the thought that this power might express the view of the movie's makers?

In "Composing English Studies: Toward a Social History of the Discipline," Richard Miller argues for "a vision of composition that places the field's special area of expertise in knowing how to solicit, read, and respond to student work." He goes on to suggest that "we reread the institutional history of English studies in light of the solicitation and treatment of student writing." As a first step in conducting this rereading, Miller suggests beginning with questions pertaining to this solicitation and treatment. These questions ask how students have been constructed by past teachings, what needs these teachings attribute to students, how the writings solicited from students relate to their teachers' commitments, and how these relationships are shaped by institutional constraints (174). To address "ways of thinking about film and composition pedagogically," film and writing teachers need to begin to ask some of the same questions. I hope that the suggestions and recommendations I offer here can be of some value, then, in the early stages of this conversation.

# Works Cited


Boggs, Joseph M. 1996. *The Art of Watching Films*. 4th ed. Mountain View, CA: Mayfield.

Bordwell, David, and Kristin Thompson. 1990. *Film Art: An Introduction*. 3rd ed. New York: McGraw-Hill.

Cook, David A. 1996. *A History of Narrative Film*. 3rd ed. New York: W. W. Norton.

Corrigan, Timothy. 1998. *A Short Guide to Writing About Film*. 3rd ed. New York: Harper Collins.

Crowley, Sharon. 1990. *The Methodical Memory: Invention in Current-Traditional Rhetoric*. Carbondale, IL: Southern Illinois University Press.

Giannetti, Louis. 1991. *Flashback: A Brief History of Film*. 2nd ed. Englewood Cliffs, NJ: Prentice Hall.

———. 1996. *Understanding Movies*. 7th ed. Englewood Cliffs, NJ: Prentice Hall.

Goldman, William. 1983. "Everything You Always Wanted to Know About Stars." *American Film* (March): 57–64.

Marius, Richard. 1989. "Reflections on the Freshman English Course." In *Teaching Literature: What Is Needed Now,* edited by James Engell and David Perkins. Cambridge, MA: Harvard University Press.

Maltby, Richard. 1995. *Hollywood Cinema: An Introduction*. Cambridge, MA: Blackwell Publishers.

Miller, Richard E. 1994. "Composing English Studies: Towards a Social History of the Discipline." *College Composition and Communication* 45 (May): 164–79.

Pollitt, Katha. 1991. "Why Do We Read?" *The Nation,* 23 September.

Prince, Stephen. 1997. *Movies and Meaning: An Introduction to Film*. Boston: Allyn and Bacon.

Sklar, Robert. 1993. *Film: An International History of the Medium*. Englewood Cliffs, NJ: Prentice Hall.

Sontag, Susan. 1996. "The Decay of the Cinema." *The New York Times Magazine,* 25 February.

# Appendix

## *(Classic) Entertainment*

*The Adventures of Robin Hood* (1938), *Casablanca* (1942), *Double Indemnity* (1944), *High Noon* (1952), *It Happened One Night* (1934), *Laura* (1944), *Singing in the Rain* (1952), *Tarzan and His Mate* (1934), *The Wizard of Oz* (1939), *Wuthering Heights* (1939).

## *Industry (Film Industry Stories)*

*Barton Fink* (1991), *Get Shorty* (1995), *The Goddess* (1958), *In a Lonely Place* (1950), *Play It Again, Sam* (1972), *Postcards from the Edge* (1990), *Stand-In* (1937), *A Star Is Born* (1937), *Sullivan's Travels* (1941), *Sunset Boulevard* (1950).

## *Genre*

*Bad Day at Black Rock* (1954), *Blood Simple* (1984), *City Slickers* (1991), *Class Action* (1991), *Forbidden Planet* (1956), *Mildred Pierce* (1945), *My Man Godfrey* (1936), *The Purple Rose of Cairo* (1985), *Reversal of Fortune* (1990), *The Usual Suspects* (1995).

## *Technology (Color/Sound/Widescreen)*

*Bonnie & Clyde* (1967), *Cat on a Hot Tin Roof* (1958), *Crimson Pirate* (1952), *Days of Heaven* (1978), *Drugstore Cowboy* (1989), *Gentlemen Prefer Blondes* (1953), *Psycho* (1960), *Touch of Evil* (1958), *Toy Story* (1995), *Who Framed Roger Rabbit?* (1988).

## *(Star) Performance*

*The Accused* (1988), *Big* (1988), *The French Connection* (1971), *In the Heat of the Night* (1967), *Moonstruck* (1987), *On the Waterfront* (1954), *Roxanne* (1987), *Runaway Train* (1985), *The Seven-Year Itch* (1955), *Shaft* (1971).

## *(Cinematic) Space*

*Annie Hall* (1977), *The Breakfast Club* (1985), *Clueless* (1995), *Driving Miss Daisy* (1989), *Fargo* (1996), *The Graduate* (1967), *Kramer vs. Kramer* (1979), *Lost in America* (1985), *Paper Moon* (1973), *Written on the Wind* (1956).

## Film Time/Movie Time

*Back to the Future* (1985), *Groundhog Day* (1993), *The Killing* (1956), *Madigan* (1968), *Peggy Sue Got Married* (1986), *3:10 to Yuma* (1957), *This Is Elvis* (1981), *The Time Machine* (1960), *The Times of Harvey Milk* (1984), *Westworld* (1973).

## Narrative

*Butch Cassidy and the Sundance Kid* (1969), *Desert Bloom* (1986), *Diner* (1982), *Invasion of the Body Snatchers* (1956), *Mission: Impossible* (1996), *Over the Edge* (1979), *Places in the Heart* (1984), *Powwow Highway* (1988), *Twister* (1996), *Zelig* (1984).

## Politics

*All the King's Men* (1949), *Bob Roberts* (1992), *The Candidate* (1972), *Dave* (1993), *Falling Down* (1993), *The Front* (1976), *Guilty by Suspicion* (1991), *Modern Times* (1936), *Roger & Me* (1989), *Tucker: The Man and His Dream* (1988).

## Criticism

*Breaking Away* (1979), *Bus Stop* (1956), *Cleopatra* (1934), *Gun Crazy* (1949), *Hannah and Her Sisters* (1986), *The Maltese Falcon* (1941), *The Naked Gun: From the Files of Police Squad!* (1988), *Rear Window* (1954), *She Wore a Yellow Ribbon* (1949), *Streetwise* (1985).

# 13

## Apocalypse Yesterday

### *Writing, Literacy, and the "Threat" of "Electric Technology"*

### Lucy Fischer

## I. A Very Touchy Subject

> To some Westerners, the written or printed word has become a very touchy subject. . . . [T]here is . . . a new electric technology that threatens this ancient technology of literacy built on the phonetic alphabet. . . . Our Western values, built on the written word, have already been considerably affected by the electric media of telephone, radio and TV. Perhaps that is the reason why many highly literate people in our time find it difficult to examine this question without getting into a moral panic. (McLuhan 1964, 84–85)

When Marshall McLuhan wrote these words in *Understanding Media* in 1964, he was engaging a major contemporary debate: whether print culture, as we knew it, was suffering destruction at the hands of the "electric media." Clearly, Signet Books (who published his work) identified McLuhan with a radical stance. Before allowing the readers to engage the central portion of his text, a page of publicity copy greets them with the slogan "Good-bye to Gutenberg." Further down the page, another paragraph, ostensibly expressing McLuhan's views, deems "modern man" a "relic of the logical, linear, 'hot' culture of movable type." At points, McLuhan himself exacerbates the humanist's paranoia. As he writes, "Electric technology does not need words any more than the digital computer needs numbers" (83).

While McLuhan's theories no longer have much academic or popular currency, his notion of the opposition between word and image (as "hot" and "cool" media) remains. Equally tenacious is his vision of a print culture humiliated, and antiquated, by visual technology. In *The Closing of the American Mind,* written more than two decades after *Understanding Media,* Allan Bloom (1987) speaks of having noticed "the decline in reading" as far back as the late sixties—precisely McLuhan's era (62). Like McLuhan, Bloom establishes a polarity between written and visual forms, valorizing the former. As he notes, "Lack of education simply results in students' seeking for enlightenment wherever it is readily available, without being able to distinguish between the sublime and trash. . . . For the most part students turn to the movies . . . " (64).

While McLuhan sees visual media as a menace to print culture, he never envisions it as a replacement. He remarks, "A new medium is never an addition to an old one, nor does it leave the old one in peace. It never ceases to oppress the older media *until it finds new shapes and positions for them*" (158, my emphasis).

In this chapter, I will examine the "evolutionary" process to which McLuhan alludes by exploring how cinema finds "new shapes and positions" for writing. First, I will review the ways in which print language has traditionally functioned within the film medium. Second, I will propose ways that the dynamic of cinema and writing can be harnessed for the composition class. Third, I will situate the conjunction of composition and film within the broader history of cinema studies.

# II. Screen/Writing

Today we can say that at last the director writes in film. (Bazin 1967, 39)

Although film viewing and reading are often imagined as antagonistic activities, they have historically been related. McLuhan sees the cinema as a "spectacular *wedding* of the old mechanical [print] technology" and "the new [visual] electronic world" (249, my emphasis). Furthermore, he sees the spectator's viewing of sequential images as parallel to the reader's following "the black and white sequences of stills that is typography" (249). Finally, for him, literature and movies are linked by "their power to generate fantasy in the viewer or reader" (249).

Clearly, the first task of teachers of composition and film classes is to make connections between cinema and writing apparent to their students, to break down the false dichotomy that has structured thought on the subject. One might point out, for example, that while the very earliest works of silent cinema had no recourse to written language, films soon had "intertitles" (written inserts between images), which provided necessary narrative exposition and dialogue. Some movies transcended a banal use of the format. In *Sunrise* (1927), when a femme fatale inquires whether her lover's wife might not conveniently "drown," her projected words sink down upon the screen, as though descending in water.

Some critics see a continuing dynamic of print and image in the contemporary cinema. For Tom Conley (1992), a film's on-screen title is to be taken seriously as a form of "inscription," which is "posed as an enigma above and before the image" (x). Also, a film's credits bear similarity to "emblematic traditions in literature" (xi). Finally, Conley is intrigued by the spectator's retrospective "matching" of movie images with print advertising slogans previously apprehended.

While, with the coming of sound, printed language came to be dominated by spoken word, certain cinematic works continued to exploit the figure of writing on screen. It can be useful for a teacher of composition and film to present excerpts of these works to the class, as preparation for future writing about film. One thinks, for example, of the films of Godard in which street signs, tabloid headlines, and packaging logos carry semiotic and dramatic weight. In *The Married Woman* (1964), as the heroine trysts with her paramour in an airport, one sign reads "Rendez-Vous Points" and another exclaims "Danger." One also recalls Robert Bresson's *The Diary of a Country Priest* (1951), in which the spectator is required to read pages of the prelate's journal on screen while simultaneously listening to the priest's voice-over narration. One might consider, as well, radically experimental works like Su Friedrich's *Gently Down the Stream* (1981), in which lyrical verses are scratched directly into the photographic emulsion—creating the effect of their being "written" on screen before the viewer's eyes. Finally, one might view a film like Hollis Frampton's *Poetic Justice* (1972), which consists entirely of sequential pages of a shooting script photographed in silence upon a coffee table. Here, the word completely subsumes the image and evacuates the latter of any threatening pictorial content. Frampton's film represents in witty form the ultimate "revenge" of print culture—its "poetic justice," as verbal scenario stands in for the film.

As part of the process of cinema making "peace" with writing, French film critics began arguing for the status of film director as "author." As Andre Bazin stated in the 1950s, "The filmmaker is no longer the competitor of the painter and the playwright, he is, at last, the equal of the novelist" (39–40). According to this logic, the act of analyzing the work of John Ford might bear similarity to that of studying the oeuvre of Shakespeare.

## III. Screen/Writing

When approaching the cinema from the linguistic point of view, it is difficult to avoid shuttling back and forth between two positions: the cinema as a language; the cinema as infinitely different from verbal language. Perhaps it is impossible to extricate oneself from this dilemma with impunity. (Metz 1974, 44)

When McLuhan references the humanist's "moral panic" (in the face of electric technology), he notes that actually "there is *more* material written and printed and read today than ever before" (84, my emphasis). Ironically, one might claim that a significant part of that ever-expanding literature is filled by writing that pertains to the electric media themselves—especially to the cinema. In addition to the tomes of newspaper and magazine reviews published about film since the turn of the century, there have been countless books written about the medium from aesthetic, philosophical, historical, sociological, and cultural perspectives. Furthermore, a plethora of specialized film journals has appeared—whether dedicated to issues of production or critical studies. Moreover, the screenplay and the ciné-roman have become autonomous art forms, creating new modes of literature with a cinematic base. Finally, one of the major branches of film theory (semiotics)—a school identified with Christian Metz—has claimed that film is a type of "language," making the ties between filmic and verbal discourse even stronger.

Hence, rather than supplant the written word, cinema has contributed to its proliferation—a fact that belies the neat division of the world into print and visual culture. It is the erroneous assumption of such a stereotypical dichotomy that causes shock to the average undergraduate who naively wanders into a film studies course and finds that, in addition to screening movies, she is responsible for readings equal to those assigned in more traditional classes. Furthermore, while film studies courses may entail some exams in short-answer format (for definitions, dates, film titles, and names of directors), most stress critical writing: term papers, take-home exams, and journals. Thus, while the object of study may consist largely of images, the assignments and methods of evaluation for the course are still mired in "ancient" print culture.

## IV. Composition and Cinema

Writing about films is one of the most sophisticated ways to respond to them. (Corrigan 1992, xiii)

But what of the class that, more *fundamentally,* combines writing and film—beyond assigning essays as means of testing knowledge of the cinema? Such is the case in a course entitled General Writing/Film regularly offered at the University of Pittsburgh, a composition class that takes film as its principal topic. Class sessions entail both discussion of writing by students and "professionals," as well as brief film screenings consisting of excerpts or "shorts." The primary assignments for the class are a series of weekly essays examining some aspect of the cinema.

As I see it, there are several pitfalls one must avoid in this class, the first being the temptation to confuse it with a course on film analysis or film history. While students in General Writing/Film will, no doubt, learn much about film style and history, given that considerable attention is spent on the process of writing, there is not adequate time to do these broad topics justice. Rather, what works best is to allow students to ponder precisely those issues that traditional film classes *fail* to consider: What has been the import of cinema in my life?

How has the star system affected my vision of the world? What actor has had some influence on me and why? What is my view of the cult of celebrity associated with the film industry? What is my favorite film genre? Such personal topics, concerning one's own relation to the institution of cinema, rarely get considered in formal film studies classes. Yet these are the questions whose answers explain our fascination with the medium and its place in our everyday lives, subjects that can best be confronted in essay form. As Corrigan (1992) notes, "If the movies inform many parts of our lives, we should be able to enjoy . . . the challenging pleasure of trying to think about, explain, and write about our experience at the movies" (3).

Beyond allowing students to deal with topics not deemed "serious" enough for traditional film studies courses, a class like General Writing/Film focuses attention on the composition process. Corrigan notes:

> Those who teach film rarely have time to discuss writing about film. Most instructors are busy presenting films and books about those films, and the usual presumption they are forced to make is that students know how to put what they see and think into comprehensible written form. (xiii)

Clearly, this is often a mistaken conjecture.

A course like General Writing/Film can also be a valuable occasion for demonstrating to students the difference between a variety of expository forms, all of which are useful in their college careers. While some of the topics indicated previously are within the autobiographical mode, students can also be encouraged to write essays that fall into descriptive, analytical, evaluative, or interpretive camps. While film theorists have long noted the incredibly dense nature of the film image, in which innumerable details are revealed simultaneously, this can be impressed upon students, quite dramatically, by having them describe a still film image. They are often quite astounded to find how much verbiage it takes to render what seems immediately perceptible on screen. Other kinds of descriptive exercises are also possible. Students might translate, to written form, a complex cinematic sequence, or write descriptive passages for an imaginary screenplay.

One of the most successful ways to merge writing and film analysis is to have students do a "shot-by-shot" breakdown of a particular film segment of some ten to twenty shots. While the first stage of this exercise is to record each shot in terms of its distance, length, content, and sound, the second part is to assess and organize the results: Is it a sequence primarily composed of long shots or close-ups? Is the duration of most shots brief or extended? Is the sequence an example of assertive montage or realistic long-take? Does it exhibit parallel editing or standard scene construction (establishing shot, to long shot, to medium shot, to close-up)?

Of course, the process of analysis generally solicits interpretation and, in such an assignment, one might also want to ask what the sequence *means,* and how its style constructs sense. For another interpretive exercise, it can be quite useful to show students a brief, enigmatic experimental film (e.g., Luis Bunuel and Salvador Dali's *Un Chien Andalou* [1928], Bruce Connor's *A Movie* [1959] or Maya Deren's *Meshes of the Afternoon* [1943]) and then ask them to compose an essay that performs an interpretive "reading" of the text. While some students are averse to analyzing poetic discourse in linguistic form, they are often open to the process when it is applied to cinema.

As for evaluative writing, the standard film review is a familiar and exemplary form. A class on cinema and writing can provide an occasion to read and discuss such a ubiquitous brand of journalism, one generally ignored in film studies classes in favor of criticism and theory. While students are aware of the typical newspaper review (and its television equivalent), they are less cognizant of its literary counterpart (e.g., the extended *New Yorker* essay by Pauline Kael; *The New York Times* "think piece" by Janet Maslin or Vincent Canby; the belle lettristic essay by Michael Woods in *The New York Review of Books*). Beyond simply reading such pieces, students can write them—from short "consumer-oriented" reviews of a film they have seen (brief description, thumbs up or down), to more considered essays appropriate to a middlebrow magazine.

There are yet more creative ways to engage the topics of composition and cinema that involve imagining the formal parallels between the media. This is a topic that has long fascinated film critics, beginning with the early musings of French theorist Alexandre Astruc (1968), who conceived of the camera-stylo (camera-pen) as "a means of writing just as flexible and subtle as the written language" (18).

Clearly, we use the term "editing" to signify both attention to the order of words on a page and to the cutting and arranging of pieces of celluloid. What if there were a way, in class, to bring these tasks together? Ideally, if the instructor were versed in the basics of film editing, it would be possible to do a class "experiment" with stock footage whereby several versions of a film (with variable shot order) made clear the transformations possible through plastic manipulation. One might also assign readings about the famous "Kuleshov effect," whereby a Soviet filmmaker alternately showed his students a close-up of a dejected person followed by a bowl of soup, and then a close-up of that person followed by a dead child. Kuleshov's pupils read the man's facial expression as either hunger or grief, depending on the version they watched. Furthermore, instructional films exist that illustrate the impact of shot choice and editing on the overall narrative. An old standard, called *Film: Interpretation and Values*, shows an episode of the 1950s television show *Gunsmoke* edited in various ways, each variation having a differing effect. Parallel to this, the instructor might prepare a fragmentary linguistic text for class experimentation, to make clear how word choice and order can entirely transform tone and meaning. One might even bring to class a novelty item such as a box of magnetic poetry, magnet-backed cutout words that can be positioned and reconfigured on any metal surface.

Attention might also be paid to the function of figurative language in both writing and film: how tropes are linguistically and cinematically constructed.

There is considerable theoretical writing on this topic (e.g., *The Figure in Film* by N. Roy Clifton [1983] or *Metaphor and Film* by Trevor Whittock [1990]), which might be assigned as reading. Furthermore, certain examples of metaphorical construction in the cinema could be examined, such as Charles Chaplin's comparison of workers to sheep in *Modern Times* (1936), Sergei Eisenstein's likening of a state official (Kerensky) to a peacock in *October* (1927), or Josef von Sternberg's use of entrapping nets, anchors, and cages in *The Blue Angel* (1930). Finally, students might be encouraged to compose their own piece of figurative writing that draws upon such tropes as metaphor, simile, and synecdoche, or to find their own examples in film.

## V. On Refusing to Be an "Audiovisual Aid"

The motion picture . . . should show you just what problems people are facing today and the different ways that these problems can be solved. They should show you the consequences of certain ways of solving problems so that you may know what to expect if you try to work out your problems as did the persons on the screen. (Dale 1935, 208)

I was once asked, in my department, to speak on a panel called "Pedagogical Uses of Film." Though it was a stimulating event, when it came my turn, I announced that I took exception to the word *uses* in the session's title. What I objected to was the familiar notion of film being placed "in the service of" something *else:* be it a demonstration of gravity, a glimpse of volcanoes, a history of painting, a view of the Andes, or a lesson in life choices, such as the one imagined in 1935 by educator Edgar Dale.

In order to explain my reaction, I drew upon biographical and historical perspectives. I noted that when I came to film studies in the 1970s, the field was emerging from a period in which its academic existence had been under the sway of the established disciplines such as literature, theater, communications, or fine arts. Thus, film studies had long been viewed as the Exotic Primitive to the Cultured Norm, and the power to define it had been given to the mainstream fields that saw it as a reflection of themselves. Hence, drama saw cinema as filmed theater; literature as visible narrative; art history as mobile painting or animated photography.

There then ensued a period in which, as a reaction to this "colonialist" appropriation, the rhetoric of academic film studies took on a militant or "liberationist" tone, and a stance of "identity politics." Hence, the field argued for its own separate departments and the recognition of a distinct history, cultural formation, and theoretical base. Perennially out of synch with established academic trends, film studies managed to avow such disciplinarity just at the moment when older fields declared disciplinarity defunct. Before long, other fields reasserted their claim to film studies, now for a new reason: not because film studies failed to be a sophisticated enough discipline to stand alone, but because disciplinarity had been found meaningless.

From this situation came a variety of consequences, some salutary and some questionable. On a positive note, there was a revived and expanded sense of vital interdisciplinary work, with such fields as literature, history, and fine arts contributing both scholarly work and methods to the investigation of cinema. Furthermore, the growth of cultural studies challenged *all* fields to examine the aesthetic or textual object in the light of other social events and artifacts.

But there was a down side as well, one that filled film studies veterans with a jaded sense of déjà vu. This entailed the tendency to, once again, employ film as an "audiovisual aid"—those most despised words to the true cinephile—to use it to teach literature or history to those reluctant to read, or to motivate students' creative expression in *another* medium, such as writing.

It is this last "use" of the cinema that constitutes the second pitfall for those teaching a composition and film class. While such a course is not entirely about the cinema, neither is it entirely about composition. It is not an occasion to "use" the cinema merely to stimulate writing, or as a discussion topic more approachable than literature. Rather, it is an opportunity to learn something central about the cinema in the act of improving one's writing. One of film's "uses" as an "audiovisual aid" is surely to teach film.

Thus, in a class on composition and film, instead of simply looking "through" the screen for an occasion to encourage student writing, one might ask students to do basic research in film history: to view a film from the past, to locate an old film review, and to write a short paper about them. Likewise, instead of suggesting that students write about a contemporary film because they like it better than a recent novel, one might require them to discuss it within a film historical frame, for instance, as an example of an established film genre.

In short, what I am calling for is a refusal to treat cinema as the academic "Other." This entails a refusal to parade it into class as the "non-literary," the "non-painterly," the "non-theatrical," or the "non-writerly." For a composition course, this requires that film functions as more than a mere stimulus for reading and writing.

# VI. "Cineliteracy"

Is it necessary, really, to learn how to read a film? Obviously, anyone of minimal intelligence over the age of four can—more or less—grasp the basic content of a film . . . without any special training. Yet precisely because the media so very closely mimic reality, we apprehend them much more easily than we comprehend them. (Monaco 1981, vii)

In recent years, scholars have made clear how notions of writing are tied to those of literacy and cultural capital. One is not simply taught to write, but to write a certain way, in a manner acceptable to academic, commercial, and/or corporate circles. Writing is also connected to literacy through the canonization of certain examples of the craft, be they the plays of Henrik Ibsen, or the novels of Virginia Woolf. While cinema's association with "popular culture" has often exempted it from such discussions, critics have argued for the notion of "cineliteracy" (Eidsvik 1978).

In light of this debate, another way in which a class on composition and film can engage its dual subject is by interrogating the concept of canonicity. The perfect text for this is E. D. Hirsch's *Cultural Literacy* (1987), which concludes with an appendix entitled "What Literate Americans Know." Rather than find an encyclopedia of brief entries of an explanatory nature on a variety of topics, one finds only a list of individual terms. For example, under *A*, this list includes "Adonis, Adrenal gland, adrenaline, Adriatic Sea, adultery, adverb, AEC (Atomic Energy Commission), Aegean Sea, Aeneas, Aeneid, The (title)" (152). While the word *Casablanca* appears on Hirsch's list, there is no parenthesis after it denoting "title," so we realize that the literate American must know the Moroccan city, but not the film of the same name. While Fred Astaire and Ginger Rogers make the list, Orson Welles and *Citizen Kane* (1941) do not.

Although a public, insecure about its intellectual status, may have qualms about questioning Hirsch's traditional selections from the disciplines of literature, fine arts, science, and history, it may be more confident about challenging his choices in popular culture: Why include Walt Disney and not Frank Capra? Why include *The Birth of a Nation* (1915) and not *It's a Wonderful Life* (1946)? Why list Chaplin but not *The Gold Rush* (1925)? Why include the phrase "Win this one for the Gipper" but not the word *Rosebud*? Curious, as well, are Hirsch's listing of certain texts without specifying their particular medium—literary or filmic—even though most Americans are familiar with them in multiple forms (for example, *Gone with the Wind* [title] or *The Wizard of Oz* [title]). It is as though Hirsch were saying, "Of course, I mean the book! How foolish of you to imagine otherwise."

What Hirsch's incorporation of references from popular culture accomplishes is to allow for the questioning of the existence of his list at all. If the "requisite" knowledge about popular culture is so arbitrary and spotty, can his construction of traditional literacy be any better?

It would make a stimulating assignment for students to take a letter of the alphabet, Hirsch's organizing principle, and formulate their *own* list of "requisite" cultural references, serious or parodic, justifying their selections in essay form. Or, they might take a section of Hirsch's extant list and dispute it, especially for its exclusion of cinematic citations.

## VII. Conclusion: "The Raw and the Cooked"

> There are a great many authors of the past who have survived centuries of oblivion and neglect, but it is still an open question whether they will be able to survive an entertaining [film] version of what they have to say. (Hannah Arendt, quoted in Boyum 1985, 8)

Whenever one considers courses that conjoin the disciplines of English and film, the question of literary adaptation immediately arises. While General Writing/Composition is not a class on literature per se, it often involves a writing assignment to consider a film version of a novel: be it one by Charles Dickens, Kurt Vonnegut, Scott Turow, or Jane Austen. In this classic binary, film risks being configured as the inferior "Other" to the superior "Norm," an attitude that Hannah Arendt's statement makes abundantly clear.

In response to this bias, many filmmakers have been understandably reluctant to work from classic literary properties. Godard once commented that "the only way he could think of filming a novel would be to photograph it page by page" (Boyum 1985, 17)—a quip that leads us to wonder if Hollis Frampton had Godard's words in mind while shooting *Poetic Justice.* Similarly, Alain Resnais once stated, "I would not want to shoot the adaptation of a novel because . . . to make a film of it is a little like *reheating a meal*" (Boyum 1985, 17, my emphasis).

But I am recommending more than the avoidance of literary adaptation as the centerpiece in a film/composition course. I am suggesting that "adaptation" of another sort be foregrounded, one that seeks to reconfigure the writing curriculum in the light of an "electric medium" like cinema. But, this must be done without simply looking through it, regarding it as the academic "Other," bracketing it in a static binary, relegating it to pedagogical "stimulus," or viewing it as an institutional "threat."

In other words, in dealing with the interface of McLuhan's "hot" and "cold" media, print or electric, academically "cooked" or "raw," we cannot simply "reheat" the curriculum, but must work to find new food for thought.[1]

## Note

1. In referring to print culture as the "cooked" and the electric media as the "raw," I am, of course, invoking the work of Levi-Strauss (1969). In *The Raw and the Cooked,* he identifies the former with the uncivilized and the latter with the acculturated. For example, he talks about the function of fire in myth: "The conjunction of a member of the social group with nature must be mediatized through the intervention of cooking fire, whose normal function is to mediatize the conjunction of the raw product and the human consumer, and whose operation thus has the effect of making sure that a natural creature is at one and the same time cooked and socialized" (336).

## Works Cited

Astruc, Alexandre. 1968. "The Birth of a New Avant-Garde: La camera-stylo." In *The New Wave,* edited by Peter Graham, 17–22. Garden City, NY: Doubleday.

Bazin, Andre. 1967. "The Evolution of the Language of the Cinema." In *What Is Cinema?* Vol. 1, 23–40. Translated by Hugh Gray. Berkeley, CA: University of California Press.

Bloom, Allan. 1987. *The Closing of the American Mind.* New York: Simon & Schuster.

Boyum, Joy Gould. 1985. *Double Exposure: Fiction into Film.* New York: New American Library.

Clifton, N. Roy. 1983. *The Figure in Film.* Cranbury, NJ: University of Delaware Press.

Conley, Tom. 1992. *Film Hieroglyphs: Ruptures in Classical Cinema.* Minneapolis: University of Minnesota Press.

Corrigan, Timothy. 1992. *A Short Guide to Writing About Film.* 2d ed. NewYork: Harper Collins.

Dale, Edgar. 1935. *How to Appreciate Motion Pictures: A Manual of Motion-Picture Criticism Prepared for High-School Students.* New York: Macmillan.

Eidsvik, Charles. 1978. *Cineliteracy: Film Among the Arts.* New York: Random House.

Hirsch, E. D. 1987. *Cultural Literacy: What Every American Needs to Know.* Boston: Houghton Mifflin.

Levi-Strauss, Claude. 1969. *The Raw and the Cooked: Introduction to a Science of Mythology: I.* Translated by John and Doreen Weightman. New York: Harper & Row.

Mast, Gerald, Marshall Cohen, and Leo Braudy. 1992. *Film Theory and Criticism: Introductory Readings.* 4th ed. New York and Oxford, England: Oxford University Press.

McLuhan, Marshall. 1964. *Understanding Media: The Extensions of Man.* New York: Signet.

Metz, Christian. 1974. *Film Language: A Semiotics of the Cinema.* Translated by Michael Taylor. New York and Oxford, England: Oxford University Press.

Monaco, James. 1981. *How to Read a Film: The Art, Technology, Language, History, and Theory of Film and Media.* Rev. ed. New York and Oxford, England: Oxford University Press.

Whittock, Trevor. 1990. *Metaphor and Film.* Cambridge and New York: Cambridge University Press.

## Films

*The Blue Angel.* 1930. Directed by Josef von Sternberg.

*Un Chien Andalou.* 1928. Directed by Luis Bunuel and Salvador Dali.

*The Diary of a County Priest.* 1951. Directed by Robert Bresson.

*Gently Down the Stream.* 1981. Directed by Su Friedrich.

*The Married Woman.* 1964. Directed by Jean-Luc Godard.

*Meshes of the Afternoon.* 1943. Directed by Maya Deren.

*Modern Times.* 1936. Directed by Charles Chaplin.

*A Movie.* 1959. Directed by Bruce Connor.

*October.* 1927. Directed by Sergei Eisenstein.

*Poetic Justice.* 1972. Directed by Hollis Frampton.

*Sunrise: A Song of Two Humans.* 1927. Directed by F. W. Murnau.

# Contributors

**Ellen R. Bishop** is currently Associate Professor of English at Indiana University of Pennsylvania. She is currently working on a book on the representations of teenage girls in American postwar film.

**Patricia M. Caille** is presently finishing her Ph.D. at the University of Pittsburgh; her work focuses on issues of authorship and, more particularly, the reception of the American independent filmmaker, John Cassavetes, and his films in France. She has been teaching various courses in composition, film, and literature at the University of Pittsburgh for the past few years.

**Kate Neale Chanock** (B.A. in Anthropology; Ph.D. in African History; R.S.A. in TESL; Dip.Ed. in TESL and Social Studies) is a lecturer in the Humanities Academic Skills Unit at La Trobe University in Melbourne, Australia. She has taught high school English and History in East Africa, adult ESL at the University of Texas, the General Education Diploma in the Texas penal system, the B.Ed. in TESL at La Trobe, and academic discourse in the Faculty of Humanities at La Trobe. She has worked for the Home Tutors Organisation as a Tutor Trainer, for the Adult Migrant Education Service as a writer and cartoonist, and for SBS TV as a writer. She is the author of *Writing "Independent" History: African Historiography 1960–1980* and of *Show Me English* (a teaching resource for Home Tutors); coauthor of *Hello, Australia* (an advanced ESL workbook for SBS TV); editor of two collections of conference proceedings; and coeditor of *Academic Skills Advising: Towards a Discipline*. She is interested in teaching students to understand academic cultures and control academic discourse.

**Dulce Maria Cruz** earned a Ph.D. in Literature, Literacy and Language at Indiana University–Bloomington. She is an assistant professor of English at George Mason University. Her areas of expertise include Composition/Literacy Theory and Pedagogy, contemporary U. S. Latina/o literature and culture, Feminist Ethnography, and Cultural Studies. Currently, she is revising a book manuscript, an ethnographic study on the ways high literacy and ethnicity intersect. Her subjects in that research are Dominican American academics teaching the humanities and social sciences in U. S. colleges and universities. Aside from screening international films, she is passionate about scuba diving and sailing.

**Donna Dunbar-Odom** is the Director of First-Year Composition at Texas A&M University-Commerce, Dept. of Literature and Languages.

**Lucy Fischer** is a Professor of Film Studies and English at the University of Pittsburgh, where she directs the Film Studies Program. She is the author of *Jacques Tati* (G. K. Hall, 1983), *Shot/Countershot: Film Tradition and Women's Cinema* (Princeton, 1989), *Imitation of Life* (Rutgers, 1991), and *Cinematernity: Film, Motherhood, Genre* (Princeton

University Press, 1996). Her monograph on the film *Sunrise* (written for the British Film Institute) was published in 1998. Another monograph (on American cinema), to accompany the British Film Institute's "Century of Cinema" series is also in press. She has published extensively on issues of film history, theory, and criticism in such journals as *Screen, Sight and Sound, Camera Obscura, Wide Angle, Cinema Journal, Journal of Film and Video, Film Criticism, Women and Performance, Frauen und Film, Film Quarterly.* She has held curatorial positions at The Museum of Modern Art in New York and The Carnegie Museum of Art in Pittsburgh and has written catalog essays for exhibits at the Wight Gallery (Los Angeles) and the Neuberger Museum (Purchase, NY). She has been the recipient of a National Endowment for the Arts Art Critics Fellowship. She has lectured abroad in Tel Aviv, Israel; Ausgburg, Germany; Amsterdam, Holland; Vienna, Austria; and on the Semester at Sea program of the University of Pittsburgh. She has twice served as host/organizer of the Society for Cinema Studies conference.

**Joseph Harris** teaches English and directs the composition program at the University of Pittsburgh. He is author of *A Teaching Subject: Composition Since 1966* (Prentice Hall, 1997) and coeditor of *Media Journal: Reading and Writing About Popular Culture* (Allyn & Bacon, 2nd ed, 1998). Harris also edits *College Composition and Communication.*

**John Heyda** teaches film and composition at Miami University in Miami, Ohio.

**Loretta F. Kasper** is Associate Professor of English at Kingsborough Community College/CUNY, where she regularly teaches discipline-based courses to developmental students.

**Edward Maloney** is a Ph.D. candidate in the Department of English at the Ohio State University, where he also works as Assistant Editor for the journal *Narrative* and for the International James Joyce Foundation. His dissertation discusses the relationship between narrative form and postimperial historical fiction. He has published in the *Encyclopedia of the Novel,* and he is currently completing an article on Gabriel Garcia Marquez's use of metafiction as a counter-cultural narrative practice.

**Paul Miller** is completing his Ph.D. in rhetoric and composition at Ohio State University. His dissertation focuses on the use of pragmatism as a theoretical framework from which to address the roles of technology in composition. He has published numerous movie reviews, and is currently completing a collaborative study of writing instruction in introductory engineering classes.

**Victoria Salmon** curently teaches a variety of English courses at Northern Virginia Community College and at George Mason University. She received her doctorate in 1997 for a dissertation on composition theory.

**Johanna Schmertz** coordinates the Basic Writing program at Southeastern Oklahoma State University. She has published essays on popular culture and viewing practices in *Postscript: A Journal of Film and the Humanities.* A doctoral candidate at Texas A&M-Commerce, she is currently writing a dissertation on the disciplinary politics of English studies.

**Robert Singer** is Associate Professor of English at Kingsborough Community College/CUNY, where he teaches literature, writing, and film courses.

**Annette Trefzer** is Assistant Professor of American Literature in the Department of English, Humanities, and Languages at Southeastern Oklahoma State University. She has recently published "'Let Us All Be Kissing-Friends?': Zora Neale Hurston and Race Politics in Dixie" (*Journal of American Studies,* 1997) and is currently working on an article entitled "Possessing the Self: Caribbean Identities in Zora Neale Hurston's *Tell My Horse.*" She is also coediting conference proceedings on Native American Studies and working on a book titled *Identity Politics in Dixie: Race, Writing, and the Canon.*

**Daniel H. Wild** is a doctoral student in the Department of English at the University of Pittsburgh, where he teaches composition and film courses. His research concerns the phenomenon of writing as it appears within film.